Learning Causality in a Complex World

Understandings of Consequence

Tina A. Grotzer

ROWMAN & LITTLEFIELD EDUCATION
A division of
ROWMAN & LITTLEFIELD PUBLISHERS, INC.
Lanham • New York • Toronto • Plymouth, UK

Published by Rowman & Littlefield Education
A division of Rowman & Littlefield Publishers, Inc.
A wholly owned subsidiary of The Rowman & Littlefield Publishing Group, Inc.
4501 Forbes Boulevard, Suite 200, Lanham, Maryland 20706
www.rowman.com

10 Thornbury Road, Plymouth PL6 7PP, United Kingdom

British Library Cataloguing in Publication Information Available

Library of Congress Cataloging-in-Publication Data

Grotzer, Tina.
Learning causality in a complex world : understandings of consequence / Tina A. Grotzer.
p. cm.
Includes bibliographical references and index.
ISBN 978-1-61048-863-1 (cloth : alk. paper) -- ISBN 978-1-61048-864-8 (pbk. : alk. paper) -- ISBN
978-1-61048-865-5 (electronic)
1. Causation. I. Title.
BD591.G765 2012
122--dc23

2012010457

The paper used in this publication meets the minimum requirements of American National
Standard for Information Sciences Permanence of Paper for Printed Library Materials,
ANSI/NISO Z39.48-1992.

Printed in the United States of America

To Annaliese, Slater, Liv, and Mikey
—in you resides my very best hopes for the future…

Table of Contents

Acknowledgments

A book that encompasses a large body of research and so many years of thought does not come about without the contributions of many groups and individuals. I have been fortunate to benefit from the collegiality of many wonderful thinkers who have directly and indirectly contributed to the ideas on the pages to follow. First and foremost, I'd like to thank Dave Perkins for being a mentor and for supporting me in my early forays into these ideas. Dave has been there from the academic beginnings of these ideas, from my dissertation to the first National Science Foundation award to study the concepts in schools. It seems exactly right to have him author the preface to this book.

I am deeply grateful to those on the Understandings of Consequence Project Team over the years who carried out the careful work in schools and with teachers. These include in alphabetical order: Therese Arsenault; Belinda Bell Basca; Maya Bialik; Nicole Brooke; Erin Carr; Ruthie Chang; Evelyn Chen; Becky DeVito; Kiki Donis; Leslie Duhaylongsod; Michael Edgar; Heidi Fessenden; Adi Flesher; Rebekah Gould; Amanda Heffner-Wong; Rose Honey; Carolyn Houghton; Jennifer James; Sheila Jasalavich; David Jeong; Sun Kim; Katya Levitan-Reiner; Molly Levitt; Rebecca Lincoln; Debbie Liu; Dorothy MacGillivray; Wendy Mages; Samantha Marengell; Sarah Mittlefehldt; Mickey Muldoon; Maritess Panlilio; Reuben Posner; Megan Powell; Daniel Record; Kristen Record; Gina Ritscher; Matt Shapiro; Susie Shaw; Erika Spangler; Margot Sudbury; and Kelly Whitney. A very special thank you to Shane Tutwiler and Lynneth Solis who have worked with me most intensely on these ideas recently and will carry them forth in coming years to bring them to a new level.

I also have had the good fortune of working with many wonderful teachers over the years. My appreciation goes out to all of them with special mention to Rich Carroll, Lucy Morris, Val Tobias, Lin Tucker, Allison Friedman-Jacobs, Jo Hendry, Linda Ryan, Elise Morgan, Sarah Blodgett, Christine Fetter, Maureen Danahy and Suzannah Carr.

I have had the great pleasure of working with and learning from many students over the years and examples of what I have learned from them pepper this book. The ideas here have been percolating since my earliest teaching days at Poughkeepsie Day School and the Arlington Public Schools to more recently through my interactions with students in the Burlington Public Schools, Cambridge Public Schools, The Banneker School in Cambridge, MA, and The Community Day Charter School in Lawrence, MA.

This work has enjoyed support from the National Science Foundation, Grants NSF#0845632, and ESI-0455664, to Tina Grotzer; REC-0106988 and REC-9725502 to Tina Grotzer and David Perkins and from the Institute of Education Sciences, U.S. Department of Education, Grant No. R305A080514 to Chris Dede and Tina Grotzer. I am deeply appreciative to Nora Sabelli, Elizabeth Vanderputten, Ken Whang, Julio Lopez-Ferrao, Gregg Solomon, Sharon Lynch, Glenn Markle, Carole Stearns, Jim Dietz, Ed Metz, David Hanych and Joan Ferrini-Mundy for their wise counsel over the years. Any opinions, findings, conclusions or recommendations expressed here are those of the author and do not necessarily reflect the views of the National Science Foundation or the Institute for Education Sciences or the Program Officers at those institutions.

I'd like to acknowledge my colleagues at Project Zero for their support and wisdom with special mention to Howard Gardner who has offered wise counsel on a number of occasions; Tom Trapnell and Faith Harvey who have made everything easier; and Steve Seidel for many deep conversations that I cherish. I'd also like to thank my colleagues at the Center for Health and the Global Environment. I am deeply inspired by each and every one of you. I was fortunate to have precious time learning from Paul Epstein before he left this life far too soon—having made many, many contributions but with so much more to teach all of us. Thank you to my colleagues at the Harvard Graduate School of Education for offering a supportive intellectual home for this work. To Chris Dede, Amy Kamarainen, and Shari Metcalf, I have enjoyed exploring these ideas in new ways and look forward to future collaborations in the years to come.

I'd like to express my appreciation to Tom Koerner, who read an article I'd written on these ideas and contacted me with the idea of writing a book. I am grateful for the leap of faith that he took and his incredible patience in what has been a longer journey than I anticipated. Thank you to Carlie Wall, Carly Peterson, and Chris Basso who have worked their magic to make all of this come together into the volume that you are now holding.

Finally, there are those around me everyday who make me smile, make the endeavor worthwhile, and offer insights into the very human nature of cognition and affect. Annaliese, Slater, Liv, and Mikey, you are the reason for this book and you represent the promise of a generation who will do better than those before you. David, it would not have happened without your love and support (and all those examples that you kept putting on my chair!) Here's to the next chapter…

Preface

David Perkins

What's worth learning? One can hardly ask a more fundamental question about education. First and last, school is not just about the results in the classroom but the results beyond. School learning ultimately delivers through what learners take away toward personal, professional, and civic life in the 21st century.

Learning Causality in a Complex World speaks powerfully to what's worth learning. The pages to come introduce us to the challenges of understanding a range of phenomena that matter– economic fluctuations, ecological tipping points, energy grid anomalies, endemic ills, and much more. Author Tina Grotzer's name for this theme is complex causality, and complex it is! Complex enough, Grotzer urges, that many of us miss what's going on much of the time, defaulting to simple linear causal models.

How learners can develop such understandings is a topic with some twists and turns. Tina Grotzer offers a revealing map of the terrain along with encouraging results from classroom approaches. She shares numerous examples to illustrate how understanding complex causality speaks to a striking range of everyday areas and experiences. We find here a rare combination of insight and, let's call it, out-sight – insight into challenges of learning and out-sight about their importance to our world and our lives.

It would be nice if this amalgam of insight and out-sight could be taken for granted in education, but it cannot. Historically, our culture has been alarmingly lazy about rethinking the mission. Over the decades, not a lot about how we answer that fundamental question *what's worth learning* has changed, at least not a lot of a fundamental character, although more content regularly gets jammed between the cracks of present content.

These days though, things are looking up. A number of individuals and consortia have stood back from education-as-usual to reconsider some fundamentals. The familiar phrases here are 21st century skills and 21st century learning. Around the world, several frameworks have emerged toward a formal education that speaks more powerfully to the lives today's learners are likely to live. Global understandings, learning to learn, self-management, entrepreneurship, critical and creative thinking, collaboration, facility with information technologies, and many other areas take a place alongside a call for deeper learning in the disciplines. The trend is heartening, and the present exploration of complex causality contributes to it.

However, *Learning Causality in a Complex World* becomes especially important for its insight and out-sight because these ambitious initiatives seem to have missed complex causal thinking. One case in point is the well-known framework developed by the Partnership for 21st Century Skills. The framework begins by urging stronger learning in a range of traditional disciplines, enriched by five 21st century themes that cut across them. The 21st century themes include global awareness; financial, economic, business and entrepreneurial literacy; civic literacy; health literacy; and environmental literacy. One could hardly think of topics that bristle more with complex causality – the dynamics of global politics, the disconcerting oscillations of the stock market, the nimble adaptations of pathogenic organisms to new antibiotics, the threat of climatological tipping points.

Yet complex causality and the challenges of complex causal thinking hardly get a nod in the framework. The elaborations of the five themes do nothing to acknowledge the tricky dances of cause and effect, where, as Grotzer notes, what's cause and what's effect often blur into a maze of looping interdependencies. Moreover, complex causal thinking has little presence in the rest of the framework. Under Learning and Innovation Skills, educators are encouraged to cultivate creative thinking and innovation, creative patterns of work with others, effective reasoning, judgment, decision-making, and problem solving. Oh yes, and *systems thinking*, analyzing how parts of the whole interact with each other to produce overall outcomes. This is the only heading in the entire elaborated framework that in any way recognizes causal complexity, and systems thinking as usually understood by no means encompasses all that Tina Grotzer has in mind.

Looking across a number of frameworks for 21st century learning, the story is pretty much the same. While critical and creative thinking, learning to learn, decision-making, problem-solving, metacognition, and similar areas figure prominently, complex causal thinking or proxies for it almost never appear. Perhaps this is further testimony to a phenomenon illustrated here again and again: causal complexity tends to be invisible to eyes not educated for it.

Please don't get me wrong about the Partnership for 21st Century Skills and other similar endeavors: I greatly admire these contemporary efforts to reframe what's worth learning. They touch on much of importance, they merit attention, and they deserve action.

However, they also require extension into neglected areas of high significance. So let's be thankful for this book. Let's appreciate its insight. And let's appreciate it's out-sight. After all, any educational agenda that makes sense *for* our intricate new millennium surely must equip today's learners to make sense *of* that millennium.

Chapter One

Introduction

The Biofuel Plan, part of the Energy Policy Act of 2005,[1] was intended to lessen U.S. dependence on foreign oil. With growing need for food from China and India and failed grain harvests due to drought, using corn for ethanol increased prices of grain and grain-based foods such as beef, milk, and eggs. Riots ensued in Haiti, Somalia, Bangladesh, and Mozambique.

According to scientists, we are already experiencing the early impacts of climate change. The anthropogenic causes of climate change are highly distributed, emerging from the collective behaviors of many—behaviors that are nonintentional with impacts that are often felt far from the contributing causes. Getting the public to connect climate change with their individual actions, particularly when changes now will not have immediate discernable effects, is challenging.

Mongooses were introduced in Hawaii by sugar farmers in the late 1800s to control rats. They are not nocturnal like rats, so they ate few rats, but devastated other native populations. They transmit a potentially fatal disease to humans and have no natural predators in Hawaii.[2] Scientists currently struggle with controlling the Asian Long Horn Beetle, Purple Loose-strife, and other invasive species that impact biodiversity.

Engineers at the Chernobyl Nuclear Power Plant were running a routine safety test in 1986. Manually controlling the system, they overshot in response to the reactor's self-dampening behavior. Then, focusing on the current situation rather than the system's dynamics, they increased its instability—setting off one of the largest nuclear-plant disasters the world has seen.[3]

We live in a complex world. Typically, we tend to simplify and miss much of that complexity so that problems come back at us in unexpected ways. We can do better. We can learn to reason more effectively about causal complexity and do a better job anticipating the ways that our world works. Very importantly, we can help the next generation learn to do so.

Why are these efforts so urgent now? An increasingly global economy, learning to live with climate change, feeding the world's increasing population, and rapid transmission of vast amounts of information via the Internet are just a few reasons. How people reason about risk, for instance, terrorism, pandemics such as SARS or H1N1, the spread of insect-borne disease such as West Nile Virus, diseases with extended onset such as mad cow disease, and events such as Hurricane Katrina hinge upon how we allocate our attention which is impacted by the types of causal complexity involved.

While it is easy to look back with 20/20 hindsight on the mistakes of the past, each generation makes similar kinds of mistakes. The reasoning patterns required to analyze complexity well are not simple, and as the chapters in this book elaborate, it is very human to err in these ways. It stems from the perceptual, attentional, and cognitive patterns inherent to the architecture of how we think.

Why do we miss so much of the complexity in our world? As the following pages will reveal, humans are equipped to notice certain types of events, relationships, and outcomes. In our daily lives, we make sense of our world, abstracting information about how it works. Much of this learning happens implicitly and efficiently—without higher order reflection—and thus, we develop a set of default reasoning patterns and assumptions to guide our behavior. Our basic survival depends upon these default patterns. However, these same reasoning patterns, unexamined, can get us into trouble.

On what basis do I suggest that we can do better? Much of what we know about our causal reasoning stems from research in psychology and early learning about how we discern patterns in our world. While this research suggests why we might employ particular default patterns, it also suggests incredible promise in terms of the ability of very young children to learn complex causal principles. It reveals that from a very young age, humans can be quite adept at figuring out causal relationships—even when the available information is limited in a variety of ways and has complex features.

Beyond this, we are just beginning to bring the power of learning about causal complexity to the classroom—supporting students in moving beyond abstracting patterns on their own to engaging in higher-order reflection upon and about causal complexity. This book reviews promising research on the benefits of helping students learn to reason about the patterns and features of causal complexity.

Over sixty years ago, John Dewey argued that we need to educate children for the world in which *they* will live—the world of the future.[4] Our world today is vastly different from the one that our children will inherit as adults. Knowledge is quickly outdated. Skills rapidly become obsolete. Technology enables new possibilities, new ways of thinking, communicating, and interacting. New problems will surface and many of the challenges our children will inherit are highly intractable.

How do educators make curriculum choices in such an uncertain world? All teaching requires a leap of faith. We trust that children will carry into the world the lessons that they are taught. *What* we decide to teach is also about trust—a pact of sorts between generations. Children work hard in school, trusting that what we teach them will pay off in their futures. Our world has never been certain, but there's more uncertainty today than in the past hundred years in terms of what really will pay off.

It is in this context that I argue for teaching children to reason about causal complexity—the patterns governing the ways that the world works and how we interact with it. These patterns exist in our interactions in our schools, homes, and communities. They govern how we think about risk, analyze actions, and make decisions. The examples in the pages that follow are drawn from science, health, social studies, the economy, the staff room, and even the playground!

Our ability to detect complex patterns promises that we can better fit our actions to the world in which we live, decreasing unanticipated outcomes. This book is filled with historical examples where we failed to do so and paid the consequences. As our world becomes increasingly complex, increasingly global, and increasingly interconnected, our opportunities for success or failure in dealing with complexity are compounded.

I anticipate that thoughtful and responsible educators may ask with healthy skepticism, "Isn't causality an esoteric concept, especially for children? What does it mean to help students learn complex causal patterns? How can I teach causal patterns for the future when I am accountable for the students' learning according to the standards we have in place today?" The paragraphs below, elaborated by each of the chapters to follow, attempts to answer these questions.

BUTTONS, PUDDLES, AND PLAYGROUND POLITICS: CAUSALITY WITHIN REACH

Causality may sound like an esoteric concept, but children think about it implicitly every day. Consider the following examples.

A toddler pushes every button and light switch that he can find. His mother thinks that he is just trying to push her buttons. He is actually finding out that causes do not have to physically touch their effects—that causes can act at a distance. Someday, he may use this knowledge to analyze the impact of nuclear waste disposal in one area on an area upwind or how carbon emissions in New York can impact polar bears in the Arctic.

A kindergartner jumps over puddles on the playground. She misjudges one and falls in with a splash. Cold and wet, she asks her teacher for her dry change of clothes. In warm, dry clothes, she resumes puddle jumping. Asked whether she is making a good choice, she responds with certainty, "I am not going to fall in again." She is learning to think about chance events and to balance those against her growing skills. Someday she may use this knowledge when judging whether to perform a delicate surgery.

A fifth grader watches two friends get in an argument. The conversation spirals out of control as each side escalates in their anger—saying things that they would never have said outside the context of the conflict. Recalling a recent lesson, he runs in to tell his teacher, "We have escalating causality and we need a cool down." Someday he might use this knowledge to help manage conflict between factions in a war-torn country.

A wealth of research in child development and education shows that children can think about different kinds of contingencies and causal patterns in their worlds. Infants in nurseries adjust their crying behaviors to the patterns of when certain nurses respond to them. If a nurse typically comes right away, they cry if she doesn't respond right away. However, if a different nurse responds more randomly, they hold off on crying. [5] Preschool children know that certain events lead to disorder, but that order involves an investment of energy. If the dog knocks everything off a table, they aren't surprised by the mess, but if everything magically goes back to its place, they are indeed surprised. [6]

However, for a variety of reasons—including tensions between efficiency and deep understanding, the ways that our minds handle massive amounts of stimuli, and familiar patterns that serve us well much of the time—we all tend to simplify and distort what is going on in the world. [7] If the world were simple, this might not matter. Simplifying a complex world can lead to misconceptions, misunderstandings, and mishaps!

It doesn't have to be this way. As the examples above illustrate, causality is a part of our everyday lives. Children have many opportunities to think about the nature of causality and to apply the principles to new learning. We can harness their implicit understanding and help children use it to build more sophisticated, explicit understandings—of their reasoning processes, of causal patterns, and of the complex world in which they live.

Currently, students seldom have opportunities to explicitly consider causal patterns and how they apply to the world. Research has documented numerous examples across the curriculum where students' inability to recognize the inherent causal patterns leads to misunderstandings and difficulties learning new concepts.[8] For over thirty years, researchers have studied the kinds of misconceptions or alternative ideas that students have in science, math, social studies, and beyond. Many of these are linked to how students structure the causal patterns embedded in the concepts.

But research shows that with support, students can learn to understand causal complexity.[9] My first foray into these ideas began in the late 1980s as a part of my own graduate studies. Since then, over years of research with K–12 students, in my work and that of my graduate students, we have seen significant gains in understanding science, understanding causality, and transferring these understandings beyond the topics taught.[10] In the past decade, a significant body of research has been growing to support the ideas here. Examples of this research are highlighted throughout this book.

The patterns presented below have important implications for learning science. I could have easily filled this book with hundreds of science examples, particularly the environmental sciences. However, the patterns are also highly relevant to other disciplines. We studied learning in biology and physics in our research, however, many of our collaborating teachers have taught their students to reason about causal complexity in social studies, language arts, health, and beyond.

Some causal patterns that we detect may depend upon our cultural context while others may stem from universal human patterns of perception. Those raised in an Asian culture are more likely to notice relational than strictly linear patterns.[11] Salish Kootenai students on the Flat Head Indian Reservation noticed cyclic patterns more readily than their age counterparts in Cambridge, Massachusetts.[12] This suggests the promise of malleability in which patterns we notice. Also, increasingly diverse classrooms will demand greater sensitivity on behalf of educators to how students structure their causal assumptions.

A CURRICULUM FOR TEACHING COMPLEX CAUSALITY

What does it mean to teach about complex causality? How would it change the curriculum and what causal concepts would it include? Below, I introduce a set of causal concepts—patterns and features—that are embedded in basic science concepts and in the science of complexity. My graduate students, our collaborating teachers, and I have focused on these to build deep understanding in science,[13] but also extended them to politics, economics, health, and so on. Though not the only ways of talking about causal complexity,[14] these had a powerful impact on students' understanding.[15]

This book has four parts. Part one discusses our tendency toward simple forms of causality and the emerging cognitive science that may explain its allure. Part two introduces a set of *causal patterns* that bring us beyond simple, linear causality. Part three introduces *features of causal complexity*. It considers default assumptions that we typically make about these features that can be in tension with noticing the complexity in our world. Part four summarizes and offers techniques and examples of how educators can address these causal patterns and features.

A Set of Causal Patterns

Six different causal patterns are introduced and contrasted: simple linear; domino; cyclic; escalating; mutual; and relational. The characteristics of each are previewed in Table 1 below and discussed in depth in part two. Consider, for instance, the causality involved when children are on a seesaw. Who goes up and who goes down depends upon the differential between their weight (assuming that they sit the same distance from the middle)—a relational form of causality. This causal pattern differs from a simple line of impact where one thing directly makes another happen.

The assumption of different types of causality departs significantly from how systems and complex causes are typically mapped. Usually "causal impact diagrams" are drawn with arrows to show the causal connections and direction of impact. Each arrow implies a causal force. Pluses or minuses accompany the arrows to signal amplification and dampening. Here, I am arguing that the essence of causality at each of those arrows can be very different and that in order to understand the world well, we need to understand how. The arrows in causal impact diagrams can gloss over these distinctions.

We used the patterns in Table 1 in our research in K–12 science classrooms. However, we didn't actually start with the patterns. We began with the science and what made it difficult for students to learn. We studied students' explanations for a range of science topics in physics and biology—simple circuits, force and motion, heat and temperature, density, air pressure, and ecosystems.

Repeatedly, students' explanations departed significantly in the underlying causal form from those of scientists—before, during, and after teaching. For each topic, we developed ways to understand the causality within the particular science concepts.[16] This set of patterns emerged with specific nuances in each of the science concepts. We also found transfer across concepts. For instance, students who studied the relational causality aspects of density performed significantly better on a preassessment on air pressure than students who did not.[17]

Teachers began asking about teaching the causal patterns separately and then applying them to the science. This question invokes a deep and significant debate in the study of learning. Are there generic thinking patterns that can be adapted to specific cases or is learning in each topic so nuanced that learning is necessarily context specific—what is called "situated learning"? There are intense and thoughtfully reasoned arguments on either side.

Further, the nature of the concept does not mandate how it is taught. As researchers Rich Lehrer and Leona Schauble have argued, the fact that a concept has wide application does not mean that reasoning about it is best taught "as a domain general form of reasoning encapsulated in a set of content-free, all purpose routines to be 'applied' as needed."[18]

As a teacher for fourteen years and then as a researcher in learning and cognition, I have worked from specific toward generalizeable patterns. However, I am not convinced that the dichotomization serves education well. I would not be content unless my students understood the nuanced characteristics of the concepts. Yet, I also aimed to help them gain generalizations about broader principles in the world. The continuum between the two is certainly to be respected and a thoughtful navigation between the poles is perhaps the most empowering educational tact in enabling deep and flexible understanding.

Noticing a broader set of patterns can help us recognize and attend to a more complex set of causal dynamics—ones that are often overlooked and where the essence of the causality is lost if it is reduced to simple linear causality. Without an explicit awareness of our tendency to reduce these patterns to simpler ones, we aren't likely to realize when we have done so. While all of these patterns can be reductionist in how they are applied, they also can help us to discern more complex dynamics as we reason about causal systems.

However, while it is important to recognize when the causal characteristics set forth in this book are present, I also believe that there is a danger in teaching these patterns as if they are *the* causal patterns. Offering initial patterns for students to reason about must be balanced against enabling emergent and organic structures to arise, lest the approach here become reductionist and not serve the purpose of reasoning about complex systems. Explanation in particular contexts captures aspects of the causal patterns and features here, but given situation-specific nuances cannot be reduced to these.[19]

Further, there are other ways to characterize patterns within causal concepts,[20] for example, as a set of constraints that one reasons within, such as how voltage, current, and resistance interact in a circuit—known as constraint-based reasoning. Or the archetypes in systems thinking that Peter Senge has written about, for instance, the "tragedy of the commons" when a resource is overused to the point where the benefits are lost by all. Or broader ways of characterizing a system, such as focusing on the structure, behavior, and function, as my colleague Cindy Hmelo-Silver employs in her work on biological systems.[21]

Features of Causal Complexity and Getting beyond Causal Default Assumptions

The book also introduces *features* of causality that are inherent to complex causality and that often are contrary to our default assumptions. Table 2 summarizes our simplifying assumptions along with a more complex pattern that it is typically in tension with. It offers examples of how each feature is important to learning. In parentheses, there is a simplified phrase for each—representing language used by the elementary and middle school students we've worked with.

It is important to keep in mind that the simplifying assumption is not always a bad choice. Sometimes it fits with what is going on. But at other times, we force fit a simpler pattern where it doesn't work and end up distorting the phenomenon.

In practice, the *causal patterns* and our assumptions about the *causal features* of a phenomenon work together in any given instance. For example, middle school students are expected to understand the concept of sinking and floating in terms of density. But they focus on the most obvious part of the problem, typically the weight of the object which can be directly perceived or felt. This reinforces a simple linear causal model and obscures the relational causality between the mass and the volume and between the density of the liquid and the object.

Each chapter in the third part takes an in-depth look at a default assumption and identifies causal features that we tend to miss. It illustrates how the assumption impacts our thinking across the curriculum and in everyday life. Suggestions are given for how to help students reframe their thinking for better learning and how to talk about the inherent causality.

This book is the result of the *Understandings of Consequence Project*, funded by the National Science Foundation (NSF).[22] It involved over a decade of research in schools—work that is ongoing with continued NSF support and related work funded by the Institute of Education Sciences (IES).[23] Many of the examples come from those classrooms and the efforts of collaborating teachers, administrators, and students. As often as possible, I include the students' voices to illustrate how these causal concepts come to life in the classroom to enrich learning across the curriculum.

In addition to the K–12 research, we have worked with preschoolers, have reviewed the causality research on infants, and investigated adult forms of reasoning. One of the scientists at a world-renowned institute for ecosystems study remarked that he had seen these default assumptions in many senior scientists, himself included! This book includes the many anecdotes that I have collected over the years to illustrate its points.

WHAT ABOUT THE STANDARDS?: TEACHING FOR TODAY AND TOMORROW

Even if the teaching of causal patterns really works, how can educators justify spending the time when they are accountable to the standards? A critical question at the outset of this work was whether it was possible to integrate the teaching of causality into the curriculum to teach for the future and still meet the current standards.

Our research in classrooms suggests that it is not an either/or proposition. To the contrary, students showed deeper understanding and increased performance across the curriculum. [24] We saw significant and substantive gains in student performance in classes where we taught the causal concepts in the context of the science curriculum in contrast to students learning the curriculum minus the causal concepts. These gains showed up on standardized tests as well as on supplementary tests given to probe for deeper understanding.

Equally encouraging were the stories that teachers and principals reported of students who returned from high school or college to talk about the difference that it had made for them. They talked about "learning to really think" and finding "those causal patterns everywhere, even in the supermarket and band practice!" When systematically interviewing students who had worked with us in earlier years, they had held onto their science gains and many reported similar life stories about the impact of their learning. [25]

Teaching causal complexity is not a curriculum just for advanced students. Some of the greatest gains were made by those students who had the furthest to go. [26] This fits with other research on the teaching of thinking and metacognition. [27] Unpacking how explanations are structured helped students who were least likely to discover this structure on their own.

In one teacher's words, "I was previewing material with my tutoring kids. I drew the sun at the top and they were able to correctly identify that the plants should go near the sun because they get energy from the sun. Next they put a row of primary consumers, a row of secondary consumers and then a row of decomposers. Then one of my girls who really struggles with anything academic says, 'Look, it's domino causality.' Another girl said, 'Yeah, it's not cyclic because it doesn't go back to the beginning.' I hadn't even asked them about causality. It was so amazing that these struggling students could really grasp what was going on because of the causality concepts that they have learned."

Adding anything to the curriculum is hard. Yet, these concepts are already implicit to understanding the curriculum that we have. Pulling them out to explicitly focus on them enhances the learning students already have to do and better prepares them for the future. We have the opportunity to help students learn to reframe their causal thinking within the context of the current curriculum. By extending their causal repertoire, we can empower them to understand their world better, choose more informed actions, and to be critical consumers of policy.

A side benefit to this endeavor is that it's possible that you will find causal default patterns and the related pitfalls that you, too, have fallen into. Thinking about the underlying causality may offer insights into the causal dynamics that you deal with and help you to choose actions that are sensitive to them. The examples can help you to envision the possibilities and to realize these benefits—from interactions in the staff room, making projections about the outcomes of curriculum decisions, to managing the noise in the cafeteria.

WHO IS THIS BOOK FOR?

The patterns put forth in this book are relevant to the general public and are about the actions that we choose in a complex world. It is relevant to the work that educators do every day. Finally, it holds relevance for the academic community as we further investigate what it means to reason well about causal complexity and how cognitive science can inform our efforts to do so.

The book speaks directly to educators—offering many examples of what teaching for complexity looks like in the classroom. This is because the broad reach of education is critical here. Children from all walks of life need ample opportunities to reflect upon their causal assumptions and to revise these as needed in their everyday interactions. Hopefully, parents will join this educational effort. I know firsthand, in my experiences with my own children, how causal patterns and language can become part of everyday life

Finally, a note to academics is in order. You will recognize the research here and the predominant discussions in causal reasoning in psychology and philosophy, such as Bayesian reasoning, co-variation, and causal mechanisms. I haven't greatly elaborated the academic debates here (and invite you to turn to other publications for the fuller academic argument).[28] Instead, I've attempted to make the best sense of what we now know in order to offer usable knowledge for educators today in service of tomorrow.

With the exception of chapter three, this book is decidedly less about the cognitive mechanisms that are behind our learning of causality than it is about the forms of causal complexity that we must learn. Those are deeply entangled questions, and as efforts on the cognitive mechanisms come to fruition, they will more fully explain the cognition involved in the patterns put forth here.

Table 1: A Curriculum for Teaching Causal Complexity: Six Causal Patterns

Simple Linear Causality	**Domino Causality**
• There is a beginning and an ending. • It is linear. • It works in one direction. • It includes only direct effects.	• There is a beginning and an ending. • It works in one direction. • It is linear but can have branching and radiating forms. • An effect can become a cause. • It entails direct and indirect effects. • Reducing it to simple cause and effect results in short-sighted predictions and/or unanticipated outcomes
Cyclic Causality	**Spiraling Causality**
• There may not be a discernable beginning or ending (unless the sustaining causes stop). • A cause can also be an effect and vice versa. • It is non-linear. • Reducing it to a line misses the inherent feedback that fuels the continuation. • There are sequential and simultaneous forms.	• There may not be a discernable beginning or ending (unless the sustaining causes stop). • A cause can also be an effect and vice versa. • It is non-linear. • Reducing it to a line misses the inherent feedback that fuels the continuation. • It is sequential and entails an increase or decrease in magnitude of effects with each turn of the cycle.
Mutual Causality	**Relational Causality**
• Typically, it entails one event, relationship, or process (differentiating it from Cyclic Causality). • There is a blurring of causes and effects in that each cause or causal agent is affected. • It is bi-directional. • It has a simultaneous quality. • Reducing it to simple cause and effect misses the bi-directional costs and benefits involved.	• The relationship between two variables accounts for the effect, typically one of balance or imbalance. • Shifts in the relationship can account for changes in the outcome. • Reducing it to simple cause and effect often is the result of ignoring the less salient variable in the relationship such that when the balance shifts, it can lead to surprising outcomes and faulty explanations.

Table 2: A Curriculum for Teaching Causal Complexity: Helping Students Move Beyond Simplifying Default Assumptions

Simplifying Assumption:	How does it work?	Reframing for Causal Complexity:	How the reframed version works ...	How we tend to get stuck ...
Simple Linear ("This Makes That Happen")	One thing makes another thing happen.	Extended or Nonlinear (Domino, Cyclic, Escalating, Mutual, or Relational Causality)	Causal patterns can be extended or nonlinear. They can include indirect or bi-directional effects.	We often adopt simple story-like patterns where one thing happens and causes something else. We miss patterns that are domino-like, cyclic as in a feedback loop, mutual as in symbiotic relationships, or relational where a relationship between two variables results in an outcome.
Event-based ("What Happened?")	Something has to happen in order for us to think about causality.	Steady State ("What's Going On?")	Systems in balance entail causal relationships even if nothing is happening at the moment.	Unless something is happening, we often don't think about the causal relationships in play. We tend to focus on the balance of forces that made a bridge stand only if it falls down. Similarly we tend to realize what forces sustained a government once it collapses.
Sequential ("Step by Step")	Causes always come before effects in a step-by-step pattern.	Simultaneous ("All at Once")	Causes and effects can co-occur in time and still have a causal relationship.	We expect that causes have to occur before effects in our explanations even when it doesn't fit the phenomenon. Gears all turn at once even though one causes another to turn.
Obvious Variables or Mechanisms ("Easy to Notice Causes and Effects")	Some causes can be directly perceived.	Non-obvious Variables or Mechanisms ("Hard to Notice Causes and Effects")	Some causes are non-obvious because they are microscopic, imperceptible, or inferred.	We focus on obvious causes instead of non-obvious ones unless there is no obvious cause to be discerned. Students are more likely to report worms as decomposers than microbes. We don't think about air pressure as the cause of earaches on planes unless we have been told to. We do reason about inferred causes such as intentions in social situations, but we reason in more complex ways about ourselves than others.

Table 2: A Curriculum for Teaching Causal Complexity: Helping Students Move Beyond Simplifying Default Assumptions

Active or Intentional Agents ("Someone Did It" and "On Purpose")	Many cause-and-effect relationships involve an actor who intends a certain outcome. Many actions have a purpose or intent.	Passive or Unintentional Agents ("No One Did It" and "By Accident" or "Didn't Mean To")	Some causal relationships don't involve action or intentionality to work. Or actors and their intentions may not correspond with effects arising at another level.	We tend to look for who made something happen and assume active and intentional agents. Seatbelts, a passive restraint system, keep us in the car when it stops without actively doing anything. Electrons are active and protons are passive, yet outcomes are caused by their attraction, not one or the other. We drive our cars intending to get somewhere, not intending to contribute to global warming. We refer to "Mother Nature" to assign agency to natural occurrences.
Deterministic ("It's Always Supposed to Work")	An effect always follows a given cause.	Probabilistic ("It Usually Works")	An effect sometimes follows a given cause.	In part, we judge whether a causal relationship exists by how reliably the effect follows the cause. While we sum across instances, allowing for some unreliability, probabilistic causes make it harder to notice and attend to causal patterns. It also can lead to risk taking. We might think, "I did it before and I didn't get sick, so I'm not going to get sick now," instead of, "Even if I didn't get sick before, I can still get sick now." Overreliance on correlation can lead to assuming that relationships are causal so that we don't seek out other possible causes.
Spatially and Temporally Close ("Local Causes and Effects" and "Immediate Causes and Effects")	Causes and effects physically touch each other or are close to each other in space and time.	Spatially and Temporally Distant or Delayed ("Distant Causes and Effects" and "Slow" or "Delayed Causes and Effects")	Causes can act at a distance and there can be delays between causes and effects. Sometimes effects need to accumulate to a certain level to be noticeable or they must reach a trigger point before which there is no effect.	We often limit our search for causes and effects to those that are close together in space and time. Thus we miss more distant causes of events. We also don't attend to effects that are at an attentional distance, for instance, we don't think about impacting polar bears when we drive to work. We misunderstand events in the Middle East because we view them in too brief a time span. Teens think, "I can't see any bad effects of getting a suntan right now," instead of, "The hurtful effects of getting a suntan accumulate and show up after a long delay between cause and effect."

Table 2: A Curriculum for Teaching Causal Complexity: Helping Students Move Beyond Simplifying Default Assumptions

Centralized and Direct ("Someone's in Charge")	A central figure or leader causes (and typically intends) the outcome.	Distributed and Emergent ("No One's in Charge")	Individuals interacting give rise to an emergent effect where the intent of the individuals may not align with the higher level outcome.	We tend to focus on centralized causes and don't attend enough to the power of distributed causality. So we think that government institutions and leaders rather than our individual, daily civilized actions give rise to a civilization. Or we wait for our leaders to enact legislation to combat global warming rather than changing our individual actions to contribute to the emergent solution.

NOTES

1. The Energy Policy Act of 2005
2. Scott, 2002
3. Dorner, 1989
4. Progressive Education in the 1940s, available: http://www.youtube.com/watch?v=opXKmwg8VQM[accessed 7-1-2011].
5. Sander, 1975
6. Friedman, 2001
7. Feltovich, Spiro & Coulson, 1993; Grotzer, 2004
8. e.g., AAAS, 1993; Driver, Guesne & Tiberghien, 1985.
9. e.g., Grotzer & Basca, 2003; Levy & Wilensky, 2008; Perkins & Grotzer, 2005; Wilensky & Resnick, 1999.
10. See Grotzer, 2000; Grotzer & Basca, 2003; Houghton et al.; 2000; Perkins & Grotzer, 2005; Grotzer, 2009
11. Nisbett et al., 2001
12. Honey & Grotzer, 2008
13. There has been considerable discussion in the academic literature by those who study learning as to whether processes of thinking are situation specific or whether there is value to teaching generic forms. The patterns presented in this work emerged both from the science, thus situation specific, and from general patterns of reasoning, the observation by Driver and colleagues that we tend to be linear in our scientific reasoning, for instance. The stance here is that dichotomizing learning between situation-specific and generic forms is not helpful and that moving on a continuum between the two enables the most flexible and adaptive learners.
14. For instance, work in Systems Thinking by the members of the Creative Learning Exchange; in Systems Archetypes by Peter Senge and colleagues, and work on reasoning about systems using a Structure-Behavior-Function approach by Cindy Hmelo-Silver, Ashok Goel, and colleagues.
15. See research reviews available at: http://www.pz.harvard.edu/ucp/causalpatternsinscience/
16. This work resulted in the "Causal Patterns in Science" curriculum series and teacher professional- development website. It can be accessed at: http://www.pz.harvard.edu/ucp/causalpatternsinscience/
17. Grotzer, 2005

18. Lehrer & Schauble, 2004; Feltovich, Spiro & Coulson (1989) have argued that presenting fuzzy, ill-structured cases such that students discern and abstract them from the nuanced contexts enables more robust, transferable concepts than "sanitized, simplified" descriptions.

19. For an example that overlaps with the patterns here and involves additional nuance, see Walker and Salt (2006), which focuses on causal dynamics in ecosystems science.

20. Other ways of characterizing causal concepts includes references to types such as resistive, facilitative, etc. (Brown, 1995); using Aristotle's four causes (Raia, 2008); focusing on additive and multiplicative causes (e.g., Kun, Parsons & Ruble, 1974); how we reason about multiple sufficient of necessary causes (e.g., Kuhn & Angelev, 1977); and so on.

21. e.g., Hmelo-Silver, Marathe & Liu, 2007; Liu & Hmelo-Silver, 2009

22. This work was supported in part by Grant No. REC-9725502 and REC-0106988 from the National Science Foundation to Tina Grotzer and David Perkins and #ESI-0455664 to Tina Grotzer for the Understandings of Consequence Project. Any opinions, findings, conclusions, or recommendations are those of the authors and do not necessarily reflect the views of the National Science Foundation.

23. Causal Learning in the Classroom Studies supported by Grant No. NSF-0845632 from the National Science Foundation to Tina Grotzer; EcoMUVE Project supported by the Institute of Education Sciences, U.S. Department of Education, Grant No. R305A080514 to Chris Dede and Tina Grotzer; and EcoMOBILE Project supported by Grant No. NSF-1118530 to Chris Dede and Tina Grotzer. Any opinions, findings, conclusions, or recommendations are those of the author and do not necessarily reflect the views of the National Science Foundation or the Institute for Education Sciences.

24. e.g., Grotzer, 2000; Grotzer & Basca, 2003; Perkins & Grotzer, 2005

25. Grotzer, 2005

26. Grotzer, 2000, Grotzer & Sudbury, 2000; Perkins & Grotzer, 2005

27. White & Frederiksen, 1998, 2000; Zohar & Peled, 2008

28. Grotzer, 2003; Grotzer, Miller & Lincoln, 2011; Grotzer & Tutwiler (forthcoming)

Part 1: The Lure of Simple Causality

We think about cause and effect every day—it is an implicit part of our lives. It is essential to having a sense that we understand and have some control over our worlds. This section considers the simple linear causality that we so commonly employ. It serves as a point of comparison as other patterns are explained in part two. It then go on to consider what cognitive science currently suggests about why we tend toward simple linear causality. This is an evolving story, but presents what we currently know from a range of literature to help us think about what that means for our actions today.

Chapter Two

Simple Linear Causality: One Thing Makes Another Happen

"For every problem, there's a simple explanation . . ."

"There must be a simple solution."

The home team just lost the play-off game? It must be the lack of depth in the pitching rotation. The cafeteria is too noisy? The students must be ignoring the rules about using "inside voices." The traffic this morning was bumper to bumper for miles? It must have been that accident off to the side.

WHAT IS SIMPLE LINEAR CAUSALITY?

Often, our explanations take on a simple linear form of "this made that happen." In cases of simple linear causality:

- The pattern of cause and effect works in one direction.
- Cause precedes effect; there is a sequential pattern.
- There is a direct link between cause and effect.
- There is a clear beginning and a clear end.
- The effect can be traced back to one cause.
- There is only one cause and one effect; extended causes or effects turn this pattern into domino causality (to be discussed in chapter four).

Simple linear explanations follow three basic principles that, historically, researchers argued fit with our conceptions of causality—both those of children and adults.[1] The first principle is temporal priority—that a cause precedes an effect. The second principle presumes a mechanism—that some entity or process accounts for the outcome. The third principle assumes that when something happens, a cause exists (determinism). These principles stem from the work of David Hume.[2]

It appears that we learn simple causality from our earliest days. As babies, we find out that *we* can make things happen—batting at a toy makes a sound, crying gets mom to come, and sucking on a bottle makes milk come out.[3] Intensified efforts are often matched by intensified outcomes—the harder we bat, the louder the sound. Through a combination of intervention and observation, babies learn a lot about the causal patterns around them.[4] As babies, we learn that we can act as agents in our world; we can make things happen and it is very empowering.

Attending to our own agency invites us to notice what we can directly manipulate and instances where the impacts are directly observable. The infant may know that mom came with a bottle, but is entirely unaware of the broader sequence of events that his or her cry set in motion—the mixing of formula, warming of the bottle, finding something to entertain a slightly older sibling, and so forth.

It also focuses our attention on the causal power of our behaviors without making salient the causal power of other factors. For instance, being able to suck milk from a bottle also depends upon the nonobvious causal factor of ambient air pressure, but babies have no way to grasp this aspect of the causal system. (However, many a frustrated parent has grappled with the balance of air pressure needed to get the liquid out of the bottle without having baby sucking only air!)

The information available to infants is decidedly limited. Even looking beyond one's own agency, an infant often isn't in a physical position to observe extended and complex effects. Simple cause and effect and a focus on one's own agency are some of our earliest forms of understanding the world and are very well ingrained.

SIMPLE LINEAR CAUSALITY IMPACTS
LEARNING IN THE CLASSROOM

Research in science education suggests how robust these early understandings are. Researchers have studied the difficulties that students have in reasoning about many science concepts and how their intuitive ideas differ from the scientifically accepted explanations. A wide range of topics has been studied, from air pressure,[5] heat and temperature,[6] electrical circuits,[7] force and motion,[8] to microscopic, nonobvious variables such as the role of microbes in decomposition.[9]

Three decades of research on how students struggle to deeply understand science concepts show that a big part of the problem relates to how students structure their explanations in science.[10] Extensive work investigating children's ideas, spearheaded largely by Rosalind Driver and her colleagues at the University of Leeds, including John Leach, Phil Scott, Colin Wood-Robinson and others, found that simple notions of cause and effect were often at the core of students' struggles.[11] Students employ these ideas in everyday science and in the science of complexity, including reasoning about emergence and self-organizing systems.[12]

In the *Understandings of Consequence Project*, we interviewed third through eleventh graders before, during, and after they were taught different science concepts. Most of their explanations took on a simple linear causal form even when the science concepts represented a different causal structure. Students said things like "the power goes from the battery to the bulb to make it light" and "the weight makes it sink." Often the explanations were agency oriented as in "I suck on the straw to make the juice come up."

From a scientific perspective, each of these cases requires a shift away from a simple linear causality in order to reach deep understanding of the concepts. The very words "cause" and "effect" can fail to capture the essence of what is going on.[13]

What might be involved in such a shift? Envision a line of dominoes. As the first one falls over, it causes the second in line to fall—an effect. The effect in turn acts as a cause as it hits the third one and then that falls over, and so on down the line. Already, we've moved beyond the simple idea of cause and effect where one thing makes another thing happen. Suddenly effects have in turn become causes. This minor shift to "domino causality" requires a big shift in our thinking about the nature of causes and effects.

Domino causality is only one example of a causal pattern that extends beyond simple cause and effect. It isn't all *that* different because it is still linear or "chain-like." But there are plenty of patterns that are quite different. Popular culture offers examples. For instance, in the saying, "What goes around comes around," there is a distinct cyclic causal pattern. "It's a win-win situation," embeds a two-way or mutually beneficial causal pattern. Clearly, we can recognize and attend to different kinds of causal patterns and they occupy an implicit place in our language and culture.

I do not mean to imply that simple linear causality never fits. Sometimes it describes the pattern of causal interaction and, at other times, it meets our needs at the moment. If I need to turn on the lights, I flip the switch, the lights come on, and that's all I need to think about. I don't need to think about the cyclic pattern of the circuit unless there is a problem.

But, at other times, our causal expectations are too simple to capture the dynamics of the causal system. Years ago, I was working with a group of four hundred students and their parents and flipped the light switch to signal the end of a group activity session. The school building was old, with sodium vapor lights that only come up to full brightness after a delay of a few minutes. While we all sat in the semidarkness, I had a moment to recall and make sense of the fleeting look of concern on the face of Al, the custodian, as he saw me heading for the lights and realized what I was about to do.

A teacher colleague of mine from long ago, Cope Craven, would quote Mencken, "For every problem, there's a simple explanation . . ." to which she would add, "And very often it's wrong." As we explore new ways of characterizing causal patterns in part two, we'll see why sometimes simple is just too simple and can't really capture the complexity of why the home team lost, the noise in the cafeteria, or the traffic jam on the highway. The remainder of this section takes a deeper look at why, from a cognitive science perspective, simple causality is so alluring and difficult to part with, even when we know that we should.

NOTES

1. Bullock, Gelman & Baillargeon, 1982; Huang, 1943. This is not to imply that these were the only principles characterizing causal reasoning. For instance, Koslowski and Okagaki (1986) found that adults take into account other forms of information relating to causal mechanism, analogous effects, and the status of potential rival causes as well.

2. Hume, 1739–1740

3. Andersson, 1986

4. Sommerville, 2007; Sommerville & Woodward, 2005

5. e.g., Engel Clough & Driver, 1985

6. e.g., Erickson & Tiberghien, 1985; Wiser & Carey, 1983

7. e.g., Fredette & Lockhead, 1980; Shipstone, 1984, 1985

8. e.g., Clement, 1982

9. e.g., Leach et al., 1992

10. A number of theories have been put forth about why students struggle with these concepts. Some focus on unsystematic assumptions that people make (diSessa, 1993). Others focus on confusions in how to treat certain concepts, treating processes as matter, for instance, (Chi, e.g., 1997) and on systematic assumptions in how people structure the underlying causality (e.g., Perkins & Grotzer, 2005). We believe that the multiple sources of difficulty exist and that different types of difficulties can be captured in part or in whole by the various theories. DiSessa (2006) summarized much of this work in his review of the misconceptions research in relation to conceptual change and the interested reader is referred to his thoughtful review and analysis.

11. Driver, Guesne & Tiberghien, 1985; Driver et al., 1993; Grotzer, 1989, 1993, 2000; Perkins & Grotzer, 2005

12. Grotzer, 2004; Grotzer & Basca, 2003; Raia, 2008; Perkins & Grotzer, 2005. This fits with other findings in the field, including the research of Carol Smith and colleagues (e.g., Smith, Carey & Wiser, 1985) on density, Shipstone (1984, 1985) on electricity, and Engel Clough and Driver (1985) on air pressure.

13. Basca & Grotzer, 2002; Grotzer, 2004; Grotzer & Basca, 2003

Chapter Three

The Cognitive Science of Simple Causality: Why Do We Get Stuck?

"I was so focused on what I was doing that I didn't even notice the storm developing outside."

"I really thought I could control the outcomes, I put all of my effort into this."

"We had done it three times before with no ill effects— it should have been fine, but on the fourth time, wham!"

So if simple forms of causality can get us into so much trouble, why do we fall into them so easily and find them so hard to leave behind? There are a number of features that contribute to their allure. Each of the causal patterns in part two and the default assumptions in part three have features that fit with patterns of human perception—pulling against our ability to reason well about complexity. Before moving on to those sections, I step back to take a deeper look at the cognitive science behind our everyday causal reasoning and what it tells us about how and why we get stuck simplifying complexity.

Some of the points in this chapter are slightly more technical than in other chapters. I have aimed to make the discussion here accessible whether or not one has a background in the material. Those who are less interested in the deeper cognitive science story might want to review the tendencies below and then move on to the next section.

In terms of human perception and cognition, there are a number of principles that guide our everyday causal learning. These principles lend insight into how we end up simplifying causality:

• Agency—making things happen and watching others make things happen—offers some of our most powerful learning experiences.

- We sum across our experiences to notice patterns or correlations between events.
- We seek out plausible mechanisms to explain the patterns that we notice. [1]
- Our attention is necessarily selective. We cannot take in all of the information in our environments. We must filter some out.
- We tend toward efficiency—impacting what we notice and where we draw boundaries. Extended searches are beyond what we attend to in space and time.
- Patterns that are meaningful are more likely to be noticed.
- We default toward "well-traveled" patterns. This invites a reinforcing quality to the patterns that we detect.

In the paragraphs below, I elaborate on each of these tendencies. Then, in the rest of this book, I aim to convince you that learning about the nature of causality can be a broader enterprise than our everyday causal learning enables. We can use our higher-order reflective processes to become familiar with and learn to detect new patterns and features—at least more often than we typically do now.

AGENCY IS A POWERFUL CONCEPT

As introduced in chapter two, we learn the power of causal agency from our earliest days. As babies in our cribs, we find out that *we* can make things happen—we get milk from bottles, make mom appear, and make sounds shaking rattles. [2] These simple, agency-oriented schemas are some of our earliest forms of understanding the world and can lead to empowering experiences. According to Susan Carey, a well-known cognitive and developmental scientist, attending to agency is a core aspect of human cognition. [3]

A significant body of research in the early causal learning literature focuses on the role of agency in how infants and preschoolers understand causal relationships. It shows that babies learn from their ability to carry out actions—to be an agent—in the most special ways. The ability to intervene and see what happens is a powerful part of learning. [4] If an effect is tied to our own actions, we are more likely to notice it than ones tied to someone else's effort or to effects that are not the result of an intentional being (such as air pressure!). It lends a sense of control over the world.

Babies also learn from watching the actions of others. [5] Abundant research shows that imitation is a powerful learning mechanism. Few parents would disagree—as the saying "monkey see, monkey do" brings to mind. According to Andrew Meltzoff, known for his ingenious studies of imitation, "the perception and production of acts is built into the mind of the human baby." [6]

When he had babies watch others perform novel acts (such as turning on a machine with their head), they were more likely to perform the act compared to babies in a control group.

Interestingly, it is not just that babies learn to do what others do. They pay special attention to the intentions of others. Meltzoff writes that they develop an "agentive framework involving intentions and goals." As early as six months old,[7] they attend more to behaviors that offer information about an actor's goals than to other behaviors.[8] These abilities become increasingly elaborate and textured.[9] In one study, Meltzoff had infants observe an adult trying to yank a small dumbbell in two, but failing. When given the dumbbell, babies did what the adult intended instead of imitating what s/he actually did.

However, even though babies learn from the agency of others, their own actions lead to the strongest[10] and most accurate causal learning.[11] Meltzoff had two groups of infants watch an experimenter manipulate novel objects, but one group of babies was also given the opportunity to manipulate the objects—which nearly all of them did. The next day, both groups were given the objects. Babies who had a chance to previously manipulate the objects imitated more of the acts than the babies who had not.[12] Our own experiences may allow us to better understand and map the experiences of others.[13]

So agency—the ability to engage in an action with the goal of an outcome—clearly holds a special place in the learning repertoire of babies. The kinds of actions that they can engage in are more limited than those of older children or adults: batting a toy; crying for food; and so on. These actions have many of the features of simple linear causality and can result in empowering and reinforcing outcomes.[14]

Prioritizing agency as a causal schema can be limiting depending upon the context. Many forms of complex causality do not involve an actor (such as a bridge that falls) or do not involve intentionality at the level of the outcomes (such as when distributed actors contribute to climate change, when they are only intending to drive to work). Some researchers describe a fully causal view as understanding that there can be natural causes that are not agent-like.[15]

Nonagentive causes do not seem to have a place in the infant's causal repertoire. According to Meltzoff, infants "draw limited inferences when no causal agent is present," referring particularly to a human causal agent.[16] When changes are revealed, but no agent is shown as the potential cause of the change, babies do not imitate the manipulations.[17] However, when a person tries to change an object, babies infer and produce the change.

The critical role of intention and intentionality in early causal learning invites reflection. What may be highly adaptive as an infant for getting one's needs met, may be less so later in life and in broader contexts. Whether it has an *enduring* privileged role in our causal reasoning repertoire is a question for empirical research. Evidence from science learning research, as discussed in chapter twelve, suggests that it does.[18] This is not surprising. Consider how often we assign agency to nonagentive causes, for instance, referring to "Mother Nature," or "the wind's fury."

Agency is also emotionally compelling. Following the terrorist attacks in the United States on September 11, 2001, it was appealing to think that the country could take swift action and return to an age of relatively greater innocence—"happily ever after time!," quoting Mr. Rogers. It appealed to the idea that we could have direct control over the kind of world that we live in.

SUMMING ACROSS OUR EXPERIENCES

Human beings are sense makers. We notice patterns in our world and use these in our reasoning. How we "make sense" is an ongoing topic of debate in psychology, cognitive science, philosophy, and the history of science. Part of the puzzle is how we can arrive at conclusions about our world inductively—using evidence to support conclusions when further evidence can contradict these conclusions. The prevailing discussions in psychology and cognitive science consider whether we use Bayesian reasoning mechanisms to sum across instances and what this implies for our causal reasoning.[19]

What does it mean to be Bayesian in summing across instances to find patterns? Imagine that you find yourself in a new world. You wake up early and the sky is getting brighter. This happens day after day and you begin to notice a pattern like the one that we call "sunrise" here on Earth. On the fifth morning, the sky is gray and doesn't brighten. On the sixth day, it brightens again. Summing across those instances, you develop an implicit expectation that the sky brightens in the morning.

This is a very simplified example of how one aspect of Bayesian reasoning—summing across probabilistic events—leads to a set of assumptions about the world. Those who study Causal Bayes Nets (CBN) reasoning make a few other assumptions which I consider below.

Notice that there is a statistical aspect to this process. We notice patterns of conditional probability between events, in this case, morning and a brightening sky. How probabilistic those events are and the nature of the probability can vary with context. In New England, the weather can vary greatly from one day to the next or you might have five days of gray before the sun breaks out again. However, humans adjust to discern the broader patterns and its exceptions. If one morning it was completely dark, as in a solar eclipse, you would view it as a departure from normal.

Considerable research suggests that children use information on how events co-vary in their causal reasoning, but that they also use other information, such as how close together events are in space and time.[20] (They also use information about plausible mechanisms as discussed below.)[21] Recent research suggests that even the youngest children follow Bayesian rules in summing across their experiences.[22] Alison Gopnik and her colleagues argue that young children can override imperfect correlation and are able to use different patterns of probability in contiguity to make accurate causal inferences.[23]

But the sunrise patterns above are those of correlation, not causation. Just because two things happen in space and time together does not make them causally linked. Relying only on patterns of correlation can get us into trouble. Usually we don't stop there (though occasionally we do); instead we call upon other tendencies in our causal reasoning repertoire.[24] Research shows that, fortuitously, humans tend to look beyond mere correlation in at least two ways, first, by intervening when possible and, second, by seeking explanatory mechanisms.

THE POWER OF INTERVENTION

Correlation can suggest the possibility of a causal connection, but it still does not tell you that one thing causes the other. A radio program recently advised that all medical students should receive piano training because it was found that a number of the best surgeons were excellent piano players. Here, a third variable, likely adept fingers, may well have been the hidden cause.[25]

Algebra was considered the "gateway to college" when it was found that students who took algebra in eighth grade were more likely to go to college.[26] It is enticing to conclude that promoting an algebra course in middle school would increase college admissions, yet other factors, such as invested parents, selection of college-track courses, and so on, are likely causal contributors to the outcome.

This is where intervention becomes important. In addition to noticing patterns of conditional probability between events, like the infants discussed above, intervening can help us to see what happens with different manipulations.

Let's look at an example. For instance, if we think that staying up late results in feeling groggy the next day, but we only stay up late when we watch the news, we can stay up late without watching the news and see how we feel the next day. We can also watch the news at other times during the day and see how we feel. We may learn that the news *or* staying up late *or* watching the news just before we turn in causes our grogginess. This type of reasoning is similar in some ways to formal controlled studies in science.

Causal Bayes Nets researchers investigate how we go beyond summing across experiences and intervene upon and partition off certain variables to assess their impact. This research suggests that we readily detect causal structure by intervening[27] and that this allows us to disambiguate causes.[28] It suggests that we "screen off" or partition the impacts of particular variables by seeing what happens if we hold certain ones constant or cancel them out, for instance, staying up late but not watching the news.

Researchers Alison Gopnik, Laura Schulz, Dave Sobel, Tamar Kushnir, and colleagues have shown that preschoolers are able to intervene to figure out the causal structure of problems with limited numbers of variables. They were able to do so both in deterministic contexts where the outcome always followed the cause[29] and in probabilistic contexts where the outcome often but not always followed the cause.[30] In one experiment, preschoolers were able to partition off which fake flowers "made" a stuffed monkey sneeze and which did not, by intervening to remove certain flowers and observing the outcome.[31]

Intervention doesn't just refer to our own actions, it can refer to those of others and to changes wrought by nature.[32] It is this broader construal that researchers in development of causal learning tend to employ. As the research above makes clear, we learn causal structure from observing interventions in the world. However, as suggested above, non-agent-oriented outcomes are unlikely to gain our attention as much as agent-oriented ones.

Further, intervening effectively in a complex world is a nearly impossible thing to do. Causal Bayes Nets theories may explain how we meet with a fair amount of success in everyday causal reasoning, but when causality becomes complex, problems arise. The problems are not necessarily with the theory. Indeed, the theory may explain why we struggle with complexity as we do.[33]

The Causal Bayesian Net theory assumes acyclic patterns and the independence of the variables except for their direct and indirect effects.[34] The real world is far more complex. Causal Bayes Net theory does not attempt to address a number of the kinds of causal patterns presented in part two. The later chapters draw upon the more extensive preexisting body of research in causal reasoning, in addition to the current Bayesian approaches, in order to consider how we reason about nonlinear, extended causal patterns and their complexifying features.

One of the essential puzzles for Causal Bayes Net theories is to explain the ontological problem—how we get from a messy, complex world to a set of meaningful variables to reason about. It asks, "How do we know what to attend to in the first place from the wealth of stimulation coming our way?" Indeed, the ontological problem poses quite a challenge. CBN researchers admit that it is one of the hardest to teach and learn and, in some studies, assume that it is solved and give the variables to the subjects.[35] Later in this chapter, I consider the problem of how we allocate attention in a complex world.

The Causal Bayes Net research tends to focus on the strong case of when we know the value of the variables—when we can measure how much we drank, the temperature of a room, what time we went to bed, etc. In everyday causal reasoning, we often do not have such information available to us and when we do, we are notoriously bad at incorporating it into evaluating interventions.[36] Even with considerable statistical information about the likelihood of an event, we tend to override it with other kinds of information— powerful images, personal experiences, and narratives that tap into our affect and impact reasoning.[37]

When causality extends beyond direct causal inference, the problems with effective intervention are exacerbated. With so many possible variables and possible interactions between them, discerning the causal relationships becomes overwhelming very quickly. The unaided human mind in everyday contexts is unlikely to be able to effectively intervene and build effective causal models of such complexity.

This may indeed explain why we override this information with narratives that are motivated by affect.[38] It may well be adaptive to do so.[39] Our brain structures evolved to prioritize certain events and once our amygdala gets our most immediate and basic emotions into the act, the neocortex may not have a chance to get beyond what the amygdala signals to be important![40]

As we are summing across instances in our everyday world and attempting to intervene to assess causal connections, the information available to us, what we attend to, and what we are able to hold in mind to reason about is fairly limited. Except for what is enabled by media and technology, most of the information is local and immediate. Not unlike the baby in the crib, this may limit the reach of our causal models and our recognition of the inadequacy of those we hold.

SEEKING OUT PLAUSIBLE MECHANISMS

Many everyday patterns are not so easily manipulated and come to us as observations, not personal experiences. Here's where seeking out plausible mechanisms becomes so important. An abundance of research shows that we seek out and use information about plausible mechanisms in our causal reasoning.[41] Reflect on the following two statements and consider how you reason about each:

"There is a high correlation between ice cream consumption and obesity."

"There is a high correlation between ice cream consumption and drowning."

Were there any differences in how you analyzed each statement? If you are like most people, you accepted the first statement with less reflection than the second. Many of us assume that a high-fat dessert can directly lead to obesity. However, most people find themselves mentally searching for a plausible explanation or *mechanism* to account for the outcome in the second statement. Mechanisms may be physical, behavioral, or mental. Intentions, forces, and mechanical devices are all examples of mechanisms.

Even children realize that mechanisms must exist.[42] They claim that seemingly uncaused events require explanation, even if they aren't able to specify the details[43] and they search for mechanisms when one is not apparent.[44] When told that two objects move together because of a hidden string, but no string could be found, like adults, four- and five-year-olds looked for another cause or accused the experimenter of playing a trick.[45] Gopnik and colleagues found that most four-year-olds posited an unobserved causal mechanism when asked why two puppets moved together and there was no obvious causal mechanism.[46]

If young children's knowledge does not afford an explanation, they may resort to "it had to be magic," particularly in cases of physical effects.[47] Paul Harris argues that this makes sense; that often phenomena cannot be understood by considering only outer physical structure—we must assume that the outward structure of events can be explained by invoking an invisible set of hidden processes that lack any known physical embodiment. He writes, "It is plausible to suppose that magical thinking is part of a wider disposition to invoke a hidden causal structure beneath the surface appearance of a phenomenon."[48]

One of the prevalent views in the literature argues that we use knowledge of types of mechanisms to reason about causality and that we amass considerable knowledge about types of causes, causal force of particular mechanisms, and situation-specific details about where this information applies.[49] Children learn about things like remote controls, telephones, and so on and use this knowledge to reason about causality in particular instances. As we shall see in part three, mechanism knowledge can be an especially important part of our causal repertoire when reasoning about causal complexity.

The tendency to seek mechanisms and to amass knowledge about types of mechanisms makes it less likely that we will mistake a mere correlation for a causal relationship. If no plausible causal mechanism can be found between two events, we may discount the relationship and consider it merely a coincidence. Or lack of a plausible mechanism may signal that we need to search for a non-obvious one as discussed in chapter eleven.

Clearly, from an early age, humans appreciate the need for a causal mechanism. We realize that some causal mechanisms can't be seen and will search for mechanisms that aren't visible. Problems can arise, however, when, a plausible mechanism is readily available and we constrain our search as discussed below without considering alternatives or multiple possible causes. How extensively we search is considered further next.

SELECTIVE ATTENTION AND THE DUAL-EDGED SWORD OF EFFICIENCY

The research on how we allocate our attention clearly shows that in our everyday lives, we tend toward efficiency. Our attention is necessarily selective. We filter out a lot of information as extraneous in just about every situation. We need to be selective or the world would be overwhelming. [50]

However, this selective process also has its costs. A growing body of research referred to as "inattentional blindness" shows that we miss information that we are not expecting, particularly when we are cognitively busy. [51] This runs contrary to our sense of what we perceive. While we might be willing to admit that we don't take in everything, most people are surprised when they find out how much they miss. Research in visual perception reveals that most of us miss subtle changes, such as those in movies including clothing changes, item brands, hair styles, even mid-scene changes to who is in the background. [52]

In 1996 Warner Bros. released an Arnold Schwarzenegger movie called *Eraser*. Days prior to its release, they learned that they had named the evil corporation in the film close enough to that of a real corporation to raise the threat of a lawsuit. So they sent the film out to numerous production houses to have it digitally altered postproduction—what folks in the industry referred to as "getting a really big eraser." All of the scenes containing the name were modified. It was on things like swinging glass doors, so fixing the problem was complicated. But most of us would never detect any oddities in the film. [53]

How our cognitive energy is focused makes a difference in what we notice. Researchers Daniel Simons and Daniel Levin did an experiment in which they had someone approach another person to ask directions. While the subject was giving directions, two "rude" door movers came by and walked in between them, at which point the direction asker was switched with a new person similarly dressed and different (though not dramatically so) in appearance. Half of direction givers missed the switch. [54]

The information that we miss is not always subtle. Daniel Simons popularized "The Gorilla Video." In it, two teams, one in white shirts, the other in black shirts, are passing a ball. Observers are asked to count the number of times that the white team passes the ball. This focuses them on noticing white shirts at the expense of noticing dark objects. Part way into the video, a large person in a gorilla suit walks across the screen, beats its chest, and walks out of view. Viewers often miss the gorilla, particularly those who do the best job counting the number of ball passes. Their cognitive attention was elsewhere.

One could argue that none of this is meaningful information to the viewer. It doesn't really matter what actors wear, the scenery looks like, the physical features of a person asking directions, or even if a man in a gorilla suit beats his chest in the middle of a scene. There may be no reason for this information to draw the focus of the viewer. However, this can also be so when considering information relevant to important causal structures. If we don't know what the problem parameters are, we might well filter out information that could be relevant.

Prey to factors of time and efficiency, we tend to choose models that "satisfice." We adopt a default strategy of efficiency—it simply isn't efficient in most instances to do an extended, unbounded search. Adults resort to automatic, less thoughtful causal processing when they are "cognitively busy."[55] We may just need a workable solution that doesn't have to be elegant or the most correct. This doesn't account for every case where we miss causal complexity (given research showing that students sometimes explicitly reject extended indirect effects when asked about them[56]) but efficiency clearly has its costs.

Figuring out what information is relevant to a given situation—the "ontological problem"—determines what we attend to, and what we don't, in our causal reasoning. As we learn about different types of causal mechanisms, we gain important information that helps us to know how to allocate our attention. Frank Keil and colleagues have argued that it helps us to constrain, in a meaningful, theory-based way, the data that we bring in and how we filter what we attend to.[57] However, as discussed next, we limit the information that we bring in well before we are aware that we are doing so, thus we may not seek mechanisms to explain complex phenomena that we are unaware of.

PERCEPTION AND ATTENTION ARE NOT THE SAME THING

Picture yourself walking down a crowded street. Focused on where you are headed, you walk past a sea of faces. Suddenly, a face breaks into your awareness, and you realize that the face is that of an old friend. You have just experienced what researchers call "attentional capture."[58] Your attention was captured by features of your friend's face and led to the explicit recognition that this is someone whom you know. But in order for that to happen, you must have been processing that sea of faces at some level of unconscious awareness.

This experience fits with the findings of research on what captures our attention. It is clear from this research that the relationship between perception and attention is anything but straightforward. Most of us believe that we perceive something and then give it our attention. We tend to think of attention as intentional.[59]

However, researchers Arien Mack and Irwin Rock[60] demonstrated that there are different levels to attention and perception. They differentiate between unconscious and conscious perception. Unconscious perception refers to the early processing of sensory stimuli prior to awareness and conscious perception to the processing of stimuli once attention is engaged. We must implicitly attend to something before we can perceive it and then we can explicitly attend to it.

Before attention is captured, the processing of the formal perceptual qualities must be complete. What kind of information is taken in at this level? It tends to be fairly low level. Research on priming, our ability to parallel process, and "subliminal awareness"[61] suggests that without explicit perception, we are limited to fairly basic-level processing.[62] Whether or not information captures our attention depends upon a number of variables including size, location, familiarity, loudness, and emotional content.[63] Very large and loud stimuli demand attention. But the magnitude in terms of size and loudness is not all that matters.

How meaningful and relevant the stimulus is to you matters a lot; this information has very "privileged" access.[64] On that crowded street, many faces did not "grab" your attention, but your friend's did. Your name is more likely to break through than other familiar words. Meaningful information matters more than how recently you were exposed to it; you are more likely to notice a friend you haven't seen in ages than someone you passed by yesterday.

Taken together, the power of agency, our tendency toward efficiency, our selective attention, and the ways that we prioritize some information makes certain patterns more familiar and more meaningful to us than others. This, in turn, reinforces the likelihood that we will prioritize these patterns in our explicit perception and attention and will default toward them. The world that is meaningful to us increasingly becomes the world that we perceive.[65]

The research on attention underscores that the ontological problem—the problem of how people figure out what causes to pay attention to in the first place—is a critical piece of the puzzle in complex causal reasoning. As certain patterns become meaningful from our earliest days, we may prioritize those patterns, selectively attending to them to the potential exclusion of others. Our robust, early causal tendencies may help to shape the world that we perceive, what we consider relevant, and the problem parameters that we assume.

Current evidence certainly supports this interpretation. Significant research is being conducted on how our minds work and how it relates to our behaviors. Further insights in the neuroscience of perception and attention and how neural networks are pruned and shaped should offer more insights in the coming years.

CAN WE GET BEYOND THE LURE OF SIMPLE?

Simple linear explanations fit with the way that we tend to allocate attention. They typically play out in a short enough time span that they hold our attention. They may engage our own agency. They are efficient in terms of how much cognitive energy they take—focusing on the aspects of a situation that most readily grab our attention, that are directly observable and nearby in terms of time and space. Events demand our attention, steady states fade from view.

What does all this mean for our ability to reason about causal complexity? A lot. We learn from the patterns that we observe over and over, but less salient information is likely it is to be edited out of the picture. Too often we draw the boundaries of a system smaller than we should. As the following chapters illustrate, we often miss spatially distant causes, time-delayed events, steady states, non-obvious causes, and so on. Our attentional apparatus makes them hard to detect. Our selective perception prevents sensory overload, but how can we prevent filtering input that offers important information about the world?

I have cast the problem in terms of our everyday causal reasoning and attentional patterns. Clearly, selective attention is built into our perceptual apparatus and is necessary to our survival. But it leads to efficiency that can be a dual-edged sword. The very tendencies that we have evolved with may not be enough to help us understand the complexity of our modern world. We might well be content to drink PCB-contaminated water while moving away from a bustling bee hive that is less likely to kill us unless we have a specific allergy.[66]

Fortunately for us, we have the advantages of our neocortex and higher-order reasoning processes that we can bring into conversation with our perceptual default tendencies. Further, as I elaborate in the final chapter, the ways that we perceive and reason about causality every day, while powerful influences, do not necessarily dictate how we must learn about it. Research suggests that teaching causal patterns and features can make a dramatic difference in achievement for all learners.[67] Learning to recognize a broader causal repertoire can lead to different interpretations, choices, and actions in everyday life.

In each of the chapters to follow, I will engage some of the most powerful means of learning known to cognitive science: analogical reasoning, the power of narrative, surprises and discrepant events, and metacognition to help share the more complex patterns and to illustrate how we might teach students to recognize them more often. I return to these modes of teaching in the final chapter.

NOTES

1. The research related to the second two bullet points has been characterized by two prevalent views. For an in-depth discussion, see Corrigan & Denton, 1996; Grotzer, 2003. One prevalent view relates to how we use regular associations or co-variation between events to detect instances of causality (e.g., Bullock, Gelman & Baillargeon, 1982; Siegler & Liebert, 1974). A variation of this view might include the current Causal Bayes Nets theories (in various formulations). A second prevalent view is a type of modular- mechanism argument that explains how one event causes another in terms of the specifics of a generative mechanism or generative transmission (e.g., Atran, 1995; Carey, 1995; Keil, 1994; Leslie, 1995; Shultz, 1982; Shultz et al., 1986). Causes are seen as particular types of domain-specific forces and research focuses on what children understand about the nature of such mechanisms. While I draw across the literature in these two traditions, some proponents of the second view may not view their findings applicable beyond the contexts in which they were studied.

Gopnik, Sobel, and colleagues have argued that Bayesian structure learning *is* a form of mechanism (e.g., Gopnik & Glymour, 2002; Sobel, 2004; Sobel & Buchanan, 2009; Sobel, Tenebaum & Gopnik, 2004) that gives rise to specific theories and understandings about the causal force of particular mechanisms and does not preclude the use of mechanism knowledge once it is gained. For instance, "These studies suggest that at least in generative, deterministic cases, preschoolers can use the conditional intervention principle to learn causal structures from patterns of evidence and to predict patterns of evidence from causal structure. Children seem to make use of differential spatiotemporal information and prior knowledge about particular causal mechanisms, and well before they can conduct controlled experiments themselves." (Schulz, Gopnik & Glymour, 2007, p. 331)

Further, the order of presentation here is not to argue that summing across happens prior to an assessment of mechanism. For instance, if after I eat a snack, I feel sick, I could consider possible mechanisms in the food such as bacteria growth that might lead to sickness and/or I might consider whether the last time I ate that food it made me feel sick. Most likely, we integrate these sources of knowledge. For instance, I would integrate information about whether or not this is a type of food that is more or less likely to hold a mechanism that could make me ill. If I had just finished a sushi dinner, knowledge of candidate mechanisms and the greater likelihood that sushi carries them than a plate of saltine crackers would play into my assessment. I might also integrate knowledge of what others had said to me, a form of trust in testimony (e.g., Harris & Koenig, 2006) about eating sushi in general, about the specific restaurant in particular, and the kinds of bacteria my sushi might have. What I know about mechanism would likely inform what I consider relevant and valid about co-variation and vice versa.

2. Andersson, 1986; Kelemen, 1999
3. Carey, 2009
4. Meltzoff, 2007; Sommerville, 2007
5. Meltzoff, 2007; Gopnik & Shultz, 2004
6. Meltzoff, 2007, p. 39
7. But not earlier, it appears. Research suggests that prior to six months, they respond in ways that are not deemed causal (Cohen & Amsel, 1998) and do not attend to the goal directedness of actions (Sommerville, Woodward & Needham, 2005).
8. Woodward, 1998
9. e.g., Woodward, 2003; Janovic et al., 2007; Baldwin et al., 2001
10. Bojcyk & Corbetta, 2004; Meltzoff, 2007; Sommerville, 2007
11. This is true for a range of ages. Gopnik et al, 2004; Kushnir & Gopnik, 2005; Kushnir et al., 2003; Sobel, 2003; Sobel & Kushnir, 2006; Steyvers et al. 2003; Waldmann & Hagmayer, 2005
12. Meltzoff, 2007
13. e.g., Harris, 1989; Goldman, 1989
14. However, while these simple causal schemas may be a staple of an infants' experience, given their environment and what is empowering to them, it doesn't dictate that babies can't do more. Meltzoff and a colleague (Meltzoff & Blumenthal, 2006) showed that fourteen-month-olds could learn how to activate a remote box by observing a grown-up do so. This is a form of "action at a distance" as discussed in chapter eight. Infants may well be capable of recognizing greater complexity than their worlds invite even if the affordances of their environments may prioritize simple linear schemas over others.
15. Woodward, 2007
16. Meltzoff, 2007
17. Ibid.
18. Andersson, 1986; Basca & Grotzer, 2003; Brown, 1995
19. e.g., Einhorn & Hogarth, 1986; Kahneman, Slovic & Tversky, 1982
20. Borton, 1979; Leslie, 1982, 1984; Leslie & Keeble, 1987; Oakes, 1993; Spelke, Phillips & Woodward, 1995; Van de Walle & Spelke, 1993
21. e.g., Bullock, 1979; Baillargeon, Gelman & Meck, 1981
22. Earlier research (Shultz & Mendelson, 1975; Siegler, 1976; Siegler & Liebert, 1974) suggested that the youngest children had trouble tracking one-to-one correspondence, not necessarily that they were willing to override it explicitly. Even so, it leaves open the question of what causal assumptions they make even if they appear implicitly Bayesian. However, it certainly impacts how they behave in accordance with probabilistic causes, as well as the possibility of their explicit awareness and acceptance of probabilistic causation.
23. Gopnik et al., 2004; Kushnir & Gopnik, 2007
24. However, confusing correlation with causation is not an uncommon mistake. For reviews of the literature indicating that adults as well as children are prone to this error, see Alloy & Tabachnik, 1984; Crocker, 1981; Kuhn, Phelps & Walters, 1985; and Nisbett & Ross, 1980.
25. In response to this research, my colleague David Perkins suggested that asking your surgeon to play a piano sonata prior to surgery might be a good way to assess adept fingers!
26. Bracy, 1998
27. e.g. Gopnik & Schulz, 2007; Gopnik et al., 2004; Steyvers et al., 2003
28. Sobel & Kushnir, 2003
29. Gopnik et al., 2001; Schulz & Gopnik, 2004

30. Kushnir, Gopnik & Schaefer, 2005

31. Schulz & Gopnik, 2004

32. Meltzoff, 2007

33. Grotzer & Tutwiler, forthcoming

34. This is known as the Causal Markov Assumption. "For any variable X in an acyclic causal graph, X is independent of all the other variables in the graph except for its own direct and indirect causes) conditional on its own direct causes." Gopnik & Schulz, 2007, p. 4

35. Scheines, Easterday & Danks, 2007

36. Hagmayer et al., 2007

37. e.g., Kahneman, Slovic & Tversky, 1982; Sunstein, 2002, ch. 2: "Thinking about Risks" (pp. 28–52), reviewed and elaborated upon this earlier research.

38. See, for instance, "Affect Heuristic," as written about by Finucane et al., 2000.

39. Scheines, Easterday & Danks, 2007

40. LeDoux, 1 996, 2000, 2007, n.d.

41. Ahn et al., 1995; Bullock, Gelman & Baillargeon, 1982; Koslowski & Masnick, 2002

42. What constitutes a plausible mechanism is a point of discussion in the research. One prevalent view argues that causes are seen as particular types of domain-specific forces and this research focuses on what children understand about the nature of such mechanisms (e.g., Atran, 1995; Carey, 1995; Keil, 1994; Leslie, 1995). By age four, they begin to a differentiated sense of mechanism (e.g., Springer & Keil, 1991; Goswami & Brown, 1989). However, some research also argues that children are developing an understanding of "impersonal mechanistic causality" whether or not they have knowledge of a particular mechanism. (e.g., Bullock, 1979, 1984, 1985; Bullock, Gelman & Baillargeon, 1982; Shultz, 1982; Shultz & Kestenbaum, 1985; White, 1995). See Grotzer, 2003, for an in-depth review.

43. Bullock, Gelman & Baillargeon, 1982

44. e.g., Bullock, 1979, 1984, 1985; Baillargeon, Gelman & Meck,1981; Corrigan, 1995; Schulz & Sommerville, 2006

45. Bullock, 1985

46. Gopnik et al., 2004

47. e.g., Browne & Woolley, 2004

48. Harris, 1997, p.1019

49. e.g., Atran, 1995; Carey, 1995; Keil, 1994; Leslie, 1995; Shultz, 1982; Shultz et al., 1986; Sobel, 2004

50. For an in-depth review, see Grotzer, Miller & Lincoln, 2011

51. e.g., Mack & Rock, 1998; Simons & Levin, 1998; Treisman, 2006

52. e.g., Simons, 1996

53. B. Campbell, personal communication, June 20, 1996

54. Simons & Levin, 1998

55. Gilbert, Pelham & Krull, 1988

56. Grotzer, 1993

57. Keil & Lockhart, 1999

58. Mack & Rock, 1998

59. Treisman, 1982; Neisser, 1967

60. Mack & Rock, 1998

61. Priming refers to the phenomenon in which earlier low-level exposure to a stimulus impacts later responses to it. For instance, subjects are shown an image that they may not be aware of and later detect that image at a higher level than images that they were not previously exposed to. Parallel processing refers to the simultaneous processing of different stimuli. Subliminal awareness refers to processing below the level of conscious perception.

62. Dorfman, Shames & Kihlstrom, 1996; Greenwald, 1992

63. Moray, 1959; Ohman, Flykt & Esteves, 2001; Eastwood, Smilek & Merikle, 2001; Vuilleumier, 2005; Yamasaki, LaBar & McCarthy, 2002; as cited in Treisman, 2006.

64. ibid.

65. Grotzer, 2011

66. Grotzer, Miller & Lincoln, 2011

67. e.g., Grotzer, 2000; Grotzer & Basca, 2003; Perkins & Grotzer, 2005

Part 2: Getting beyond Simple: A Set of Causal Patterns for the Curriculum

This section considers five causal patterns that capture greater complexity than the simple causality that we employ so readily. It introduces each pattern, its characteristics, and why it is important to attend to it. It offers examples from the curriculum and for helping students develop deeper understanding of phenomena structured by each pattern.

As per the caveat in the introduction, these are not the only ways of characterizing causal patterns. Rather these are a set that teachers found to be powerful in the classroom—ones that emerged from the situated contexts that they were teaching. While they are presented as generic forms here, as you consider them in relation to the world, you'll find that they often hold nuances particular to the situation. You'll also notice that they seldom are found in a mutually exclusive manner. There are aspects of more than one in any given instance and they are complexified by the features discussed in the third part of this book.

Chapter Four

Domino Causality: Effects That Become Causality

"One thing leads to another and another . . ."

"Pay it forward."

"It was like a game of Mousetrap."

In the 1950s, the people of Borneo suffered from malaria. So the World Health Organization sprayed large amounts of DDT to kill the mosquitoes carrying the malaria. The mosquitoes died and malaria declined. But that wasn't the end of the story. Soon, the thatched roofs of people's houses fell down on their heads. The DDT had killed a parasitic wasp that had controlled thatch-eating caterpillars. The DDT-poisoned insects were eaten by geckoes which were eaten by cats. As cats died, rats flourished, and resulted in outbreaks of sylvatic plague and typhus. In response, the World Health Organization parachuted live cats into Borneo. [1]

WHAT IS DOMINO CAUSALITY?

Most people have played with dominoes and know the patterns that they create. One domino causes the next domino or set of dominoes to fall down. Those dominoes, in turn, cause other dominoes to fall, and so on. Dominoes are interesting for students to think about in terms of cause and effect. When dominoes fall, the falling is both an effect (of the domino that fell into it) and a cause (of the fall of the next domino). This is so for all of the dominoes except the last one (which is just an effect). We refer to causal patterns with these characteristics as "Domino Causality."

Simple cause and effect focuses on a primary cause that has a direct effect. But instances of domino causality—where effects become causes of new effects—are *very* common. Consider when school is let out early due to unforeseen events; a water main break, snow, or electrical outage. This affects the students, who go home early. That affects parents, who leave work early to care for them. That affects people who were planning to meet with the parents and so on. Effects can branch out. Domino causality invites us to consider extended effects and to recognize indirect effects of an initial cause.

What other images conjure up domino causality? Billiards, cars starting and stopping on the highway, missing a plane, shortening the allotted time for science class, and so forth, all involve domino causal patterns. The game Mousetrap[2] invites us to play with domino causality. Paying kindness forward is domino-like, either a long causal chain or a branching pattern in the cases where a kindness begets more than one act of kindness.

Rube Goldberg inventions or those of Wallace in the Wallace and Gromit films—where one thing leads to another to another to another and so on—are domino-like. Searching the Internet yields many more examples. A Honda car commercial shows a set of domino-like events developed out of car parts, which eventually leads to a car rolling off a ramp.[3]

WHAT ARE THE CHARACTERISTICS OF DOMINO CAUSALITY?

Domino causality[4] works in one direction. It typically has a clear beginning, middle, and ending (though we may not be aware of the actual ending). Effects act as causes of other effects. The causes can be similar to each other (as in the dominoes where each domino falling over causes the next one to fall) or they can be quite different (as in the events following Hurricane Katrina that led to a rise in gasoline prices nationally).

Some examples of domino causality have one-to-one correspondence between causes and effects—so one cause is followed by one effect. Variations on domino patterns include branching patterns ,where each effect in turn causes one or more effects, and radiating patterns, where one event has many direct outcomes and then many indirect outcomes.[5]

In cases of domino causality:

- There is a beginning and an eventual ending.
- It works in one direction.
- Causes occur before effects.
- Effects can become causes.
- There is a sequential unfolding of effects over time.
- There are direct and indirect effects of a given cause.

- There can be branching instances with more than one effect of a cause ✗ (and these may go on to have multiple effects and so on).
- Branching forms can be traced back to "stem" causes.
- Anticipating outcomes involves deciding how far to trace effects. Short-sightedness can lead to unintended effects.

One of the challenges of understanding domino causality is that the distinction between what is an effect and what is a cause is blurred. Effects can become causes in turn. This blurring of the role of causes and effects makes the patterns harder to grasp.

Research shows that as early as seven months, babies pay attention to what is a cause and what is an effect and reversing their roles is quite puzzling to them.[6] Some researchers have argued that as early as one year of age,[7] children reason about causality by attaching specific actions to specific causes, for instance, certain kinds of agency, such as launching another object, are seen as enduring properties. Affording special status to causes and attaching some forms of agency to particular objects makes instances where one event or entity is both a cause and an effect conceptually difficult.[8]

In the row of toy dominoes, the chain of effects is expected. We know that pushing the first one over eventually makes the last one fall. In fact, if it doesn't, there is disappointment and a realigning of the dominoes.

However, in other instances, we don't necessarily anticipate that an effect can become a cause. This can happen even when we *have* had the opportunity to think through our actions and believe that we have done our best planning. For instance, we administer a new test to make certain that students are learning to read at a higher level, but given constant resources in terms of funding and time, teachers begin reallocating their efforts to accommodate the test and we end up with unanticipated effects on other areas of learning—math, science, conflict resolution, and so on.

Research shows that children develop the ability to reason about indirect and mediating causes around three to five years old[9] and, in at least one study, as early as fifteen months old.[10] The research involved physical apparatus with visible intermediate effects[11] like the row of toy dominoes. However, domino causality in real-world contexts typically involves effects that are not physically present within the attentional context of the person reasoning about them. Further, often they are not so salient in that they involve non-obvious causes: germs, forces, populations, and so forth.

Thus the actual links may not be easily detected—making them harder to realize in retrospect or to keep in mind looking forward. When applying pesticides, most of us realize the direct impact on the insects in the lawn. We may realize the indirect impact on primary consumers—rodents and birds—of the insects. We may not be aware of the links that connect the pesticide to future hawks. Rodents eat insects and plants with small amounts of pesticides in each, concentrating it in their bodies. They, in turn, are eaten by birds of prey, which lay eggs with weakened shells and are unable to produce new generations of hawks.

Research shows that students don't reason about indirect effects in many instances when they should. For example, students typically miss the domino-type connections within ecosystems and even high school students think that changes in one population will only affect another population if the two are related in a direct predator-prey relationship. [12] Dissipation effects have been found in which students' ability to reason about causal connections decreased with increasing distance of the item from the target item in the problem. [13] These difficulties are partially, but not entirely, age related. [14]

Even experts can miss domino causality, as in the example above. The story of how the World Health Organization sprayed DDT in Borneo and set off a domino of effects that literally brought down people's houses was popularized by Amory Lovins, a renowned thinker in systems dynamics. But there are many more stories just like that one. It can be hard to look far enough ahead and anticipate all the possible dominoes that may fall in response to a given action.

Ask yourself:

- What are some recent examples in which I confronted unanticipated outcomes?
- Might analyzing the situation using domino causality have helped me to anticipate the outcomes?
- A rumor spreads through the school. How might I help the student who appears to have started the rumor to think about the role he or she played in the outcome?

WHY IS DOMINO CAUSALITY IMPORTANT TO LEARN?

Why should we pay attention to domino causality? With simple cause and effect, we consider immediate effects, but we are less likely to consider the effects of the effects. Reducing phenomena to simple cause and effect can result in shortsighted predictions and unanticipated outcomes. Given our tendency toward efficiency, we are not naturally inclined to engage in the extended search that would reveal potential domino causality. Doing so invites us to reason about indirect effects as well as direct effects. Tracing out extended causes and effects can avoid unanticipated outcomes.

Reasoning about domino causality can help us to predict the magnitude of impact for various actions. Imagine the branch of a tree. If you cut off a twig, less of the system is impacted than if you cut off the entire branch. Cutting off the tree at its base disrupts the entire system. Thinking about domino causality can also take us back to the initiating sources of a problem.

[handwritten margin note: mistake intern for root]

In lab research asking people about the causal chains describing real world and artificial causal connections, they tend to intervene on immediate or root causes as opposed to intermediate causes. When told to seek a long-term solution, they prefer to intervene on the root cause.[15] In treating disease, we try to treat the "root cause," tracing it as far back as we can. Analyzing where in the system connections fall helps us reason about various outcomes.[16] This research does not address the critical, real-world problem of attending to and anticipating in advance what those connections are because the causal chain is given.

In the real world, we don't always anticipate the causal connections or have the opportunity to go back and address causes at the "stem." They may play out in time so that such opportunities are lost. Residents of Nantucket Island off the coast of Massachusetts know this well.

The story goes that in 1922, some men on a fishing sloop found a deer paddling in the ocean and took pity on him. Nicknamed "Old Buck," he was helped ashore and a few years later, two does were imported on his behalf. Even though Old Buck was hit by a car in 1936, with few predators on the island, his progeny have flourished. So has tick-borne illness, Lyme Disease, Babesiosis, and Ehrlichiosis.[17] More than one resident has probably longed to go back in time to those stem causes and make sure that Old Buck stayed off-island or, at least, remained a lonely bachelor.

Domino causality also carries with it the possibility of social cascading or "snowballing." These refer to an avalanche of eventual effects from one cause and the potential amplification of effects along the way. This can be seen in examples of contagion or stampedes. Like spiraling causality in chapter six, both are very difficult to stop once they start. Paying careful attention to actions, events, and situations early in the pattern can help to stem the tide before it is too late to avoid the avalanche.

Some phenomena involve tipping points where accumulation of causes and effects suddenly reach a point where subsequent effects are of a substantially different magnitude than the apparent causes.[18] We often see governments attempt to move early in cases of civil unrest to keep "the rest of the dominoes" from falling or quick attempts to quell rumors during political campaigns before the rumor takes on a "life of its own." Climate-change predictions suggest that at some point, CO_2 accumulations will reach such a point, with dramatic changes occurring all at once.

If simple cause and effect is so well ingrained, can students learn to think about domino causality? Research offers a resounding "yes." Research shows that even preschool children can learn to think about the causal chains and mediate transmission of effects involved in domino causality.[19] They understand that the links in the chain are part of the causality involved and can explain them above the level of chance.[20]

In our work, students learned domino causality and revealed deeper understanding of domino-like concepts as a result. From third grade through high school, students developed good mental models and met with a lot of success talking about domino causality. In fact, we adopted the name "domino causality" from the third graders we worked with who used it to describe how the sun was important to the food web. Further, the students who were taught to reason about the food web in terms of domino causality significantly outperformed the students who were not on a test of ecosystems concepts.[21]

WHAT ARE SOME EXAMPLES OF DOMINO CAUSALITY IN THE CURRICULUM?

Examples of domino causality can be found across the curriculum. Consider language arts, for instance. Jerome Bruner argued that the mind structures its reality through narrative as a cultural product of life.[22] For students whose cultures stress linear narratives, domino causality can be a logical extension for considering the "longer view."

Many narrative structures are linear and often involve domino causality where one thing causes another thing to happen. Think of the unfolding of events in stories like *Charlotte's Web* by E. B. White. Wilbur, the pig, befriends Charlotte, the spider, who, in an effort to save Wilbur's life from the butcher, weaves words into her web so the farmer will believe that he is special. One thing leads to another and soon Wilbur is famous, crowds of people come to see him, and his longevity is assured.

Choose Your Own Adventure books, where readers make choices at various points in the story and then turn to a certain page to continue, have a branching domino structure. In these books, the story unfolds based on the choices the reader makes and the causal links along that branch of the domino. Helping students think about both direct and indirect effects as they plot out their own story lines can help them create richly textured narratives.

Some of our collaborating teachers have found that literature can be a great way to teach domino causality. They have used books such as *The Lorax* by Dr. Seuss, where building a Thneed Factory leads to pollution and extended domino effects, and *Because Brian Hugged His Mother* by David Rice, where an act of kindness is paid forward throughout the day, to invite students to think and talk about domino causality.

We see many events in history that can be described as domino-like. Religious persecution in England led the Puritans to seek a new land and the eventual establishment of the American colonies. History books in New England tell the story of how the colonists, so angered over the taxes levied by King George, dumped tea into the harbor, setting off a domino pattern of other events. Where civilizations are founded and how they develop can also follow domino-like patterns of causality. The Nile River Valley and how the riches of the valley enabled civilization to develop is one such example.

Teaching domino causality only in terms of history can make it harder to realize how difficult anticipating future "dominoes" can be. When teaching about domino causality though history, a concurrent focus on current events, such as policy decisions, weather events, and so on, can help students consider the challenges of anticipating domino causal patterns. Hopefully, this can lead to a thoughtful, proactive consideration of potential outcomes for developing problems before they get out of hand and lead to other problems. It can illustrate the very different challenges involved in description and prediction.

There are many examples of domino causality in science, such as the transfer of kinetic energy at the particle level in the process of reaching thermal equilibrium during conduction. Domino causality also describes the transfer of energy in ecosystems from the sun to green plants through the primary and secondary consumers until it dissipates as heat energy.

A common misconception that many students have about the food web is that the green plants are only important to the things that directly eat green plants. They reason that if all the green plants disappeared, the secondary consumers would be okay because they don't eat green plants.[23] Focusing on the domino transfer of energy in ecosystems helps students to view the food web as a connected system of relationships based on the transfer of energy, not individual feeding relationships. It underscores the critical connection between the food web and the sun as a source of energy.

Domino causality *often* comes into play in environmental science as in the Borneo story above. Consider the case of climate change. Certain effects quickly become causes of other effects. Increased greenhouse gases lead to melting ice sheets which in turn cause flooding, displacement of certain populations, and loss of biodiversity, and these in turn cause further effects and, eventually, result in an avalanche of massive effects.

Recognizing domino causality in the curriculum may also incur benefits in the classroom. When students better anticipate the direct and indirect effects of their actions, they may be more sensitive to the potential chain

reactions that one set of actions can set in motion. They may be more inclined to take the "long view"—a tendency that will help them in the classroom community and beyond.

NOTES

1. This story is based on an actual event reported in the *New York Times*, November 13,
1969. It has been retold in various places. There is a book by Pomerantz, C. (1971), *The Day
They Parachuted Cats on Borneo: A Drama of Ecology*, Reading, MA: Young Scott Books. It
has also been told by Amory Lovins, director of research at the Rocky Mountain Institute, Old
Snowmass, Colorado.
2. Invented by Marvin Glass and associates and brought out by Milton Bradley in the
1960s.
3. Honda: *The Cog*, YouTube video: Available: http://www.youtube.com/watch?v=_
ve4M4UsJQo[accessed 6-23-2011].
4. Grotzer, 1989, 1993; Perkins & Grotzer, 2005; Van Orden & Paap, 1997
5. Grotzer, 1989, 1993
6. Golinkoff, 1975; Leslie & Keeble, 1987
7. Cohen & Oakes, 1993; Cohen et al., 1999
8. Indeed, some researchers have argued that causation is defined by a unidirectional
generative mechanism (see Bindra, Clarke & Shultz, 1980, for a discussion).
9. Baillargeon & Gelman, 1980; Shultz, Pardo & Altmann, 1982
10. Cohen et al., 1999
11. Other research with preschoolers used electrical pulleys and switches that are less
obvious in their function but still physically present (e.g., Koslowski, Spilton & Snipper, 1981).
12. e.g., Barman, Griffiths & Okebukola,1995; Griffiths & Grant, 1985; Webb & Boltt,
1990
13. White, 1997
14. Grotzer, 1989, 1993
15. Edwards, Burnett & Keil, 2008
16. People also use information about the differences between outcomes in a branching
causal structure to infer whether or not they are likely to have a common root cause (Kim &
Keil, 2003).
17. Belluck, 2009
18. As written about by Malcolm Gladwell, 2000.
19. Baillargeon & Gelman, 1980; Shultz, Pardo & Altmann, 1982
20. Baillargeon & Gelman 1980; Koslowski, Spilton & Snipper, 1981
21. Grotzer & Basca, 2003; Grotzer, 2009
22. Bruner, 1991
23. Grotzer, 1989; 1993; Grotzer & Basca, 2003

Chapter Five

Cyclic Causality: Loops and Feedback

"What goes around comes around."

"I felt like I was on a merry-go-round."

"It will come back to you."

In a well-known children's story by Dr. Seuss, the Plain Belly Sneetches want bellies with stars like the snooty and exclusive Star Belly Sneetches. So they pay Sylvester McMonkey McBean to put stars on their bellies in his wondrous machine. This in turn causes the Star Belly Sneetches to remove their stars in McBean's machine, and then the original plain bellies (now with stars) follow suit and the cycle goes round until their money runs out. In a classic example of cyclic causality, each has an effect on the other, which continues the cycle. They spur each other on until something intervenes (in this case, depletion of the Sneetches' bank accounts) to change the pattern.

WHAT IS CYCLIC CAUSALITY?

In cyclic causality, actions, events, or situations are connected in a loop. Someone drops a newspaper into a recycling bin, the recycling truck picks the bins up, the paper goes to a recycling facility where the paper is recycled, soon we see another person taking their newspaper out of a paper box, reading and then putting it in the bin again, and so it goes. Or consider a home thermostat. Just about the time that we feel cold, we hear the heat come on, soon the room warms, and the thermostat switches the heat off. As the room cools, the thermostat turns the heat back on again, in a repeating cycle.

Cyclic causality is common in social interactions. Pen pals engage in a form of cyclic causality. You send a letter in response to the letter you received and then your pen pal sends one back in response to the letter you sent. It's a pattern that can be uncomfortable if you like to keep lists and check things off. While you expect your friend to write back, a response too soon certainly undermines one's sense of accomplishment!

Sometimes there's cyclic causality in less friendly circumstances. For instance, you say something that hurts your friend's feelings; your friend turns a cold shoulder your way so you get mad and treat your now-former friend similarly, and so on. Cyclic causality can characterize unhealthy social patterns such as the connections between a mom's yelling and teenager's withdrawal. [1]

WHAT ARE THE CHARACTERISTICS OF CYCLIC CAUSALITY?

Cyclic causality is best characterized by the old question, "Which came first, the chicken or the egg?" Breaking a circle into linear parts loses essential elements of the inherent causality. In its purest form, it can be difficult to say how it got started or if it will ever end.

In variations, we might know where it started, as in the comment that one makes to a friend and then regrets for a long time afterward. It may have a clear ending, as in the Sneetches who run out of money and end the cycle of painting stars on and off. For many instances of cyclic causality, there is no clear beginning or ending. (Sometimes you can look back in time to try to find a beginning, but this often invites the chicken or the egg problem.)

Cycles are inherent to cyclic causality, but not every cycle encompasses cyclic causality. For instance, in the cycle of the seasons, each season precedes the one that follows, but doesn't cause it. Cyclic causality involves some form of feedback or reciprocity that makes the cycle continue. The circle can be as simple as two events with recursiveness between them or it can have many events embedded within the circle. Feedback loops can perpetuate the status quo or they can amplify or dampen the effect as discussed in the next chapter on "Spiraling Causality."

Typically, the pattern of feedback unfolds in time where one event happens after another. But, there can be instances where the inherent reciprocity does not necessarily involve a sequential pattern. Imagine a simple circuit filled with electrons. A greater density of electrons on one side repels those on the other side of it while being repelled by those on the other side of it, such that it turns in a circle. The whole circle turns at once like a bicycle chain.[2] The pattern is not sequential (and students who characterize it sequentially have difficulty understanding how circuits work[3]). Chapter 13 considers sequential versus simultaneous causality in depth.

In cases of cyclic causality:

- There may be no clear beginning or ending.
- A cause can also be an effect and vice versa.
- Feedback perpetuates the cycle.
- A impacts B impacts C and so on, and eventually impacts A again.
- There is an inherent repeating pattern.
- The pattern is often sequential, but it is possible to have simultaneous cases.

Research shows that students often break cyclic causality into simple linear patterns. For instance, when learning about simple circuits, students are taught that the circuit is a circle and that it must be closed. However, many students still revert back to explanations in which only one wire brings a substance to the bulb and the other is extraneous to the lighting of the bulb—a ground, for instance.[4]

WHY IS CYCLIC CAUSALITY IMPORTANT TO LEARN?

Why should we attend to cyclic causality? Breaking apart the cyclic dynamic ignores the role of feedback and how the causes and effects are locked together. Reducing it to a line misses what fuels the continuation. Shifting responsibility to one side or another for the outcome ignores the reinforcing aspects where each response calls for a response. Any child who has been caught up in a playground scuffle intuitively knows this. Any teacher who has tried to "get to the bottom" of what happened has experienced how hard that can be as they go through a seemingly endless series of "well, first he did . . ."

When cyclic causality is inherent in a pattern that one wants to sustain, it is important to understand the role of feedback and how failure in any part of the cycle can undermine the pattern. If there is a failure to reciprocate, eventually the pattern is unsustainable.

On the other hand, if there are patterns that we seek to end, and we don't understand the causes that sustain them, it can be difficult to end them. The tensions in the Middle East, while complicated and involving many other causal features, have elements of cyclic causality that are difficult to escape.

Cyclic causality and reciprocity often characterize global affairs and interactions— countries may support other countries with the expectation of gaining something in return either at present or in some future point of need.

What do we know about students' ability to develop an understanding of cyclic causality? Understanding cycles is a prerequisite to thinking about dynamic cycles—they must understand "circular connectivity"—that there is an endless revolution through a circularly connected system as in, for instance, the hydrologic or matter cycle.[5] But they also need to understand that the relationships in the cycle are causal—the difference between the seasons and pen pals is that spring doesn't cause summer, but pen pals write back in response to each other and this sustains the cycle.

Research suggests that students develop some understanding of uncomplicated forms of cyclic causal patterns between nine and twelve years of age.[6] However, even when students are *able* to understand cyclic causal patterns, they often break them apart into lines.[7] They are not sensitive to the possibility that cyclic causality might be in play.[8] Cyclic causality is seldom taught so whether these patterns are due to development, cultural tendencies, and/or the lack of learning is an open question. Teaching students to reason about cyclic patterns in social studies[9] and science[10] produced significant learning.

As in domino causality, one of the conceptual challenges is that the distinction between what is an effect and what is a cause is blurred. In cyclic causality, once the cycle is started, each event in turn causes the other to reoccur.

Ask yourself:

- Can I think of any examples where my students were reasoning about cyclic causal patterns and reduced these to simple linear causality?
- If I notice that two students are caught up in a pattern where they incite each other to unpleasant behavior and yet each thinks that the other is solely to blame, what might I say or do to help them see the inherent patterns differently?
- Can I think of any examples where I was involved in a reinforcing cyclic pattern and found it hard to "break the cycle"?
- What are some places in my curriculum where a cyclic causal pattern is in play?

One of the puzzles with cyclic causality is figuring out how to talk about it, given that our language is so linear. A third grader in our research struggled with this as she reasoned through the differences between domino and cyclic causality and how each applies to what happens to the energy from the sun and the animals in an ecosystem:

"It's like the food web. If you set up your dominoes and you knock down the first one, then the second one will knock down as the effect to the cause of the first one, it's just gonna keep on going. But with dominoes you don't have enough unless you put it in a circle because the earthworms are the end of, they also, they're the end AND they're the beginning of the food web because they end one part with one generation of the food web and they start the new generation for the new plants to grow because that's what their job is. So they're the end and the beginning of the food web. . . . With the things that break down dead matter, then it would be a circle."

You can hear her struggling with how to talk about cycles with language on beginnings and endings and trying to contrast the characteristics of the two causal patterns to figure out how they might fit. Hearing this, her teacher realized the need to help her understand the difference between matter recycling (which involves cyclic causality) and energy transfer (which involves domino causality).

Mercer Mayer's *Frog Where Are You?* is a picture book that opens with a boy and his dog staring at a frog in a jar. As the boy sleeps, with the moon in the sky and an open window nearby, the frog climbs out of the jar and the boy awakens to an empty jar. The boy and dog search high and low and come to a pond where they meet a family of frogs and take a small frog home. The story is equally sensible laid out as a circle as it is in a line.

Research suggests some cultural variation to how readily we detect cyclic patterns.[11] When given just the pictures of the Mercer Mayer story and asked to "put them in a line from beginning to ending," students from a Navajo reservation found it very hard to do so and kept moving the last one to the beginning.[12] The cyclic pattern seemed more salient to them. As discussed in chapter one, Salish Kootenai students were more likely to notice cyclic patterns in a video about decay than students in Cambridge.

While predominant Western culture often stresses linear narrative patterns, as our schools become increasingly culturally diverse, attending to other narrative patterns is increasingly important. It is also important for teachers to be cognizant of when students may interpret the patterns in tasks differently than they might be intending.

WHAT ARE SOME EXAMPLES OF CYCLIC CAUSALITY IN THE CURRICULUM?

Cyclic causality is enjoying a newfound popularity in children's literature. Witness the recent growth of books with cyclic causal patterns, for instance, the books by Laura Numeroff, including *Give a Mouse a Cookie, Give a Moose a Muffin*, and so forth. In each story, the "initial" event leads to a series of other events that eventually lead back to the "initial" event—presumably precipitating the cycle again. These books offer great opportunities to talk about cyclic causality with young children.

Great works of literature often entail cyclic patterns where one generation repeats the mistakes of another or where someone finds it hard to escape his or her reinforcing life circumstances.

Cyclic causality is an essential component of deep understanding of many science concepts—the water cycle, the rock cycle, matter recycling, and so on. In ecosystems, plants grow and then die. Decomposers consume them and release the nutrients within the plant back into the soil affecting the growth of other plants.

Convection currents entail cyclic causality. Warm air rises to float upon cooler air until it cools and sinks below the air that is then warmer, and if there is a continual heating source, for instance a dark-sand beach, it reheats and rises again. If you've witnessed the thunderstorms that develop in the afternoon on tropical islands, you've seen this pattern in motion.

Climate change involves many positive feedback loops, where one event triggers other events that feed back into the cause of the initial event, introducing further complexity into understanding and reasoning well about climate-change solutions. There can also be multiple feedback loops in operation at the same time. Use of pesticides in soils lowers the diversity of the organisms in the soil, decreasing resistance to pests and the unwitting use of more pesticides, whereas a more sustainable solution demands breaking the cycle and seeking other types of solutions.

Cyclic patterns are not hard to detect in other parts of the curriculum either. Performance in sports can be enhanced by understanding physical and psychological patterns that are cyclic in nature, for instance, performance anxiety that leads to overly active reflection that leads to worsened performance that leads to more reflection and so forth. As I've mentioned above, cyclic causality is common in social studies and current events. Many of these also contain spiraling aspects as discussed next.

NOTES

1. Koplowitz, 1984
2. Shipstone, 1984, 1985
3. e.g., Grotzer, 2000, forthcoming; Grotzer & Sudbury, 2000
4. Barman & Mayer, 1994; Grotzer, 2000, 2009; Perkins & Grotzer, 2005; Shipstone, 1984, 1985
5. Chandler & Boutilier, 1992
6. Chandler & Boutilier, 1992; Grotzer, 1989, 1993; Smith & Anderson, 1986
7. Barman & Mayer, 1994
8. e.g., Andersson & Karrqvist, 1979; Fredette & Lochhead, 1980; Osborne & Gilbert, 1980; Shipstone, 1984, 1985; Tiberghien & Delacotte, 1976; Westbrook & Marek, 1992

9. Roberts, 1978
10. e.g., Grotzer, 2000; Grotzer & Basca, 2003
11. Honey & Grotzer, 2008
12. Thomas R. Bidell, personal communication, January 18, 1986

Chapter Six

Spiraling Causality: Escalation and De-escalation

"Soon it just spiraled out of control."

"Beforehand, he never would have anticipated getting so angry."

"As Earth warms, the more quickly it will warm as increasing amounts of its dark surface are exposed."

From the 1940s through the 1990s, the United States and the former Soviet Union engaged in a period of intensifying military buildup and maneuvering to gain international support, while attempting to avoid direct conflict and mutual nuclear annihilation. Known as the Cold War, each side built up increasingly large nuclear arsenals, mainly in response to each other.

Watching the slow, calculated steps unfolding over half a century was like a nightmare that never ends; there seemed to be no way out of the spiraling patterns. For those of us who grew up in the shadow of the Cold War, the concepts of escalation, spiraling causality, and the dynamics behind the arms race are pretty well engraved in our collective memories.

WHAT IS SPIRALING CAUSALITY?

Spiraling causality is a form of cyclic causality where events necessarily unfold over time and there is a corresponding increase or decrease in the magnitude of the effects. This causal pattern is also referred to as escalating causality. Here it is referred to as spiraling causality because the middle school students participating in our research argued persuasively that it did a better job capturing the idea of increase *or* decrease in magnitude. [1]

Consider the school cafeteria. In order to be heard by the person next to them, each student raises their voice ever so slightly. Then students near them need to raise their voices ever so slightly, and so on and so on. (This example also includes distributed agency with emergent causality as discussed in chapter 15.) The cafeteria gets louder and louder until some intervening event occurs, usually an adult blowing a whistle or blinking the lights in order to be noticed above the din.

Or consider the case of a bully and his or her victim. Bullies often engage in escalating patterns of causality. They typically have low self-esteem and may not have a sense of control or power in their lives. So they may attempt to control someone else to gain a sense of power and if they find a willing victim who acquiesces, they can become emboldened to increase the magnitude of the control that they exert.

We often think about spiraling causality in relation to conflict, such as in the example of the Cold War, where each side intensifies their response to the other side. Dr. Seuss's *The Butter Battle Book*, where the Yooks butter their bread butter side up and the Zooks butter their bread butter side down, is an allegory to this escalation. It ends with the Yooks and Zooks at a point in escalation that is unimaginable at the beginning.

Understanding how spiraling causal patterns can take on a life of their own is critical to conflict resolution. Particularly in examples of escalation, people are sometimes surprised at how quickly things get out of control and how one's initial intention and resulting actions can be so far apart.

But escalation doesn't have to involve conflict. Most kids will recognize the phenomenon of escalating goofiness and how each action is a reaction to the one before it. Kids will also confess that they do things in the context of escalating goofiness that they wouldn't have done outside that context.

Cases of de-escalation involve a de-intensifying pattern. One can choose to progressively back off in a conflict (as in the end of the Cold War), or for a non-conflict-based example, a teacher might begin speaking more and more softly to encourage her class to become quieter in order to hear what she is saying.

WHAT ARE THE CHARACTERISTICS OF SPIRALING CAUSALITY?

Spiraling causality has an underlying cyclic causal pattern. Therefore, it includes many of the characteristics of cyclic causality. However, a key feature involves intensification or de-intensification of causes, and amplification or dampening of effects as part of a feedback loop that unfolds over time.

In cases of spiraling causality:

- There is an inherent feedback loop.
- Feedback amplifies or de-amplifies the spiral.
- A impacts B, B impacts A, and so on, with amplification or de-amplification of effects and intensification or de-intensification of causes.
- There is a sequential unfolding of events in time.
- Effects, in turn, become causes so there is a blurring between causes and effects.
- There may be a clear beginning and ending, but this is not necessarily the case.
- It is difficult to anticipate outcomes of later feedback loops during earlier feedback loops.

It can be argued that spiraling causality is merely a subset of cyclic causality. However, the dynamics that differentiate it can often be so dramatic and can unfold so quickly that calling attention to these features by separating it out can make good educational sense.

WHY IS SPIRALING CAUSALITY IMPORTANT TO LEARN?

Spiraling causality is important to recognize because it can rather quickly lead to outcomes of staggering proportions. If one fails to include feedback mechanisms in models, the predictive capacity of those models is undermined and a sense of false comfort can be derived from thinking that there is more opportunity to deal with a problem than actually exists.

This was the case with the early models of climate change. Climate change involves multiple feedback loops in operation at the same time. Early models did not incorporate some of these loops so the time frame for various impacts was believed to be longer. Albedo, the surface reflectivity of the sun's radiation, is a central concept in current models of global warming. There is a feedback loop between the decreasing amount of ice and the increasing amount of radiation that is absorbed by the Earth. The more ice melts, the more radiation is absorbed in a spiraling causal pattern.

Spiraling causality is also important to recognize from an emotional stance. If you have ever gotten involved in an incident of conflict, either on the road or otherwise, you may have been surprised at how quickly events can escalate and you can get carried into actions that you would not have anticipated outside the spiraling loop. Recognizing these emotions early and learning how to de-escalate or step back from them can help cooler minds to prevail. Helping children to learn how not to "fly off the handle" in these situations is important for all students.

It can also be important to recognize spiraling patterns in non-urgent instances. For example, noticing that parental support for fund-raising activities is slowly falling off at school might spur administrators to consider what is contributing to it. "Falling off" patterns can also have a spiraling causality at their core. For instance, as the number of parents who are excited about engaging in certain activities drops, the contagion of their energy falls, inciting fewer other parents to join in and so on.

Social contexts can offer avenues for helping students understand spiraling causality. Our experience in K–12 classrooms suggests that kids can learn to understand spiraling or escalating causality with examples from their everyday experiences. The playground example in the introduction about the fifth grader who ran inside to tell his teacher of the escalating causality amongst his playmates came from a group of fifth graders who had studied it in the classroom.

The research supports this observation. By nine years of age, students are able to reason about multiple facilitative causes in social problems[2] rather than merely using an additive schema.[3] It appears to be easier to understand instances where one cause facilitates another, resulting in escalation, than where one inhibits another, resulting in de-escalation.[4]

Helping students learn the characteristics of cyclic causalities to cue them to the possibility that one is in play may be an important part of teaching about escalation. Students are often unaware that a reciprocal or cyclic model might describe the causal dynamics that are unfolding.[5] Nancy Roberts found significant learning in fifth and sixth graders who were taught to read dynamic feedback system causal loops and to develop feedback diagrams in social studies.[6] We found similarly promising outcomes in relation to ecosystems concepts.[7]

Ask yourself:

- Can I think of any examples where I was caught up in an escalating pattern of conflict? What was it like? Were there actions that I took that I might not have taken outside of the spiraling pattern?
- What are some places in my curriculum where a spiraling causal pattern describes the causal dynamics?

• Are there ways that I use escalation or de-escalation to capture and hold students' attention?

WHAT ARE SOME EXAMPLES OF SPIRALING CAUSALITY IN THE CURRICULUM?

I've already mentioned the example of climate change and Albedo Effect. This is a really important pattern for students to grasp. Ice and snow are good reflectors of the sun's rays. But as ice around the world begins melting, it exposes more of the land and water. This, in turn, absorbs, rather then reflects, heat from the sun, increasing the magnitude and speed of atmospheric warming. Animations of this causal dynamic can be found online at NASA and other environmental organizations. [8]

Patterns in evolution can exemplify spiraling causal patterns. Consider increased drug resistance. As we increase our arsenal of antibiotics, we manage to kill off the weakest forms, and the strongest ones go on to reproduce. We then seek out antibiotics to defeat these "superbugs" and the escalation goes on. Recognizing the spiral was an important step in recent efforts to curtail how, when, and to whom we administer antibiotics, in at least slowing the escalation.

History contains many examples of spiraling causality. Understanding patterns in war involves reasoning about escalating patterns of causality. Studying the Middle East conflict involves considering patterns of retaliation and attempts to address the problem. There is typically a pattern of escalation or de-escalation in play as each side reacts to the other. The process of invention also can involve escalation of efforts to get one's discoveries out there. Historical examples exist in addition to many current day examples such as Microsoft and Apple.

What about exponential growth patterns in math? Exponential growth patterns describe a form of increase or decrease in magnitude that may underlie some spiraling causal patterns. However, an exponential growth pattern in and of itself is not causal and doesn't necessarily describe a pattern that involves inherent feedback.

So if a child's parents agree to pay him or her a penny to do the dishes and to double it each night, paying the penny isn't the "cause" of the next night's payment—it goes back to the original agreement. In other systems, there may be inherent feedback that fuels the pattern so that a spiraling causality is in play. So each time my daughter's guppies reproduce, there are more guppies to reproduce, so the exponential growth is inherent to the cause.

Learning to detect cyclic and spiraling forms of causality can pay off in classroom and school-wide interactions as well. From noise in the cafeteria to scuffles on the playground, encouraging students to realize when cyclic causality is in play and is beginning to spiral can help them in their social interactions in school and beyond.

NOTES

1. With appreciation to the students at the Marshall Simonds Middle School in Burlington, Massachusetts, and their teachers at the time, Lucy Morris, Rich Carroll, and Val Tobias.
2. Baldwin & Baldwin, 1970; Karniol & Ross, 1976; Sedlak & Kurtz, 1981; Smith, 1975
3. Sedlak & Kurtz, 1981
4. Shultz & Mendelson, 1975; Sedlak & Kurtz, 1981
5. e.g., Green, 1997; Shipstone, 1985; Westbrook & Marek, 1992
6. Roberts, 1978
7. Grotzer & Basca 2003
8. http://www.archive.org/details/CIL-10023 [accessed 7-19-2011].

Chapter Seven

Mutual Causality: Symbiosis and Bi-directionality

"It's a win-win situation."

"It was a symbiotic relationship."

"Your gain is my loss."

During World War I, Ben May, a lumberman from Alabama had the idea to use lumber as ballast in ships as a means to transport timber to Europe where it was needed in the war effort. The navy, needing a cheap or free supply of ballast, agreed to the idea. May received free transport for lumber that he then sold once the ships got to Europe. This illustrates an instance of mutual causality—a clear win-win situation.

This particular instance also went on to have many domino effects as Ben invested his earnings into land and in 1939 founded Gulf Lumber in Mobile Alabama. By age thirty-two, he was a millionaire. [1] May became an important philanthropist as he, in turn, supported, and through endowments continues to support, significant medical research including the work of Sir Alexander Fleming, the discoverer of penicillin, and cardiology and cancer research. The Ben May Laboratory for Cancer Research at the University of Chicago bears his name. [2]

WHAT IS MUTUAL CAUSALITY?

Mutual causality is a type of two-way causal pattern where one event, act, process, or relationship has mutual, and typically simultaneous, effects. Each component has an effect on the other, so each acts as both a cause and an effect. Mutual causality[3] can be seen in symbiotic relationships where an action (such as a bee pollinating a flower) results in effects (albeit different) on both organisms (the bee gains pollen; the flower is fertilized). The event, act, process, or relationship does not always have positive effects in both directions. A tick sucking blood from a dog gets nourishment and the dog is weakened.

Historic homes are sometimes sold by towns very inexpensively so that the town saves the cost of demolition and the person buying the home gets a bargain and invests in fixing up the home, thus enhancing the neighborhood. This was a common pattern during the foreclosure crisis of 2009. "One man's junk is another man's treasure" involves mutual causality in that one person gets rid of something that they don't want while another person gains something that they do.

What fuels win-win situations in an evolutionary sense has received recent attention from scientists. According to evolutionary biologist Megan Frederickson, the prevailing consensus in the field had been that "host species have evolved to punish cheaters and to reward cooperators."[4] However, it now appears that the benefit derived offers the evolutionary advantage, so that "simple self-interest" fuels the relationship—helping a host leads to a healthy host that the investing partner benefits from.[5] This doesn't change the outcome, but it leads to a deeper understanding of what sustains symbiotic relationships.

WHAT ARE THE CHARACTERISTICS OF MUTUAL CAUSALITY?

The images conjured up by mutual causality include bi-directionality, symbiosis, and two-way causal patterns.

In cases of mutual causality:

- There is one event, act, relationship, or process where two things impact each other.
- The impact can be positive for both, negative for both, or positive for one and negative for the other.
- There is a blurring of causes and effects in that each cause or causal agent is affected.
- The effects for each entity are often simultaneous, but can be sequential. (Some sequential versions are better characterized by cyclic causality.)
- It may be event based (an act such as a bee pollinating a flower and gaining food) or may involve a relationship or process over time (such as the moss and the algae in lichen).

Mutual causality differs from cyclic causality in that it isn't characterized by a feedback loop where one event causes another which in turn impacts the initial cause and so on. If Guy has cookies and Tim has milk and they decided in advance to share, mutual causality would strongly apply. That said, even if Guy spontaneously handed over a cookie and then Tim responded by pouring a glass of milk for the first person, we might still call it a "win-win situation." Mutual causality is most strongly characterized by simultaneity, but it is not impossible for the mutual impact to play out over time.

Some mutual causal relationships can have outcomes that are positive at one level but not at another. For instance, in a food web, mice cause energy to be present for owls and the owls help to maintain the size of the mouse population such that it is in greater balance with its food sources. While the owls benefit at both the population and the individual level, the mice benefit only at the population level (presuming it never benefits the individual to be eaten).

Joanna Macy has written about the centrality of mutual causation to Buddhism and to General Systems Theory. She argues that each attends to the self-organizing nature of the world and involves patterns of reciprocal and mutual causation. Following from this, she explains that the self, in Buddhism, is not the knower and actor but part of a process or flow. "When we recognize our participation in its co-arising patterns, we can claim our power to act. We can then, through our choices give expression and efficacy to the coordination at play in all life forms."[6]

WHY IS MUTUAL CAUSALITY IMPORTANT TO LEARN?

Recognizing mutual causality often alerts us to costs and benefits. Breaking apart the mutuality into simple linear causality when mutual benefits exist can result in a misperception of the incentive structures in play. Analyzing the mutuality where there are negative consequences in one direction and positive ones in another can help us reason about the magnitude of the costs and benefits. It doesn't typically help a parasite to kill its host so the costs may be understood best in the context of the relationship. (It may not matter if the parasite needs its host only temporarily.)

Focusing on only the "active" side of a relationship, as many of us tend to do, can also disguise what sustains it. There are many social examples where we might think that one person is deriving all of the benefits of an exchange, but the other person is getting something that they need or feel is worthwhile. Breaking these relationships down to simple cause and effect misses much of the causal story.

As in domino causality, one of the conceptual challenges is that the distinction between what is an effect and what is a cause is blurred. In mutual causality, something can simultaneously act as a cause and be an effect. As discussed above, the developmental literature shows that this blurring is conceptually difficult.[7] The science- education literature also demonstrates the conceptual difficulty. For instance, learning to reason that forces act in pairs and about equal and opposite effects as per Newton's third law is notoriously hard for students and they typically think of one object as having more force.[8]

Research shows that students often miss mutual relationships.[9] Instead, they typically impose a simple cause-and-effect pattern and miss instances of interdependence. Students aged twelve to sixteen rarely used the concept of ecological interdependence when explaining preservation of species.[10] Researcher David Green found that without cueing, only 16 percent of twenty-year-olds gave two-way accounts of predator-prey relationships. If cued, then 60 percent of those tested gave two-way accounts, but this number went down again when more complex problems were posed.[11]

In addition, when there is a more active player in the relationship, people often notice only that side of the equation. In thinking about how gears work, students typically consider the driving gear as active and the other gears in the train as passive recipients of motion. They miss the *interactive* causality in which gears push against each other.

It is easier to see that a bee gains pollen than that the flower is fertilized. *The Bee Movie*, written by Jerry Seinfeld and animated by DreamWorks Animation in 2007, explored what might happen if bees suddenly had no need to gather pollen or nectar. Despite some liberties with the science, it drove home the point that there are two sides to this causal equation.

Ask yourself:

- What are some recent examples where mutual causality might have been in play?
- In these cases was there a cause that was more active than the other?
- How might thinking about it explicitly as mutual causality have changed your reasoning or action in the situation?

WHAT ARE SOME EXAMPLES OF
MUTUAL CAUSALITY IN THE CURRICULUM?

Mutual causality is common in biology, so much so that different types have different names. Symbiosis is an overarching term that refers to the interaction of two species that are in direct contact and affect each other. How they impact each other is captured by more specific terminology.

Mutualism is a form of symbiosis where two organisms mutually affect each other in beneficial ways. Parasitism is a form of symbiosis where one organism lives off another organism, usually to the detriment of the organism being lived off of. A third type, commensalism, refers to a situation where one species benefits and the effect on the other species is neutral. These relationships can be easy to show in the classroom in a big community fish tank. Algae eaters eat algae from the fish-tank walls, helping to keep the algae in balance, while the algae keeps the algae eaters well fed.

Mutual causality is also inherent to many physics concepts. Heavenly bodies are attracted to each other in a manner described by mutual causality, not simple linear causality as many students think. For instance, students think that the gravity of Earth pulls the moon into orbit around Earth—impacting the moon. But many students don't realize that the gravitational attraction of the moon impacts the earth as well, resulting in the ocean tides, for example.

In the case of electrons and protons, while electrons may play a more active role, the attraction is between protons and electrons. If you pull two socks out of the dryer and hold them up in the air, they attract toward each other rather than having just one pull the other one toward it. If during a thunderstorm, you feel your hair beginning to stand on edge, you're becoming a part of the mutual attraction that results in a lightning strike, so it's time for action.

Mutual causality is a powerful lens through which to examine events in history. In each case, asking who was mutually impacted, how they were impacted, and attempting to examine the answers to those questions through the perspectives of those involved may lead to more sensitive and informed policy decisions. It can also be a useful lens to consider the incentives that have led to alliances, colonization, and other patterns of interaction between political entities—people or countries.

Mutual causality plays a role in classroom life as well. Helping students realize situations when their benefit has a cost for someone else invites greater sensitivity to our impact on others. Encouraging them to seek win-win situations creates incentive structures that are on everyone's side—whether the discussion is about leaving up buildings in the block corner, sharing art supplies, writing a report in ways that build on each other's strengths, or resolving playground disputes. This learning serves them well in many aspects of adult life—setting policy, resolving conflict, developing new products, and so on.

NOTES

1. Fosgate, 2002
2. http://mobilealabamahistory.blogspot.com/2010/06/ben-may-library-downtown-mobile-alabama.html [accessed: 11-20-2010]; http://www.cba.ua.edu/hall_of_fame/75BEM.html [accessed: 11-20-2010].
3. Koplowitz, 1984
4. Bradt, 2010; The first theory is known as the "host sanction" theory. The second theory is called the "partnership fidelity feedback" theory. The article, written by Bradt, outlines the work of E. Glen Weyl and colleagues.
5. Interestingly, the advance in theory grew out of collaboration between economists and evolutionary biologists which leads to the possibility that it will advance theory in each field.
6. Macy, 1991, p. xiii
7. Golinkoff, 1975; Leslie & Keeble, 1987
8. e.g., Brown & Clement, 1987
9. Barman, Griffiths & Okebukola, 1995; Barman & Mayer, 1994; Grotzer & Basca, 2003
10. Palmer, 1996
11. Green, 1997

Chapter Eight

Relational Causality: Balances and Differentials

"The balance tipped so the scales shifted."

"My identity was defined by which sibling I was with."

*"It's not how many votes you have, it is
how many more than your opponent."*

Lake Nyos is a lake in Cameroon about two hundred miles northwest of the capital of Yaoundé. It has earned the distinction as being one of the "killer lakes." In August of 1986, gases from the lake escaped into the atmosphere displacing the oxygen and nearly eighteen hundred people died. While the investigation of what happened was complex and difficult to study, scientists have pieced together enough evidence to suggest the following explanation. They call the phenomenon "lake overturn." [1]

The area of Cameroon where Lake Nyos sits is volcanically active. This means that carbon dioxide gas escapes into the environment. Gases with different densities form layers in the atmosphere as denser gases sink on less-dense gases. Carbon dioxide gas from this underground volcanic activity builtup at the bottom of Lake Nyos over time, like the dissolved carbon dioxide in a can of soda.

A disturbance in the lake, possibly from a landslide, caused the carbon dioxide to be released, the way the bubbles in a can of soda rise to the top when shaken. Because the pure carbon dioxide was denser than existing air around the lake, the carbon dioxide gas sank and the air containing breathable oxygen rose above it. The pure carbon dioxide suffocated most of the people who lived in the area overnight. There's more to this story which I revisit in chapter ten but the relevant point here is the relationship between the two sets of gases and the outcome, which is characterized by relational causality.

WHAT IS RELATIONAL CAUSALITY?

✓ Relational causality involves recognizing that outcomes can be caused by a relationship, one of balance or imbalance, between elements of a system. Neither element is the cause by itself. You can be a younger sister in relation to some siblings and an older sister in relation to others. Who goes up or down on a seesaw is caused by a relationship. When my twins clamber on, they balance each other perfectly, but if their older sister replaces one, the remaining twin goes up. If their oldest brother replaces the other twin, their older sister will go up—it all depends upon the relationship between their masses.

✓ How could our team have lost when they played so well? Why does oil float on water—making it so hard to clean out a vegetable-oil bottle? Why do we float better in salt water than fresh water? How do we get the liquid out of a juice box? How do planes get the "lift" to fly? Why do balloons fly out the windows of moving cars? These are all questions that have relational causality at their core.

✗ The concepts of balance and differentials between variables are pervasive in our world, particularly in science. Whether something sinks or floats depends upon the relationship between the density of the thing (whether vegetable oil or a person) and the density of the liquid it is placed in (whether fresh or salt water). As elaborated below, drinking juice from a straw depends upon the imbalance of the air pressure acting on the juice and that within the straw and mouth. Planes achieve "lift" due to a differential in air

✓ pressure between the top and bottom of the wing (Bernoulli's Principle).

But relational causality extends far beyond science. Why does the home team go into a summer slump? It is easy to frame the problem in terms of simple cause and effect. You might think about how we need a better pitcher or the defense has been lacking or that the team is simply getting worse!

Now consider the problem using a relational causal lens. The outcome of each game is the performance of one team in relation to the other (although we may just want to blame it on the refs!). This leads one's attention to other sets of variables. Perhaps other teams are starting out the season more slowly than the hometown team, but due to coaching, are coming together better as a team. Perhaps they are experiencing steep improvement and their performance in relation to the hometown performance has shifted. Perhaps the hometown team hasn't gotten worse at all. Perhaps they just haven't improved as much.

Relational causality accounts for why some kids make the soccer team and others don't. Students are sometimes offered a simple cause-and-effect model ("do your best and you will succeed" or "it's all about practice"— incredibly important messages about the incremental nature of learning[2]). As educators, we may believe that the most important thing is that each child did his or her personal best and/or demonstrated learning. But then they may find themselves having to perform against others and not meeting with the success that they expected. They've been misled about the causal rules of the game.

WHAT ARE THE CHARACTERISTICS OF RELATIONAL CAUSALITY?

When looking for instances of relational causality, one looks for balance or imbalance (are the two things equal, or is one greater or lesser than the other?) and what happens in each case.

In cases of relational causality:

- The relationship between two variables or sets of variables accounts for the effect. ✔
- There is more than one variable in play. ✔
- There may be a relationship of balance/equivalence or a relationship of imbalance/difference. ✔
- Shifts in the relationship can account for changes in the outcome.
- Changes in both variables that maintain the relationship between them do not cause differences in outcome.

In considering instances of relational causality, it is important to ask whether the relationship between the two variables (how much you have of one compared to how much you have of the other) causes the outcome. It is NOT an example of relational causality if one cause can result in the effect without the other cause or you have two causes, but there is no comparison between them (for instance, you just add them up or one occurs and then the other).

One of the reasons it can be difficult to detect relational causality is that if one variable changes, the outcome may change proportionally, so one might attribute what happens to just that variable.[3] However, it is important to realize that if one variable changes, often the relationship changes as well. If two variables change but keep the same relationship, the outcome doesn't change.

WHY IS RELATIONAL CAUSALITY IMPORTANT TO LEARN?

Why should we attend to relational causality? When the outcomes depend upon a relationship, if we focus only on one set of variables, we lose predictive power. We only know one side of the equation. Some of the time, we'll be right and other times, we will be surprised! We may be very impressed with our team, but if we don't know anything about the other team, it's hard to predict the outcome. Beyond this, many concepts in math and science depend upon a grasp of relational causality. The habit of reducing relational phenomena to simple cause and effect accounts for many misconceptions in both subjects.

Ask yourself:

- Are there instances of balance or imbalance that lead to outcomes in the curriculum?
- What language could I introduce to help students to be aware of the inherent relational causality?
- How might thinking about the example explicitly as relational causality shift what the discussion focuses on?

For example, relational causality is often overlooked in instances of sinking and floating. When asked what makes something sink or float, students typically respond with a focus on the object referring to its weight or size.[4] "The bigger one will sink" or "The heavier one sinks."

In one of our curriculum activities, we show students two pieces from the same candle, one larger and one smaller. The two pieces are each dropped into separate beakers. The larger piece sinks and the smaller piece floats. Students typically nod in affirmation. Then we switch which candle is in which beaker. Now the larger one floats and the smaller one sinks. Students are very surprised and they begin to focus on the liquid. "Are the liquids different?" they ask. The students' focus has shifted to the relationship between the object and the liquid.

Whether an object sinks or floats depends upon the differential in density between the object and the liquid (or between two fluids as in the Lake Nyos example.) Here, the candles float in water and sink in isopropyl alcohol. Students then begin to make connections—realizing, for instance, that they float more in salt water than in regular water. How they reason about the nature of causality in sinking and floating has shifted. In our curriculum work, we call this kind of activity a RECAST activity because it REveals the ✗ underlying CAusal STructure of the phenomenon.

Developmentally speaking, the existing research suggests that late childhood and early adolescence are times when students should be able to grasp relational causality because they have an ability to hold more information in their heads and are able to think about relationships between multiple variables.[5]

However, we don't yet know what is possible if we offer children optimal scaffolds. More typically, children's simple linear models are reinforced despite research to suggest that they are capable of more complex causal reasoning.[6] In the preschool and primary grades, teachers often create lists of "sinkers" and "floaters." This reinforces students' simple linear models instead of inviting them to realize the underlying relational causal structure. Alternatively, teachers might encourage experimentation with more than one liquid, water and salt water, for example.

In a program for four-year-olds, we set up a pulley on the ceiling with a string attached to another pulley just over a water table filled with rice. We put two water bottles upside down on the strings on either side. Lines on each bottle enabled easy measurement of how much rice was in each one. Children realized that they could not manipulate one bottle without impacting the other. Any kind of differential would make one go up and the other go down. They had fun carefully adjusting the amount of rice to even up the bottles. While playing, they were building causal concepts relevant to science class in the coming years.

WHAT ARE EXAMPLES OF RELATIONAL CAUSALITY IN THE CURRICULUM?

Examples of relational causality are abundant across the curriculum. In social studies, election results involve relational causality. In the end, the number of votes is less critical than that number in comparison to your opponent's votes. It is possible to lose by one vote. Outperforming a warring faction underlies many historical outcomes. Economies of scale are often built up when one competitor slightly outperforms another even if the difference between the products is minimal.

The examples at the outset of this chapter establish how pervasive relational causality is in the sciences. Here are a few more examples. A differential in air pressure is what enables us to take every breath, how fish regulate where they are in the water, how puffer fish and submarines rise and fall, and how a syringe works.

The examples are not just in physics. The relationship between different animal populations leads to balance or flux. Duckweed seems to magically disappear from ponds in the winter, reappearing every spring. How? It appears that as it collects sugar in the waning summer days, it becomes denser than the pond water and sinks. As it uses up the sugars to sustain itself, it becomes less dense and appears at the surface again.

Math involves abundant relational concepts, however, they are definitional rather than causal per se.[7] Fractional and *per* quantities in math are defined by relationships—a one over a two (½) is a bigger number than a one over a four (¼) even though four is a bigger number than two. These are descriptions of relationships of balance or imbalance.

Relational causality has a strong place in the curriculum, but students will find many examples outside the classroom as well. Some of these examples connect to science in everyday life. It may be comforting to know that when the heat comes on and you hear a door gently close or the shades in your window move, a differential in air pressure is the only causal "agent" likely responsible for the outcome. It may also encourage reflection and different ways of thinking about competition in sports, social interactions, and beyond, and help students understand the causal rules of the game with greater complexity.

NOTES

1.   Source: http://www.biology.lsa.umich.edu/~gwk/research/nyos.html. Information from a description of the research of George W. Kling, Department of Ecology & Evolutionary Biology, University of Michigan.

2.   Dweck, 2006

3.   This is the case with the density of pure substances, for instance, if you cut them in half. The volume and mass are proportionately impacted.

4.   e.g., Perkins & Grotzer, 2005; Grotzer, Powell & Carr, 2011; Smith, Carey & Wiser, 1985; Smith et al., 1997

5.   Work by the well-known developmental psychologist Robbie Case (e.g., 1991), suggests that concepts of this type are understood by early adolescence, during the Vectorial Stage, when they are able to coordinate dimensional structures.

6.   e.g., Gopnik et al., 2004; Kushnir & Gopnik, 2007; Sobel, 2004

7.   Whether definitions of "how things are" can be causes has been the point of many a discussion with the middle school students with whom we worked. While some students argued that it could be, even appealing to Aristotle's four causes including material causes as definitional, most students differentiated between definitional relationships and causality.

Part 3: Features of Complex Causality and Our Related Default Assumptions

This part of the book discusses *features* of complex causality and considers how these interact with our default assumptions about the nature of causality. While these assumptions can serve us well, they can also lead to problems—they are often too shortsighted and do not capture the bigger picture. All of these can contribute to reducing more complex causal scenarios to simpler ones to missing more complex causal patterns such as those in part two.

Each chapter in this section looks at a feature of causal complexity and explains the default assumption that is in tension with it. The features of spatial gaps (or "action at a distance") and temporal delays are grouped together because they interact so closely. The default assumptions that we make about each feature are a consequence of the cognition of everyday causal reasoning discussed in chapter three in relation to the complexity of the world around us. The interaction of the two is described for each feature.

These features impact how we think about complexity in terms of the triadic aspects of thinking dispositions introduced by David Perkins, Shari Tishman and Eileen Jay: (1) *Sensitivity*—whether we notice causal patterns and realize opportunities to think differently about them; (2) *Ability*—how well we are able to respond to them when we do notice them; and (3) *Inclination*—whether or not we actually do; how inclined we are both in the sense of everyday inclination in the moment and in the more reflective sense of making a commitment.

When it comes to dealing with causal complexity, each of these presents unique challenges. I come back to this discussion in part four to elaborate upon what it suggests for issues of teaching and learning.

Chapter Nine

Across Time and Distance: Detecting Delayed and Distant Effects

"How could we know that it would have an impact a world away?"

"Generations later, they were still dealing with the effects."

A block from Appian Way toward Harvard Square, on the corner of Farwell Place and Brattle Street in Cambridge, if you look down when you walk, you'll pass a brass plaque near a storm drain with an image of a fish on it and the words "Don't dump, drains to Charles River." In other places in and around Boston and Cambridge, there are similar plaques and signs painted onto the sidewalk. I walk by this plaque on a daily basis and each time, I contemplate our human need to be reminded of effects that we can't see—those that are beyond our reach in terms of space and time.

Why do we tend to notice immediate and local effects and to miss delayed and distant ones? Research shows that our default assumption is to attend to events that are close in space and time over those that are not.[1] If a bee is stinging you, the cause is local and the effect is immediate, and it is unlikely that you'll ignore it! Pain is a great motivator. But even if the bee doesn't sting you, you aren't likely to settle down to eat your lunch next to a bees' nest.

However, consider sitting in the sun without sunscreen. The sun, a distant cause, is slowly burning your skin and you are building up your likelihood of skin cancer, a delayed effect and, unless you are allergic to bees, a more catastrophic effect than bee stings. Yet there's a much greater likelihood that you'll ignore the problem and perhaps even discount it.[2]

Many causal patterns have delayed effects. A deer-tick bite today can result in the circular rash of Lyme disease weeks later. We invest in our students today with the hope that they will use what they've learned in the future. Many causal patterns also have distant effects. When Hurricane Katrina hit New Orleans in 2005, in addition to the local, tragic effects, gas prices soared across the entire country as it knocked out gas production in the Gulf of Mexico. Following the 1980 eruption of Mount St. Helens in Washington state, the finest ash impacted weather patterns all the way around the globe. How does the delayed and distant quality of these patterns impact our perception of causality and how we allocate our attention? What does the research say about each case?

DEALING WITH SPATIAL GAPS

Spatial gaps between causes and effects are a common part of everyday life. Many electronic devices involve remote controls. Life on Earth is possible because of energy from the sun. A magnet can pull a pile of pins toward it without touching them[3] and electrical circuits offer the appearance of a spatial gap if one does not consider the circuitry behind the walls as a switch is flipped and a light elsewhere comes on. Bad weather in one part of the world can impact the world food supply. Legislative decisions about the price of oil in the United States impact production and pricing elsewhere.

When generating explanations, we often give local ones when distant ones apply. The orbit of a planet results from the forward movement of the planet in a frictionless environment combined with the gravitational attraction between the sun and the planet. Yet students often describe a local force or inertia within the planet that "drives it."[4] They think that plants get their food from the soil rather than producing it through the process of photosynthesis using energy from the sun.[5] They believe that the eye sends out a ray[6] instead of light being reflected to the eye from the object one is viewing.

Understanding that causes can have effects even when they are not in physical contact has been referred to as "action at a distance." Research in cognition shows that "action at a distance" is more difficult to grasp than cases where causes and effects are touching or are in close proximity. From our earliest days, we expect physical contact between causes and effects, at least in inanimate cases.

In an interesting set of studies, Liz Spelke and colleagues showed that infants were surprised by how shadows behave.[7] Picture a shadow on a wall. What happens when you move the object making the shadow? The shadow moves. This is surprising to infants. After all, the shadow and the object are not touching, so why would moving one, also move the other?

Now consider what happens if you move the wall that the shadow is projected onto. The shadow does not move with the wall. This also surprises infants. The shadow is touching the wall so they expect the shadow to move with the wall when it is moved, when in fact it does not.[8] Certain causes that can act from a spatial distance or without physical contact with their effects clearly violate babies' rules for how the world works.

Interestingly, however, babies can override the expectation of "no action at a distance" when it comes to humans or other animate objects such as the family dog.[9] They are not surprised when they cry and mom or dad comes to them, for instance. This ability to accept action at a distance in some cases suggests the malleability of our causal assumptions and that, even at a very early age, we have the flexibility to map them to certain instances and not others.

The developmental trend is toward understanding how specific causal patterns interact with specific contexts.[10] At four months old, my son would stare at the lamp when I flipped the switch across the room and it came on. By ten months old, when I picked up the remote control for the CD player, he and his twin sister would both turn their heads toward the CD player across the room in anticipation. They had, at the very least, made an association between the remote and the eventual music despite the distance between cause and effect.

Across the preschool years, children reveal increasing understanding of the contextual nuances of where there may be spatial gaps.[11] Early research by Thomas Shultz found that two- to four-year-olds could detect when a tuning fork in front of a box made a sound as opposed to one touching it.[12] Five-year-olds, but not three-year-olds, could override spatial gaps using knowledge about how flashlights work.[13] Dave Sobel and colleagues found that when four-year-olds are familiar with the mechanisms, they can override lack of physical contact, but that physical distance makes a causal inference less compelling.[14]

More recently, researchers Tamar Kushnir and Alison Gopnik tried to distinguish between whether children were just engaging in imitation when they, for instance, flipped switches to make lights come on. Or were they able to make a causal connection between the switch and the light despite the physical distance between them?

They found that four-year-olds were more able to override instances where there was a spatial gap than three-year-olds. Children were able to use information about how causes and effects co-varied (even if it was not completely one to one) to make causal assumptions even when a cause and an effect were not touching spatially. However, children were correct more often when there was no spatial gap (even if the relationship was not one to one).[15]

This learning continues as children encounter new instances of "action at a distance" and have opportunities to revise their "spatial proximity" assumptions. Kindergarteners in our research studies understood that the voice over the loudspeaker in their room was generated by the woman in the office down the hall, even if they could not explain in any detail the mechanism that connected the cause and effect.[16]

Fourth graders realized that information on their Nintendo DS could be generated by anyone else with a DS who was within the thirty-foot range required by the technology.[17] Some of them used their iPods to work distant webcams, manipulating the camera to see waves on a beach in Florida or to follow the antics of a goat in western Massachusetts. From kindergarten through grade six, students used their knowledge about the nature of different causes to make the link, despite not having access to the cause and effect at the same time (ruling out the use of co-variation).[18] Clearly, children allow for action at a distance.

An explicit focus on learning "action at a distance" can result in increased understanding. Researchers have tried training first through fourth graders to perceive causal action at a distance using magnets. Before the training, none of the children's responses acknowledged action at a distance, but afterwards there was a significant increase amongst the older children's responses.[19]

However, even if we *can* recognize causes despite a spatial gap, it doesn't appear to be our default tendency. If given a choice, preschoolers are still less likely to pick a spatially remote event than a spatially local one as a cause.[20] Even adults, who override temporal and spatial gaps with co-variation information in research contexts,[21] and have more information about the world,[22] tend to be shortsighted and to look for local causes before searching for remote ones.[23]

As a search pattern, efficiency can make sense. However, if we are satisfied with an explanation that involves local causes, we are less likely to search for and consider distant ones and this can get us in trouble. We end up needing reminders such as the fish plaque on the street or the one on the napkins in a Starbucks coffee shop that read, "These come from trees."

Having expertise in an area doesn't make us immune to this tendency. How locally we define "the problem space" can impact what we view as both the problem and the potential solutions. Judah Folkman, once the head of surgery and a researcher at Children's Hospital Boston, eventually became recognized for discovering the important role that the recruitment of blood vessels play in the growth of cancer cells. The process that he called angiogenesis involved a shift in focus, not on the cancer itself, but less locally on the tissues surrounding the cancer.[24]

Folkman's work initially met with much skepticism in the field, albeit for a variety of reasons. As a surgeon, he was viewed as an outsider by the research community. But one of the key reasons that his ideas were so contrary to the existing views of the day was that everyone else was focused directly on the cancer cells themselves.

How far apart the causes and effects are from one another interacts with how difficult it is to detect a causal relationship between them. A particular area of difficulty appears to be dealing with "action at an attentional distance."[25] Often causal connections fall outside our everyday experience and thus escape the parameters of our everyday causal reasoning. When we get into our cars to drive to work, we don't typically think about polar bears and melting Arctic ice. A clever television ad for the new electric car by Nissan, the Nissan Leaf, aimed to bridge that attentional gap by having a polar bear travel to hug a driver of the new vehicle in his driveway.

In our research, children relied on mechanism information to connect cause and effect when action at an attentional distance was in play. They could not use co-variation information because the cause and effect were in different attentional frames.[26]

However, even when alerted to spatially distant causes, we still struggle with how to deal with the inherent complexity of spatial distance. In May of 2009, the Obama administration declined, as had the Bush administration before it, to allow the Endangered Species Act to be used to restrict emissions of greenhouse gases that were threatening the polar bear and its habitat.

The arguments hinged on whether it was appropriate to limit greenhouse gases outside the bear's Arctic range. Ken Salazar, the secretary of the interior agreed that greenhouse gases, which are generated worldwide, were connected to climate change and that climate change was the single biggest threat to the bear's habitat. But he cited the difficulties of evaluating the impact of cement plants in Georgia and Florida on the polar bear's habitat. He argued for pushing for broader rulings, while many environmentalists expressed dismay at the decision.[27]

Timing can help us detect causes even when a spatial gap is present. A set of interesting experiments showed that when the timing of a possible cause is just prior to an event, children will choose it as a cause even if there is a spatial gap.[28] This was so even when children stated prior to the event that a potential cause that was spatially separated could no longer act as the cause and gave distance as the reason. When timing cues suggested a particular cause, children were able to choose it, but expressed uncertainty and discomfort in choosing spatially separate causes.

While timing can offer useful hints to help us detect spatially distant causes, there are many instances where a time delay exists between causes and effects. In terms of recognizing causal connections, conceptually, how do we deal with time delays? To further complicate matters, often time delays go hand in hand with spatial gaps.

DEALING WITH TIME DELAYS

Time delays between cause and effect are also part of our everyday existence. A CD player typically begins to play approximately three to five seconds after pushing the play button. Thunder lags behind lightning. Ecosystem effects often take a long time to become noticeable, health benefits or costs occur after a delay, effects of acid rain and other forms of pollution accumulate such that there is a delay of the most dramatic effects.

It is much harder for us to make a connection between causes and effects when there is a time delay in between. Research shows that when one event immediately follows another, children are more likely to infer that there is a causal connection between them.[29] This is so even when two events turn out to be merely correlated with one another.

There are changes across childhood in how we deal with time delays. Time delays make it difficult for preschoolers to successfully realize a causal relationship.[30] They are more likely to choose inconsistent events that are close in time and space over events that consistently co-vary but are delayed or distant.[31]

Robert Siegler and colleagues found that when no delay was present, preschoolers could successfully make a causal connection. However, when a five-second delay was introduced, they failed.[32] By age five, children were better able to handle the delays, particularly when there was an identifiable explanation for the delay,[33] though they could still be distracted by the delay.[34] By age eight, children judged the regularity of the delay in forming their causal impressions[35] and could override time delays if the events regularly occurred together.[36]

In similar contexts, while adults typically treat all delayed events as non-causal, they are able to override temporal delays and spatial gaps when specific information suggests the need to—for instance, that there may be a more complex interaction between what appear to be two competing causes.[37] Further, adults are more likely to have and therefore use information about how often two events typically co-occur.[38]

Most of the above studies used various mechanical devices—switches, boxes, and lights— so they tap into reasoning about certain types of physical causation. In psychological and physical domains, children appear to accept time delays more easily into their causal models. Charles Kalish asked children what would happen if you drank something contaminated with "doggie doo-doo." He found that five-year-olds, but not three- and four-year-olds understood that there would be a delay in getting sick from contamination even if the emotional effects of feeling disgusted would be immediate.[39]

Clearly, the ability to detect causes that are temporally or spatially remote grows over childhood. As discussed in chapter three, children also grow to use more information than timing or spatial proximity between causes and effects to judge a causal connection. They consider whether there is a plausible mechanism that can account for the outcome,[40] they judge the consistency between causes and effects,[41] and rely on information from others.[42]

As helpful as this overall body of research is in suggesting what we are capable of, it doesn't straightforwardly translate into what we *will* do in the real world. The information on how causes and effects interact is not as readily available as in carefully controlled experimental contexts. It may be difficult to abstract or it may compete with many irrelevant or potentially relevant variables for our attention. A time delay or spatial gap increases the likelihood that the relationship will fall beyond our attentional edges. Thus we tend to miss these connections—unless there's a plaque on the street to remind us.

When spatial and time delays go hand in hand, the causal complexity increases exponentially. Try explaining the need for sunscreen to a three-year-old and you'll get the idea. If you don't put the sunscreen on, a distant object in the sky will mysteriously do something to cause painful sunburn even though you aren't anywhere near it. And it won't happen now, but later in the day. How, exactly, the sunscreen stops the sunburn is equally mysterious. My colleague, Paul Harris, studies how children learn from adult testimony. It's a good thing that they do because the sunscreen explanation is enough to make a thoughtful preschooler look at you cross-eyed![43]

DOMINO CAUSALITY AND TIME DELAYS

When a domino causal pattern is in play, often there are time delays involved as impacts that are further from the initial cause take time to unfold. Think back to the Borneo cat story from chapter four. There was a time delay between the initial spraying of mosquitoes and outbreaks of sylvatic plague and typhus, as DDT-poisoned geckoes were eaten by cats and the rat population increased over time. We often miss effects that we have to trace out over time. Our attention shifts elsewhere, we miss the connections, or don't realize that they are related.

Dating back to the ancient Greeks, a distinction has been made between proximal and distal or ultimate causes. It captures the difference between the cause closest to the outcomes, the proximal cause and the cause that initially set the pattern in motion, the distal or ultimate cause. So in the Borneo story, the proximal cause of sylvatic plague and typhus is increased rat activity, but the spraying of DDT is the distal cause or ultimate cause that set the pattern in motion.

Whether a cause is proximal or distal in practice is not always easy to determine. Sometimes it depends upon how you break the causes down.[44] But tracing causes back when there are decision points along the domino pattern can be useful in thinking about future choices.

ACCUMULATION: FIRST YOU DON'T SEE IT, THEN YOU DO

When effects have to accumulate to a certain level before they become noticeable, it gives the appearance of a time delay between causes and effects because there are no observable outcomes early in the process. This makes it easy to discount the impact of a particular action. If releasing carbon dioxide into the atmosphere has made no measurable impact for a long period of time, it is easy to see it as benign. When the levels are high enough that the impact becomes obvious, the habits are well established and it is easy to justify them with, "Well, we've always done it that way and it has never mattered before."

Accumulation can be particularly challenging to note because many biological systems have the ability to absorb a certain amount of impact before it is felt. So the early effects are non-obvious even though the system is dealing with them. Some effects accumulate straightforwardly—they become increasingly perceptible as the effects aggregate—and the effects increasingly become obvious.

THRESHOLD LEVELS, TRIGGERING CAUSES, AND TIPPING POINTS

In some instances where effects accumulate, they can suddenly trigger effects when a certain level of one variable is reached or a certain configuration of variables occurs together. This can cause a dramatic impact. It can be an accumulation where one more event triggers a cascade of effects. It can be an outcome that only appears if the right event occurs at the right time, such as a propensity hidden in our genes that unfolds if the environment interacts in the right way at the right time.

The idea of threshold levels and triggering causes relates to the phenomenon that the author Malcolm Gladwell popularized in his book *The Tipping Point*.[45] So, for instance, if one or two kids in a class have lice, we think that it may slowly spread to others, but rather, it reaches a point where it spreads precipitously. In its early stages, it appears that there will be a slow increase. You can even be lulled into thinking, "We have time to handle this." Suddenly, the pattern over time looks anything but regular and you are dealing with rapid, precipitous change.

Certain impacts of global warming have this characteristic, making it hard to come up with an adequate timeline for how events might play out. Once a certain level is reached, it triggers many other kinds of effects.

Some causes can trigger outcomes larger than one might expect. For instance, Gladwell wrote about crime in New York City in the 1990s. Changes in how smaller crimes were handled impacted the level of more violent crimes. Tolerating smaller crimes in essence sent a message about the societal tolerance for crime and triggered an attitude that one could get away with more violent crimes. Triggering causes can reach across time and distance to enable unexpected outcomes.

THE IMPACT OF TIME DELAYS AND SPATIAL GAPS ON ANALYZING RISK

Time delays and spatial gaps increase the likelihood that unintended outcomes will come back to bite us. However, there's another just as problematic side to the issue. Time delays and spatial gaps shift how we allocate our attention and how we think about risk. It is much harder to ignore effects that are immediate and local to their causes than delayed, distant ones. So risks where the effects are delayed or distant such as mad cow disease, heart disease, and global warming are much less likely to get our attention and motivate behavior change than the bee we might have sat on at lunchtime!

The extent of a delayed effect can be in tension with how salient one perceives a risk to be. People are more likely to go off of their statin heart medicine despite the risks of heart attack than they are to go off their arthritis medicine given the immediacy of the resulting pain.[46] The result of stopping statin medication is a higher risk of heart problems in the long term, but no immediately perceivable effects. This pattern is common in our individual and collective choices. Some individuals don't take the full regimen of their antibiotic prescription once the symptoms subside, subsequently breeding resistant strains of bacteria.

PICTURES OF CLASSROOM PRACTICE: WHAT DOES IT LOOK LIKE TO HELP STUDENTS LEARN TO THINK ABOUT TIME DELAYS AND SPATIAL GAPS?

The students in Ms. Jaccoby's sixth-grade class are studying ecosystems and the nature of decay—topics in the national standards. They have been talking about what happens to the leaves from the trees in the forest after they die. Many of the students think that the leaves just stay there and that unless someone takes them away, they accumulate. Located in an urban environment, the students don't have much opportunity to witness what would happen over a long period of time.

Ms. Jaccoby decides to do three things. First, she brings in some leaves and sets them up in a tank in the classroom where class members water them periodically. She also brings in pieces of rotten log at three different points of decay to discuss. Finally, she downloads time-lapse video from the Internet of fruit rotting. She uses all three to encourage a conversation about decay that she revisits at different points in the school year.

Toward the end, she plays the time lapse and discusses with students what the time lapse helps to reveal. One student remarks, "It really shows what happens. Even though our leaves are changing, it is happening so slowly that you forget how different it is now." Another student suggests, "We could put lines on the tank to show the difference." Ms. Jaccoby agrees that putting lines would be a good idea. A third student adds how "yeah, but the time lapse really makes you go whoa!"

An eighth-grade health class is discussing why some teens go to tanning parlors. Along with important discussion about issues of peer pressure and concern with appearance, Mr. Gomez, the teacher, engages students in a conversation of considering short-term outcomes against time-delayed ones. As one student puts it, "It's hard to think about what might happen in twenty years, when I'm trying to decide what to do today."

The teacher reminds the teens of an ad campaign on local television, with each ad focused on a person who wants to look "cool" in high school—particularly of one who chose to smoke and in her early thirties had to deal with lung cancer and other related health effects. The images made very clear the high cost of her earlier actions. Mr. Gomez then invites them to imagine their lives ten years from now, twenty years from now, and so on. He talks about time-delayed causes and how hard it is to attend to them in the moment, but also how important it is for when the future becomes their present.

The eleventh grade is debating the move to create legislation that makes developed countries legally accountable for climate-change impacts in underdeveloped countries that are due to the actions of the developed nations. A hot topic in the press in the spring of 2009, solutions range from allowing law suits to setting aside funds for impacted people. Mrs. Jackson asks, "What makes this such a contentious topic?" With the students, she considers how people are not used to being accountable for impacts that are far away and that they cannot necessarily see.

The students debate both sides of the accountability issue. "Can we get countries to accept their responsibility for the distant (and often delayed) outcomes of their behaviors?" "Why do people find this so hard?" "Why is it so important?" "How does it impact our ability to live together in a global world?" One student comments, "It makes you think about the saying, 'Think globally, act locally' in a new way." To Mrs. Jackson, knowing that her students can think about these things is an important part of encouraging them to become global citizens.

NOTES

1. e.g. Driver, Guesne & Tiberghien, 1985; Michotte, 1963; Perkins & Grotzer, 2005; Schlottmann et al., 2002; Siegler & Liebert, 1974
2. Grotzer, 2009; Grotzer, Miller & Lincoln, 2011
3. Shultz & Mendelson, 1975
4. e.g. Camp, Clement & Brown, 1994; Grotzer, 2004
5. e.g., Barker & Carr, 1989
6. Boyes & Stanisstreet, 1991
7. Spelke, Phillips & Woodward, 1995
8. Rubenstein, Van de Walle & Spelke, as cited in Spelke, Phillips & Woodward, 1995
9. Premack, 1990; Gelman, 1990; Woodward, Phillips & Spelke, 1993
10. e.g. Bullock & Gelman, 1979; Kushnir & Gopnik, 2007; Leslie, 1982, 1984; Sobel & Buchanan, 2009; Spelke, Phillips & Woodward,1995
11. e.g., Borton, 1979; Leslie, 1982, 1984; Leslie & Keeble, 1987; Oakes, 1993; Spelke, Phillips & Woodward, 1995; Van de Walle & Spelke, 1993
12. Shultz, 1982
13. Ibid.
14. Sobel & Buchanan, 2009
15. Kushnir & Gopnik, 2007
16. Grotzer, Solis & Tutwiler, forthcoming
17. Ibid.
18. This relates to what Shultz, 1982, has referred to as using "generative transmission."
19. Lesser, 1977
20. e.g., Koslowski, 1976; Koslowski & Snipper, 1977; Lesser, 1977
21. Michotte, 1963; Shultz & Mendelson, 1975
22. Kelley, 1973; Nisbett & Ross, 1980
23. Grotzer, 2004
24. Judah Folkman Speaks; NOVA; http://www.pbs.org/wgbh/nova/cancer/folkman. html[accessed 11-16- 2010].
25. Grotzer, Solis & Tutwiler, forthcoming
26. Ibid.
27. Revkin, 2009
28. Bullock & Gelman, 1979
29. e.g., Michotte, 1963; Schlottmann et al., 2002; Siegler & Liebert, 1974
30. e.g., Michotte, 1963; Schlottmann et al., 2002; Siegler, 1975; Siegler & Liebert, 1974
31. Mendelson & Shultz, 1976

32. Siegler & Liebert, 1974
33. Mendelson & Shultz, 1976
34. Siegler, 1975
35. Siegler, 1975
36. Siegler & Liebert, 1974
37. Michotte, 1963
38. e.g., Kelley, 1973; Nisbett & Ross, 1980
39. Kalish, 1997
40. e.g., Atran, 1995; Carey, 1995; Gopnik & Sobel, 2000; Keil, 1994; Leslie, 1995
41. e.g., Bullock, Gelman & Baillargeon, 1982; Siegler, 1975; Siegler & Liebert, 1974; Kushnir & Gopnik, 2007
42. e.g., Harris & Koenig, 2006
43. Ibid.
44. And in some domains, not considered helpful, see Thierry, 2005.
45. Gladwell, 2000
46. Jackson, 2000; Pepine, 2003

Chapter Ten

"What Happened?" vs. "What's Going On?": Thinking about Steady States

"I feel like I run around putting out fires all day."

"All of a sudden the bridge simply collapsed."

Recall the story of Lake Nyos that I introduced in chapter eight as one of the "killer lakes" of Cameroon. This is the lake where, in 1986, gases from the lake escaped into the atmosphere displacing the oxygen and killing nearly eighteen hundred people. But the whole story of what happened at Lake Nyos involves telling a related story—the one about how people attended to events at the lake prior to the disaster of 1986 and how they attend differently now.

Scientists figured out that because Lake Nyos sits in a volcanically active region, carbon dioxide gas had been collecting over time and had gradually built up in the bottom of the lake. Think of it as similar to the bubbles in a can of soda. They are dissolved and distributed in the soda but when the can is disturbed, they are released and they bubble to the top.

Two other facts are important. Colder water has the potential to support more dissolved gas than warmer water and carbon dioxide is denser than oxygen. Prior to the event, the lake water appears to have had stable stratification. Whether there was a particular trigger (the lake was saturated, and/or the warm August weather contributed) or a number of factors interacted to result in the gas release is unclear. What is clear is that the process of gas buildup is ongoing.

In studying the event, scientists realized that the whole scenario could play out again—that carbon dioxide was again collecting in the lake. Therefore, they built an extraordinary fountain in the lake that is designed to disperse the gas over time—in essence, managing the state of the lake rather than focusing on events as they happen. You can access a live webcam focused on the lake over the Internet to observe the fountain.[1] While the level of carbon dioxide continues to be a concern, managing the gas levels may well prevent another catastrophic event.[2]

This story illustrates a major shift in thinking. Often we focus on event-based causality—both in everyday reasoning and in science education.[3] When something happens, it catches our attention, and we focus on it as a cause-and-effect relationship.

However, our human attention is rarely drawn to a causal system in steady state. In order to break into our everyday awareness, to cue us that our attention is needed, an outcome has to be dramatic enough. We habituate to the normal state of many of the systems around us, and attentional capture depends upon having a strong enough signal to break through everyday patterns and background noise.

HOW EVENT-BASED CAUSALITY GRABS US

What is the lure of event-based causality and why do we attend to events at the cost of noticing the status quo? In chapter three, I discussed the phenomenon of walking down a crowded street focused on where you are headed when suddenly a face breaks into your awareness, and you realize that the familiar face is that of an old friend. This experience of "attentional capture"[4] led to the explicit recognition that this is someone whom you know.

As discussed in chapter three, research on attention differentiates between different levels of perception. Before the capture of attention, perceptual processing is occurring but it is at a low level. Our explicit perception is much more selective—we filter information from the senses to prevent sensory overload.[5] This suggests that the "causal status quo" is unlikely to gather our attention unless we make a proactive effort to focus on it.

In cases like that of Lake Nyos, when we fail to monitor steady states, there is often nothing noteworthy to capture our attention until a dramatic event occurs. However, when events do occur, in 20/20 hindsight we can sometimes detect the signals that may have led up to the event. Noticing those signals and recognizing their *relevance* to a developing problem before a catastrophic event occurs is much harder to do. Once an event has played out, the relevant cues are there for the discerning, but prior to the event they exist in a sea of background noise, any of which could be relevant depending upon what actually happens.

Also, when we are focused elsewhere, it is easy to miss other information. The gorilla video example from chapter three, where viewers are so focused counting ball passes between team members wearing white shirts, illustrates this. Viewers have filtered out the team members in dark shirts thus missing the six-foot gorilla beating its chest in the middle of the screen and revealing how difficult it can be to break through into our awareness when we are cognitively busy. It is unlikely that nonevents will break through our awareness without a profound shift in how we process information on a daily basis.

A focus on causality as event-like is fundamental to how many philosophers and causal theorists define causes and effects.[6] The pattern of causality unfolding over time also underlies the notion of co-variance, and Bayesian accounts for how people sum across instances of correlation over time to discern instances of causation.

However, this focus leads to a host of difficulties when reasoning about causal systems in steady state. These difficulties have been documented in science education.[7] Our attention may well be riveted by what causes a bridge to fall down, but in science and engineering, we need to be equally invested in the balance of forces that cause a bridge to stay up. The next generation needs to be able to look beyond causes as events to reasoning about causal systems.

Cognitive scientist Michelene Chi has argued that students often categorize concepts incorrectly—they assign the wrong "ontological status." One way in which this plays out is that they treat all processes as event-like. She divides processes into two types, events and equilibration. Events often have distinct actions with a beginning, middle, and an end. The actions are contingent or causal and unfold in a sequential order. Chi views events as "goal-directed' and to be complete when the goal is achieved. In contrast, according to Chi, equilibration often involves many actions occurring at once. The actions can be random, independent, and have a net effect at a systems level. A continuous dynamic is in play.[8]

A focus on events can make it difficult to reason about processes over time and to recognize the relevant time scales in play. This is especially so for environmental issues. A spell of exceptionally cold weather is event-like and may lead people to question global warming.[9] Yet in a longer time frame, a very different pattern is occurring. The public may not know how to think about appropriate time scales when there are no points of reference. For instance, it is easier to assess whether a baseball player's batting average is high or low because there are many other baseball players to compare to, unlike the temperature on our one and only Earth.[10]

An event-based focus can lead to considering only event-based solutions. According to Dietrich Dorner, a professor of psychology and cognitive behavior at Max Planck Institute, this can result in managing the crisis of the moment rather than the system dynamics that give rise to the current event.

Dorner recounts the disaster at Chernobyl, which I shared in the introduction, where during a test designed to improve the safety system, engineers planned to take the reactor down to 25 percent of its operating capacity. In manually controlling the system, the operator overshot dialing to take in the reactor's self-dampening behavior. According to Dorner, when the system dropped to 1% of capacity, the operator began to focus on correcting the current situation, rather than the systemic processes in play, acting in ways that increased the instability of the system and setting in motion the catastrophic events of that day.[11]

FOCUSING EVENTS

This event-based causal focus is common enough that policy makers refer to "focusing events."[12] A focusing event is when a sudden disaster or outcome garners people's attention such that there is a great push for attention and action and, often, public willingness to expend resources and energy toward solutions.

Policy makers are often able to use such events to build support for various initiatives. For instance, the events of the launch of Sputnik and of 9/11 each garnered support that would have been unlikely without such a focusing event. Atrocious events can unfold over time such as those in Rwanda, Darfur, and Tibet, and inaction is often common unless a particular event demands intervention and fuels public support.

We are likely to prioritize events that capture our attention in this way without necessarily considering other candidate issues that may need our attention but have not yet demanded it. Sometimes no recognizable "event" has yet happened that can be attributed to a causal system and still we should be minding the state of the system.

In *An Inconvenient Truth*, Al Gore drew our attention to the state of the CO_2 in our atmosphere. Yet the recognizable effects or "events" that the state of the CO_2 signaled were not yet noticeable to the average citizen. We supported the allocation of resources toward terrorism following 9/11 without a public dialogue on whether terrorism or climate change constituted a greater public enemy. The causal features of phenomena interact with whether they will demand our attention—influencing how we consider and manage risk—but the defaults that we adopt are not necessarily the most adaptive in the twenty-first century.[13]

A corollary of attending to events over processes is that we often don't take note of what *was* working in the steady state of a system, until it is disrupted and that disruption functions as an event to focus our attention. For example, when looting occurs following a catastrophe, people wonder what happened instead of considering what was happening all along to make things run as smoothly as they did. The levy system in New Orleans was a system that was working, but was in serious need of attention and didn't capture the necessary attention to address it until it failed.

It's not that we *never* pay attention to systems in steady state—it's just not our human tendency to do so. In fact, there's a healthy market for devices that monitor the steady state for us and alert us before something goes wrong. Carbon dioxide level detectors, systems that monitor your heating pipes in the wall and call you when the temperature dips too low, and monitors in Newborn Intensive Care Units (NICUs) that signal when the rhythm of an infant's heart beat or breathing deviates from normal are all examples of steady-state monitors. Unfortunately, often a focusing event is needed to motivate their use.

The Interstate 35W bridge over the Mississippi that failed in the summer of 2007, sending people plunging to their deaths, was determined "structurally deficient" two years earlier. Six years prior, a study conducted by the Minnesota Department of Transportation had found "several fatigue problems" in the approach spans and "poor fatigue detail" on the main truss of the bridge. [14]

A headline in *USA Today* the week that the bridge failed read, "New Bridge-Monitoring Devices Go Unused." It reported on dozens of new technologies that can help monitor bridges and bemoaned the fact that states had been slow to spend money on them. [15] Following the "event," bridges across the country became the focus of new inspections and allocating funds for bridge repair became the national priority—at least for a time.

PROACTIVE BEHAVIOR CHANGE IS HARD TO COME BY

Does the story of the change in focus at Lake Nyos signal that monitoring the steady state of systems is likely to become prevalent in everyday thinking anytime soon? Unfortunately, it does not. Lake Kivu in Rwanda has two million people living around it. The lake sits in an earthquake zone surrounded by active volcanoes including Mount Nyiragongo. It has a similar gas buildup, this one of carbon dioxide and methane. There is enough methane to fuel the United States for a month. These gases could result in another deadly "lake overturn" and become the next tragedy.

The *New York Times* drew attention to the problem in November of 2009 with a story that told of the problem that local villagers call *mazuku* in Swahili, or "evil wind." [16] The methane has recently been viewed as a potential source of revenue, so perhaps the economic incentive to de-gas will overcome the tendency to gamble on when the lake might overturn.

Why is a proactive focus on steady states so hard to gain? As discussed in the previous chapter, it is hard to pay attention to effects that involve time delays. It is also hard to allocate attention to things that *might* happen or at least that haven't happened yet. For instance, attention to heart health is routinely problematic. Heart disease is an epidemic in our country and yet health-care providers struggle to get people to attend to it and to modify their behaviors.[17]

In congestive heart failure, the heart is starting to give out and is not able to pump enough blood to the body. It relates to high blood pressure. Patients are put on diets to avoid salt and given diuretics so that the heart has less fluid to push. In the emergency room, these patients often do fine but monitoring the state of their system at home takes a shift in thinking and action. Equipment can help them to monitor their situation but they need to shift from event-based responses toward managing more subtle events or even the absence of events. A patient not attentive to these things often crashes quickly.[18]

LEARNING TO MIND THE STEADY STATE

There are some activities that *require* attention to the status of the system— where you must learn to monitor the state of the system. Learning to scuba dive is one of them. In order to avoid getting the bends, you have to pay attention to equilibrating the level of oxygen in your system as you go deeper. This involves developing sensitivity to balance rather than to events. Of course with scuba diving, getting it wrong can be deadly. Are there more benign opportunities to focus on such steady-state monitoring and to help children learn to think about systems in this way?

When I first observed children playing with Tamagotchi toys, I must admit that my first reaction was, "What will they think of to sell to kids next?" A Tamagotchi is a handheld digital pet that children need to feed, clean up after, and play games with to keep it happy. They need to monitor its weight level and keep track of other vital statistics. In its first ten years of existence, the company, Bandai, sold over ten million of the digital pets. So much for my initial thought that kids can just feed real pets instead!

But as I watched children playing with them, I realized that the value of the Tamagotchi as a learning opportunity for children to focus on managing the steady state of a virtual, biological system surpasses that of a real pet. After all, most parents won't let a kid starve the family pet in service of learning. With the right kinds of conversation, Tamagotchi pets invite an opportunity to learn to manage the steady state of a system (and once children have mastered that, then it might be time for a real pet!).

What other activities involve minding the steady state? Consider an aquarium with plants, snails, small fish, and a lot of micro-organisms. A healthy balance of ammonia and biofiltration bacteria is needed so that ammonia, which can be toxic to the fish, is converted first to toxic nitrite and then to much less toxic nitrate. Often this balance only becomes obvious to us as we disturb it. If too many fish are added to the tank, the lack of balance reveals itself through an event. The ammonia level spikes, the balance in the tank crashes, with the fish gasping for air at the top of the tank, and the fish eventually die if the balance is not restored.

Steady states aren't just scientific phenomena. Systems of production in balance with demand are critical to healthy lives—food-production systems in balance with need stave off starvation.

Look around your community. What kinds of social balances contribute to the way things work? Educators can often point to many examples in their school communities—collaborations between younger and older students that contribute to the learning of each or the silent contributions of support staff that mostly go unnoticed until they are out sick and chaos breaks loose before everyone acknowledges how things really were working.

If our default is event-based causality, how can we teach students to reason about steady states? A dramatic event such as all the class fish dying will certainly get their attention. It is what happens before and afterward that matters here. An explicit focus on the proactive attention to balance as part of the causal system, as well as discussions about what was happening before the crash and a reflective look at how events grab our attention, are important parts of the conversation. The EcoMUVE example in the last chapter illustrates positive results in terms of helping students to learn about steady states.[19]

PICTURES OF CLASSROOM PRACTICE: WHAT DOES IT LOOK LIKE TO HELP STUDENTS LEARN TO MIND THE STEADY STATE?

Take the example of the fish tank from above. How might the teacher turn it into a teaching opportunity? Consider this example from Ms. Bell's third-grade class. The alarm was evident in the children's voices. "Some of the fish are gasping for air in our tank and one of them is floating upside down!" Ms. Bell sighed, the tank had been fine for so long, that she really hadn't paid it much attention. Clearly something was out of balance. Testing the water, she noticed that the ammonia levels were very high.

With the benefit of 20/20 hindsight, the students started to realize that there may have been some earlier clues. "Remember that fish who died and we couldn't figure out why? Maybe the ammonia levels got to that fish first." "Oh yeah, the snail died a few weeks ago, too." Together, the class decided that they should check the tank regularly and record their observations and data on a chart. This would allow them to monitor the status of the tank instead of waiting for an event to get them to pay attention to it.

Ms. Bell used this as an opportunity to talk about the difference between paying attention to things along the way—minding the steady state—versus waiting for an event. She asked, "Why did we notice the problem in the tank?" "We saw the fish at the top and another one died," a student replies. "How is that different from keeping track of the tank all the time like in our new plan?" "Well, it's like waiting till you have a big problem and then trying fix it. Maybe it's too late." replied one student. Another added, "It's like you are always going up and down, problem, fix the problem, problem, fix the problem, problem, instead of just a straight line."

A third student connected the concepts to other kinds of experiences, "It's like what you tell us about the playground, that if someone is doing something that is not safe, tell a teacher *before* someone gets hurt. We should pay attention to our behavior, not wait for a problem." The conversation continued as students talked about the importance of monitoring processes since it is hard to pay attention to things without an event to grab your attention.

In physical education class, the sixth graders played a game called "the lap game" or "chairless." In this game, the students stand in a circle and then all slowly sit on the lap of the person behind them. As long as they all sit at once and no one falls over, the forces are balanced around the circle and the circle stays up. Around the same time, in their project-based classroom, they were building bridges. Their teacher, Mr. Freedman, saw it as an opportunity to help them to think about the bridges as a balance of forces just like the lap game.

Mr. Freedman asked the students to think about the following questions, "In what ways is the lap game like the bridges that you are building in science? In what ways is the lap game different from the bridges that you are building?" After much discussion of how different students are from the building blocks of the bridge, they realized a key similarity. It is easy to think that something happened only when the circle of students or the bridge falls down, but the causal system is "in action" all the while the circle or the bridge stays up—something is happening then, too—when a system is in steady state.

The eleventh graders study the African continent. During their study, they talked about Rwanda and the spread of violence into the Congo. One student commented that it is frustrating that the world's focus shifts away from problems when a new problem catches our attention. "It's like something bad happens and the whole world pays attention, then something bad happens somewhere else and we forget to pay attention to the first problem. The problems in Rwanda and the Congo have a long history but they demanded world attention only sporadically," she remarks.

Ms. Morris used the student's comments as an opportunity to talk about how events capture our attention, but that it is very important to focus on processes over time, to monitor more minor events that may lead to more dramatic events. Another student drew a parallel to 9/11. He commented, "Now we are more actively monitoring potential terrorist activity to prevent a big event like 9/11 from happening again. It certainly got our attention, but we don't want our attention to wander away from monitoring it."

NOTES

1. http://pagesperso-orange.fr/mhalb/nyos/webcam.htm
2. http://www.bbc.co.uk/science/horizon/2001/killerlakes.shtml
3. Driver, Guesne & Tiberghien, 1985
4. Mack & Rock, 1998
5. Ibid.
6. e.g., Sloman, 2005
7. Driver et al., 1984
8. Chi, 1997
9. Jacoby, 2008
10. For a lesson plan focused on helping students think about how we reason about time scales and what it means for a time scale to be relevant, see Causal Patterns in Ecosystems, 2nd ed., sec. 6, p. 177, at: http://www.pz.harvard.edu/ucp/causalpatternsinscience/pdfs/revised_ecosystem.pdf
11. Dorner, 1989
12. e.g., Birkland, 1998
13. Grotzer, Miller & Lincoln, 2011
14. CNN, August 2, 2007
15. USA Today, August 6, 2007
16. Kron, 2009, p. A8
17. Personal communication, Julie Bradley, Harvard School of Public Health, April 12, 2007.
18. Personal communication, David M. Freeman, general manager, Parameters, G.E. Medical Monitoring Solutions, April 19, 2008.
19. Grotzer et al., forthcoming

Chapter Eleven

What You Can't See Does Matter: Attending to Obvious and Non-obvious Causes

"Sticks and stones may break my bones,
but names will never hurt me."

"There was no obvious explanation for the problem."

"Out of sight, out of mind."

When a baby cries on a plane, parents may well check to see if the baby is wet or hungry before considering the possibility that air pressure is impacting the baby's ears. At two years old, my daughter was hit hard in the stomach by her three-year-old cousin. When she later started throwing up, she *and* her parents first thought it was linked to the hit rather than the Norwalk virus that it turned out to be. If a tree falls, students tend to assume that lightning struck it or carpenter ants have eaten it, not that microscopic organisms have caused it to decay.

Each of these examples appears to have an obvious cause—one that we can perceive and conjure up a clear image of. It is a common human tendency to look for obvious causes and a sensible tendency at that. It often makes sense to first search for what you can see before you search beyond the limits of unaided perception.

This is not to argue that we don't or can't search for non-obvious causes. There is compelling research reviewed below to suggest that even young children look for obvious causes first and, failing to find one, look for not-so-obvious causes. [1] However, if an obvious, possible cause is present, children generally will not search further whether or not it is the actual cause. Even adults do not seek a non-obvious or hidden cause when an obvious one exists.[2]

Many common phenomena are the outcome of imperceptible causes—ones that we can't perceive without special means to help us. Examples from the physical and biological worlds abound—from sunsets, soap bubbles, shapes of the clouds, patterns in our weather, the viruses that can make us sick, to the beneficial organisms that allow us to digest our food. The social domain is also full of non-obvious, inferred causes—motivations, intentions, beliefs, perceived slights, political moves, and so forth. We're actually not so hesitant to reason about social causes, but I'll come back to that in the next chapter.

Visualize a rainbow. If you ask what causes a rainbow, people typically report background conditions—it has to be raining when the sun is out. Moving beyond background conditions is harder. The actual, physical cause is completely non-obvious. A rainbow is the result of thousands of tiny water droplets acting as prisms, dispersing the light into colors arranged by their frequencies. Different colors of light travel at different frequencies. These different frequencies move at different speeds in transparent materials, causing each to refract, or bend, at a different angle. This results in dispersion, or the separation of light into different colors.

Sometimes, non-obvious causes are accompanied by non-obvious effects—at least at first. Patterns of accumulation can behave this way. In its natural state, gas is odorless and colorless. Its existence would be completely non-obvious to an observer.

In New London, Texas, in the 1930s, a new school had been built. Positioned on sloping ground, it contained a large dead-air space beneath the school structure. The story is told that the school board cancelled the gas contract, opting instead to install a residue line from the local gas company, which was both free and common at that time.

Soon after, the students began complaining of headaches. The probable cause was a leak in the residue line that had filled the dead space under the school with gas. This non-obvious cause of headaches made itself entirely obvious when a wood-shop teacher turned on a power sander and set off a tragic explosion that killed about half of the six hundred students and the teachers in the school, injuring many others.[3]

The non-obviousness of the cause made it undetectable until there was a tragic, attention-grabbing effect—a focusing event as discussed in the previous chapter. There was a non-obvious pattern of accumulation over time until the sander triggered the explosion (as considered in chapter nine). Unlike instances where you are trying to explain an outcome that you can observe, here there was little to observe until it was too late.

Gases are often non-obvious. Radon gas that emanates from granite and other natural sources can't be easily detected, yet it can cause lung cancer in humans. It's one of the variables that one might not think about when buying a new house or installing a new kitchen counter—it's just not obvious to most people that they should. Gas companies now add a distinct odor to natural gas so that it can be more easily detected and radon tests are typically included in the home-inspection process when a sale takes place.

When accumulating effects have a non-obvious quality such as those discussed above, it adds another level of complexity to discerning the causal dynamics. Those of us who are old enough to remember when people threw garbage out of car windows and how it accumulated will relate to the value of being able to see the accumulation in motivating us to clean up our act. Contrast this example to the accumulation of non-obvious greenhouse gases. Getting people to attend every day to something imperceptible is vastly more complicated than the highly visible reminder in the garbage piling up along the highway.

Of all the features that contribute to causal complexity, non-obvious causes is one of those that suffers the most from lack of attentional capture. After all, how can we pay attention to causes that we can't perceive? In the paragraphs that follow, I further explore the nature of non-obvious causes, and consider what children understand about them at different ages and how educators can help students to be more aware of non-obvious causes as potential players in causal systems.

TOO TINY TO SEE

In the ecosystems unit that we developed with our teacher collaborators,[4] we set up two tanks of the same size and shape with essentially the same amount of soil, vegetable compost, and dead leaves. We add fifteen worms to one tank, but not the other. Then we ask the students what will happen to the compost and leaves in each tank. They typically answer that the one with worms "will break down into soil." For the other tank, they say that it "won't break down" or it "will fall apart by itself." Adults give similar answers. Yet, vegetable compost and leaves do turn into soil and they don't do it just by falling apart on their own. Rather they are consumed and excreted by scores of tiny microbes.

We often don't realize that causes exist when they are too small to see. Further, we tend to have little understanding of the importance of the microscopic world. In an article entitled *The Undiscovered Planet*, writer Jonathan Shaw quotes Robert Kolter, professor of microbiology and molecular genetics at Harvard Medical School: "Our planet has been shaped by an invisible world. . . . Microbes mediate all the important cycles on Earth and have played a defining role in the development of the planet. . . . They form clouds, break down rocks, deposit minerals, fertilize plants, condition soils and clean up toxic waste."[5]

Shaw also quotes Dan Schrag, professor of earth and planetary sciences at Harvard University: "Almost all of the reactions on the earth's surface are catalyzed by microbes—in soils, in waters, in swamps. . . . [Unless you know] what microbes are doing, you don't really know what is going on."[6]

Recognizing the existence of tiny microbes in our world isn't necessarily helpful if people simply declare war on them—both beneficial and hurtful microbes. The assumption that all microbes are harmful has fueled the popularity of antimicrobials. Shaw goes on to argue that people have little sense that their own bodies are full of microbes, many specific to their bodies, and essential to their life processes. Further, even in the case of potentially harmful microbes, people tend not to view them as evolving and thus do not realize the role that human actions can play in the natural selection of the most resistant micro-organisms.

The microscopic world, despite being out of sight and out of mind, is extraordinary. It is vast and centrally involved in many of the causal processes that we attribute to more obvious causes that exist at a larger scale.

INVISIBLE AND INFERRED

Some causes can't be directly observed—not even with a microscope. It's not a matter of being too small, they are just not visible. Instead, we infer the cause based upon what evidence we can see. Take gravity for example. Scientists have models to help them think about how gravity behaves and these are inferred from the behavior of objects that gravity is inferred to act upon.

Consider air and air pressure. Air is around us all of the time, so we are accustomed to the presence of air pressure. Beyond this, our bodies continually adapt to the sea of air in which we live. Therefore, the behavior of air pushing on us is unlikely to capture our attention. We are usually unaware of our bodies' adaptations; they only become obvious when air pressure changes rapidly, such as when our ears pop in an ascending airplane.

The discovery of air pressure offers a good example of how we search for obvious causes first and, upon exhausting those, might then consider the possibility that a non-obvious cause could be involved. James Burke, in his book, *Connections*, relays the story of how in the late 1500s, miners struggled with a problem.[7] Once they had excavated mines to a certain depth, water began flowing in and filling up the mine. Yet, there were still valuable minerals to be excavated—silver, iron, salt, alum, and more.

Burke explains that of the various approaches to removing the water, three were most common. One used cloth balls on a circular chain that soaked up the water at the bottom of the shaft. Then it was squeezed out at the top. A second method used a giant screw that forced water upward as it turned. A third method used a rotating waterwheel shaft with a crank attached that operated a piston which was partially in the water. As it was understood then, it would "suck" water into the cylinder. Then a valve would close at the bottom and open at the top and as the piston came down, the water was forced upward.

The third method was the best of the three, but oddly it could not "lift" water more than thirty-two feet. What could be going on? People tried to solve the problem in many ways, each focusing on obvious variables, such as imperfections in the pumps themselves or fluid that seeped in from outside the pump. Eventually, Evangelista Torricelli, a mathematician who had studied with Galileo, became convinced that the weight of the air pushing on the water had something to do with the height to which water would rise. He tested the idea through experiments that led to the formal recognition of air pressure in 1643.

Just like the miners above, students often turn to concrete, obvious variables to try to explain air-pressure-related phenomena. We asked students why a balloon might deflate a little when driving from the top of a mountain to the bottom. Most students suggested that there could be a hole in the balloon, rather than focusing on non-obvious causes, such as changes in the surrounding air pressure.[8] Research shows that students from age six to university level fail to recognize air pressure when engaged in science activities focused on it.[9]

There are many causes that must be inferred. If when handed two cylinders of exactly the same size and shape, your hand drops in response to one because it is dramatically heavier than the other, you could infer that they are made up of different kinds of material. It has to do with density, the amount of mass per unit of volume, or more simply put, how much stuff is in how much space. Density must be inferred by holding either mass or volume constant. Without such experiences, which the world does not readily offer, you are unlikely to detect density.[10] Instead, you would be drawn to the more obvious variable of weight.

TINY, INVISIBLE, AND INFERRED = EASY TO IGNORE

Why do we focus more on obvious than non-obvious causes? For the most part, we are accepting of the possibility of non-obvious causes. Given that we do not allow for causeless effects,[11] when we see an effect we search for a cause. However, if an obvious possible cause exists, we are likely to stop there in the service of efficiency and given the limits of attention. Only in instances where there is no obvious cause might we follow a long path to seek less obvious potential causes—given the ability and inclination.[12]

A primary issue is the lack of awareness of non-obvious causes—we need to figure out that they exist. With the miners in the 1600s, they faced a clear problem and tried to solve it. Or, as discussed in the last chapter, an event occurs and people attend to the causes in a thorough investigation. In 2006, when people started falling ill and some started dying after eating spinach and spinach products, extensive investigations were conducted to determine the cause. Aware of the possible mechanisms, when people began falling ill from a highly virulent strain of E. coli bacteria in Hamburg, Germany, in 2011, investigators investigated produce.

Often, non-obvious causes don't garner attention and have silent impact while more event-based, dramatic causes draw significant resources. In the spring of 2008, when a deadly earthquake hit China killing fifty-five thousand people, the world responded with aid. Yet according to *New York Times* reporter Nicholas Kristof, as many as three hundred thousand to four hundred thousand Chinese die prematurely each year due to the effects of air pollution. He wrote about the village of Badui, known to the locals as "village of dunces" due to the high levels of mental retardation that appears connected to the polluted water supply.[13]

In Fryeburg, Maine, citizens are growing increasingly alarmed at the removal of water by Poland Spring, the water bottler, from underground aquifers, and at recent changes in the quality of a local lake, Lovewell's Pond, which would otherwise be the recipient of that water. The author of a local citizen's paper tried to fathom why Poland Spring was able to divert so much water for so long before people reacted. He writes: "The fact that all this water being diverted away from its natural course to Lovewell's Pond is from an *underground* body of fresh water makes this activity much less noticeable or objectionable to most people. Try to imagine what it would look like if this same water were above ground, and visible to everyone. It would look just like another lake, right next to Lovewell's Pond. Now imagine tanker trucks, lots of tanker trucks, parked next to this lake with big hoses dropped into the water, pumping away. Day and night, pumping water out of the lake and shipping it out of town. It seems impossible that this would ever happen and be widely accepted here in Fryeburg, but isn't that just what actually *is* happening, only in a lot less obvious way?"[14]

Attentional capture is one problem with non-obvious causes. Another has to do with how easily nonvisibility can lead to denial of risk even in cases when we are aware of them. In the early 1990s, two transformers burned and released contamination, PCB and dioxin, into some residence dormitories at the State University of New York (SUNY) at New Paltz. Dioxin is one of the most poisonous substances on Earth, creating damage at the level of chromosomes, birth defects, hormones, and organs.[15]

According to Eric Francis, a reporter who has studied the incident extensively, the dormitories were reopened a month later. As the students walked into their dormitories, it wasn't the non-obvious dioxin that would have caught their attention. It might have been the men in hazmat suits and air tanks working just outside their windows.[16] Yet reportedly the students were told it was safe to live in the dorms.

The causal link to potential ill effects would at least be hard to draw. The non-obviousness of the dioxin certainly played into the equation. If there had been a more visible danger, such as a fire burning right outside their windows lapping at the walls or a large ticking bomb, would the students have walked on in? It's pretty unlikely.

DEVELOPING AN UNDERSTANDING OF NON-OBVIOUS CAUSES

How children develop an understanding of non-obvious causes has largely focused on instances where we have an effect and are attempting to explain it. This is not surprising given the challenges of attending to non-obvious causes. As discussed above, people do not allow for causeless events, compelling a search for hidden, less obvious causes. It appears that this ability develops around ages three and four.

As discussed in chapter three, by about four years old and perhaps earlier, children realize that a mechanism is necessary for bringing about an effect and search for it when one is not apparent.[17] When told that two objects move together because of a hidden string, but no string can be found, four- and five-year-olds (and adults) looked for other possible causes or accused the researcher of playing a trick.[18] Most four-year-olds suggested an unobserved causal mechanism when asked why two puppets moved together and there was no obvious causal mechanism.[19]

Between ages three and nine, children's explanations develop toward a deeper sense of elaborated causal mechanisms. They become increasingly able to look beyond the more perceptually salient surface features toward internal mechanisms.[20] They also use knowledge of mechanisms to reason about how certain nonvisible causes behave, for instance, the wind.[21]

COOTIES, INTENTIONS, AND INSIDES

From a developmental perspective, children are *able* to reason about a variety of non-obvious causes, even if it is not their first impulse. Evidence comes from a wide variety of reasoning tasks—social interactions, thinking about the transmission of germs and illness, and inferring how the insides of things work. Research has explored how children handle these reasoning tasks and they appear much more competent than one might have thought.

Consider the social domain and how children learn to think about their own minds and those of others. A wealth of research shows that children develop ideas about how the minds of others work and how beliefs can influence what someone does.[22] When my nephew was four, I found two matching cards when playing lotto. He asked, "Did you know that was there?" I said, "I got a match." He then asked insistently, "But did you *know* that one was there?" He was clearly asking about what was in my mind and if I intentionally had picked that card.

Reasoning about such intentions is an example of reasoning about what you can't see.[23] Can you recall an instance where a preschooler said that something was "an accident"? They may have learned that this answer avoids punishment. However, as discussed in chapter three, very young children can distinguish between intentional and nonintentional outcomes.[24]

Children begin talking about desires as early as eighteen months old.[25] By age three, they are beginning to address their intentions in relation to outcomes. Feinfeld and colleagues[26] found that four-year-olds systematically distinguished between a protagonist's intention and desires. In the next chapter, I discuss our willingness to reason about intentionality as a powerful cause.

Children also can reason about causes that are obscured from them. By age four, children reason about the internal parts of animals, such as blood or bones, and of toys such as batteries and motors, as explanations for their movement.[27] Children as young as five also realize that things like sounds, wind, or light can act as causes even where there is no physical connection between the cause (wind) and effect (a candle going out, for instance).[28] This suggests that even if the specific information is not yet available, young children reason about internal parts as causes.

Further evidence for how children reason about non-obvious, nonvisible causes comes from reasoning about contamination. Can you recall the first grade when all of a sudden, you could catch "cooties"? A mere touch could confer the dreaded "cooties" whereas just a year or so earlier, it never crossed one's mind. Children's ideas about contamination as non-obvious and nonvisible causes are developing as early as three years old.[29] Young children realize that physical contact with these invisible particles is necessary for contamination[30] and that germs are responsible for contagion.[31]

Our awareness of what children understand has shifted with time. Earlier research had suggested that before age eight, children did not understand that contaminants can exist as invisible particles and maintain their potency as a contaminant.[32] In one clever (though perhaps nauseating) study, Fallon, Rozin, and Pliner[33] found that children ages three to seven would not accept a drink if a small lump of what was labeled "doggie doo" fell into it, but if the child saw the lump removed, they then accepted the drink.

However, more recent research suggests that contamination awareness is an earlier development. Other researchers[34] found that by eliminating extraneous task demands, children as young as three showed some contamination awareness. By age four, children reconciled the apparent invisibility and continuing existence of contamination by using a concept of tiny particles. By age five, most children showed an appreciation that contaminants can exist as tiny, nonvisible, non-obvious particles that still have causal potency.

The sum of this work suggests that, from an early age, children are learning to seek out and consider causes even if they are not obvious. The level of sensitivity that different studies attribute to different ages varies. Some have found that three-year-olds will not consider a cause if it is not obvious,[35] and that causality is dominated by perception.[36] However, a compelling amount of evidence suggests that as young as three, and by age four, preschoolers do not rely entirely on perceptual cues and features to reason about causal mechanisms.[37]

However, what children *can* do with the supports provided in the research studies and how they reason in everyday contexts often tell two different stories. If you mix some sugar into a cup of hot water and dissolve it, most young children will tell you that it has disappeared, melted away, or turned into water, as research in science learning has found.[38] They no longer see it, so they consider it gone, unless of course, you let them taste the water and offer another way to perceive it.

Extensive findings in science education show that students have a hard time grasping non-obvious causal mechanisms[39] Most students are unaware of the fundamental role that microbes play in life as recyclers of carbon, nitrogen, water, and minerals.[40] Before ages five and six, they think that water disappears when it evaporates[41] and by ages thirteen to seventeen, only 14 percent of students mentioned particles or molecules to describe what happened to water evaporating.[42]

The broader story here puts aspects of ability and tendency in juxtaposition. So while children are able to detect non-obvious causes, they do not pursue them in instances where they do not perceive an effect to be explained, where there is a more salient candidate, when attentional factors limit the information available to them, or they just do not have the information basis to compel a search for a non-obvious cause.

LEARNING TO KEEP THE NON-OBVIOUS IN MIND

Despite our tendencies, we do know that what we can't see, can hurt us. After 9/11, some New York City residents kept parakeets as a means to alert themselves to the potential of poisonous gases in their environment. A dead bird is a lot more obvious than an imperceptible gas. Acknowledging that we need help attending to non-obvious causes, is a first step toward making changes and setting systems in place to help us—at least for causes that we have an awareness of.

Governments, businesses, and insurance companies put policies in place to make sure that we attend to non-obvious causes. For instance, a law in Massachusetts recently went into effect requiring carbon monoxide detectors in homes. Similarly, after a certain age, if females haven't had a yearly mammogram, they may hear from their health insurance company. And gas companies add odor to odorless gases so that we can detect them. Recall as a child when your dentist had you chew red tablets to make the plaque on your teeth show up? He or she was making the non-obvious bright red to get your attention.

How can we help the next generation learn to attend to non-obvious causes? Making discussion about non-obvious causes a regular part of classroom conversations is a great place to start. As Sita,[43] one of the eighth graders in our study commented, "I think we only notice it [pressure] when there is a difference in it. 'Cause right now we don't feel all the pressure pushing on us . . . but when we go up in a plane, the difference in air pressure causes our ears to pop." These kinds of conversations integrate understandings in science with helping students realize why it may be harder to think about certain kinds of causes.

Even with the youngest students, when trying to figure out what makes something happen, ask, "Think about things that we can't see—are any of those things possible causes?" As early as preschool, you can talk about how you can't see some things but you can find ways to know that they are there. I tell preschoolers that you can't see air, but you *can* feel it when it moves, then I have them blow into their hands.

Another way to help students reason about non-obvious effects is to find ways to make them obvious. For instance, research has found that high school students do realize that the pressure of enclosed air in a syringe increases with compression.[44] This is not startling since students feel the effect of the increased pressure on their hands. The effect is obvious. When the syringe was not compressed and they could not feel an effect, 70 percent of students thought the enclosed air did not have air pressure. A group of second graders pushed so hard on the end of a syringe trying to compress it further that they nearly knocked me over.

Non-obvious causes can be made obvious by offering students the tools that enable them to see microscopic causes. They are often amazed at discovering the microscopic world, as in the classroom example below.

We can encourage students to think about and play with scale. In the book *Zoom*, the camera pans out at different levels in each picture.[45] *Powers of Ten* is a 1968 film by Ray and Charles Eames that quickly achieved pop status. It reveals a man picnicking and then invites us along as the film continues to pan out to reveal the relative scale of the universe.[46] There are other versions of such films available on the Internet. A movie called *Microcosmos* and a book called *The Smaller Majority* invite us into the world of insects, helping us to be aware of the complexity and wonder of these worlds.[47]

PICTURES OF CLASSROOM PRACTICE: WHAT DOES IT LOOK LIKE TO HELP STUDENTS LEARN TO CONSIDER NON-OBVIOUS CAUSES?

A group of first graders were talking about the book *Horton Hears a Who!* by Dr. Seuss and the "world" that Horton tries to save on the tip of a flower.[48] "It's just made-up," says one. "You can't have a whole world on a flower." Recalling that earlier in the year, the students had also been wondering what the salamander larvae in the tank in their room were eating ("There's nothing in the water," they said, and yet the larvae were growing), their teacher, Ms. Carroll, decides to build on that conversation.

Ms. Carroll hooks up a microscope to the classroom computer and projects the image on the wall. She asks the students to take a drop of water from the tank of pond water in their room. In a tiny drop of water, the students see paramecium swimming around eating tiny bacteria and algae. A hydra, looking plant-like, reached out with its long arms and shrank back. A number of tinier organisms dart through the image. One student gasps, "Is all that in a drop of water?" Another student wants to know, "Is that in the water that we drink?"

Eventually Ms. Carroll poses a question: "Remember the salamander larvae that we had a few months ago and how they kept growing and getting bigger? Some of you wondered what they could be eating. What do you think now?" Later she asks, "Could you see the cause without a microscope? Is it possible that there are things going on around us—even causes and effects—that we cannot see?" When Ms. Carroll was done with the slide, the first graders panicked when they thought that she didn't get ALL of the water off the slide back into the tank. They had clearly come to see the pond water in a new way!

With the onset of an especially dangerous and contagious flu season, the eighth-grade health teacher, Ms. Rodriguez, wanted her students to learn more than the importance of thinking about germs in relation to this flu. She wanted them to be more aware of non-obvious causes and to better realize how the non-obviousness of the microbes may interact with their risk-taking behavior in the coming years if they aren't reflective about it. So she engaged the class in a discussion about the new school policies about hand washing and the idea that hidden causes can encourage us to take risks that we otherwise might avoid.

The students consider obvious and non-obvious risks, such as walking in front of a car or not engaging in safe practices around germs. A boy laughs and says, "Well, it would be dumb to walk in front of a car." A classmate challenges him, "But it can just as easily kill you to share germs by passing around one bottle of soda, but you guys do that all the time."

The conversation continues with great passion as students contrast what it means to take chances with an obvious, imminent cause such as the car to that of a non-obvious, somewhat delayed cause such as dangerous germs. The students realize that the probability that the cause leads to ill effects plays into their accounting (as discussed in chapter fourteen) but that the non-obviousness of a cause certainly makes it easier to discount.

NOTES

1. Schulz & Sommerville, 2006

2. e.g., Karniol & Ross, 1976; Kuhn & Ho, 1977; Kushnir et al., 2003; Kun & Weiner, 1973; Sedlak & Kurtz, 1981. For a review of related research on Multiple Sufficient Causes (MSC) and Multiple Necessary Causes (MNC), see Sedlak & Kurtz, 1981.

3. The New London School Explosion, en. wikipedia.org/wiki/ New_London_School_explosion, [accessed: 4-18-2008].

4. Grotzer, 2002

5. Shaw, 2007, p. 44

6. Shaw, 2007, p. 53
7. Burke, 1978
8. Basca & Grotzer, 2003
9. Tytler, 1998
10. e.g., Smith, Carey & Wiser, 1985
11. Bullock, Gelman & Baillargeon, 1982; Kosugi et al., 2009
12. Schulz & Sommerville, 2006
13. Kristof, 2008
14. Dearborn, 2007
15. One of the challenges in reasoning about toxins is the complexity in understanding them in terms of what different concentrations mean. Some people adopt a "no level is safe policy" and this makes sense for some toxins (Kraus, Malmfors & Slovic, 2000). Dioxin is an example. Any level of exposure has biological effects and dioxin is everywhere—in the air we breathe, the food we eat, the water we drink. Other toxins are not associated with biological effects until they reach a certain level. For instance, non-obvious radon gas is naturally occurring in our environment. Below certain levels, it is considered benign, above certain levels, it has been associated with lung cancer.
16. Francis, 2000
17. Bullock, 1984; 1985; Corrigan, 1995
18. Bullock, 1985
19. Gopnik et al., 2004
20. Lehrer & Schauble, 1998; Metz, 1991; Schlottmann, 1999
21. Shultz & Kestenbaum, 1985
22. e.g., Wellman & Gelman, 1988. The "Theory of Mind" research is an extensive body of literature with many contributors. See the work of Janet Wilde Astington (e.g., 1993) for an overview.
23. Kalish, 1998
24. Meltzoff, 2007
25. Bartsch & Wellman, 1995
26. Feinfeld et al., 1999
27. Gelman & Gottfried, 1996; Gelman & Kremer, 1991; Gelman & Welman, 1991
28. Shultz & Kestenbaum, 1985
29. Au, Sidle & Rollins, 1993; Siegal & Share, 1990
30. Springer & Belk, 1994
31. Kalish, 1996; Carey (1995) argues that while this research shows that preschoolers have learned that germs are the cause of disease, we do not know if this goes beyond merely naming germs as the cause of disease as a type of input/output (something they learned / something that they can tell you) rather than knowledge of mechanism.
32. Fallon, Rozin & Pliner, 1984; Rozin, 1990; Rozin, Fallon & Augustoni-Ziskind, 1986
33. 1984
34. Au, Sidle & Rollins, 1993
35. Bullock, 1985
36. Cohen, Amsel & Casasola, 1997; Cohen & Oakes, 1993; Leslie, 1982, 1984, 1988; Leslie & Keeble, 1987; Oakes & Cohen, 1990
37. Schlottmann (1999) argues that children's understanding of causality appears to progress from perceptually dominated to dominated by an appreciation of mechanism; the development is not smooth and continuous. Frederiksen and White (2000) argue that abstract, inferred entities are an ongoing source of difficulty for students.
38. e.g., Longden, 1984; Holding, 1987
39. e.g., Driver, Guesne & Tiberghien, 1985
40. Brinkman & Boschhuizen, 1989; Leach et al.,1992
41. Bar, 1986
42. Osborne & Cosgrove, 1983
43. The names of students are pseudonyms to protect their anonymity.
44. deBerg, 1995
45. Banyai, 1998

46. A 1968 film by Charles and Ray Eames. It was based on a book from Kees Boeke and later resulted in a book by Phillip and Phyllis Morrison in 1982; http://www.powersof10.com/ [accessed 7-5-2011]; Morrison & Morrison, 1982

47. Nuridsany & Pérennou, 1996; Naskrecki, 2005

48. A version of this story appeared previously in Grotzer, 2011, in the Science Teachers' Association of New York State newsletter about the importance of supporting scientific and causal reasoning for our youngest students.

Chapter Twelve

It's Not Always a Case of "Who Did It?": Minding Passive and Unintentional Causality

"I suck the juice up the straw to drink it."

"Lightning strikes from above hitting the ground below."

"The electrons want to go to the protons."

Walking around the edge of the pond, my children and I noticed lots of dead crayfish along the banks. Their brown, decaying bodies contrasted with the verdant playing fields leading down to the water. "Why are there so many dead crayfish?" I wondered out loud. My daughter, then seven years old, offered an answer, "Something must be eating them. There must be a bigger creature in the pond." Her twin brother concurred but then wondered why the creature had left so much of each crayfish behind.

I've had many such conversations with children in which their responses have had a similar underlying feature—an intentional, active cause. These conversations range in the specifics from noticing a sand castle that had fallen apart ("Why did someone go and wreck it?") to the sweater that fell out of a cubby ("A kindergartner probably did it.") to taking care of the earth ("But it's not like a big monster is going to wreck it, why would we have to protect it?") A well-supported finding in the research literature, [1] when the cause of an outcome is not obvious, children often appeal to an intentional agent.

To some extent, adults share this tendency. When Mozart died at age thirty-five in early December of 1791 while at the height of his musical prowess, the early reports were that he had been poisoned. Fueling this notion was the fact that he had been in good health, had been productive in composing *The Magic Flute*, and was writing the *Requiem* when he very suddenly took ill on November 22nd.

Later hypotheses eventually focused on non-obvious, nonintentional causes, and scientists currently suspect that he died of a strep infection, a very common cause of death at the time and the cause of 5011 other deaths in Vienna in the nine-month period surrounding Mozart's death.[2]

When so many people died around the shores of Lake Nyos, Cameroon, in the 1986 event with no obvious cause, as discussed in earlier chapters, one of the first reactions was that this must be the work of terrorists. The effect was clear for all to see and yet nothing looked different in the community except for all the bodies. Those who survived talked of a deep sleepiness— falling in and out of consciousness. No one saw anyone.[3] Still, the initial response was that someone did it.

Yet many causes are not characterized by intentionality. In these examples, a nonintentional cause eventually surfaced; a common strep infection probably killed Mozart and the density of the gases released from the bottom of the lake in relation to the density of breathable air caused the deaths at Lake Nyos. As for the dead crayfish, it's likely that the fertilizer on the soccer fields nearby (non-obvious and nonintentional as well as spatially distant and temporally delayed) may have leached into the pond impacting the crayfish.

Not only do we tend to ascribe intentional causes, intentional causes tend to grab our attention more readily than nonintentional ones. As Cass Sunstein has written, when a pair of snipers were terrorizing metropolitan Washington, D.C., in 2002, it got people's attention and caused them to change their behaviors dramatically even as heart disease, which kills many more people, does not garner the attention that it deserves.[4]

We also judge causes that are intentionally aligned with their outcomes much harsher than nonaligned ones. David Lagnado and Shelley Channon found that intentional outcomes are rated as "more causal" as are outcomes that are foreseeable.[5] Juxtapose pilgrims who came to the New World bearing diseases that killed many of the indigenous people there[6] to Hitler who intentionally and systematically exterminated millions. Both had similar consequences, but we weigh the intentionality of Hitler heavily in evaluating the crimes.

In the paragraphs to follow, I consider what is so compelling about active, intentional causality. I contrast it to passive and nonintentional causality. I explain how this may impact the causal patterns that we notice and how we assess risk.

THE PULL OF AGENCY

Our tendency toward active, intentional causes has its roots in infancy, when we learn the power of agency. As discussed at length in chapter three, our earliest and most empowering experiences of causality typically involve our own agency. Batting a toy makes a sound. Crying makes someone come. Causes that involve agency typically also involve intentionality—the two often go hand in hand.

The research discussed in chapter three on how we learn agency and intentionality makes a compelling case that we learn to discern goal-related behavior and to assign intentions at a very young age.[7] As cognitive scientist Susan Carey has argued, attending to agency is a defining feature of our cognitive architecture.[8] We are social beings, and as infants, we learn in special ways from our ability to carry out actions—to be an agent. Making things happen and goal-oriented, intentional behavior is a powerful feature of how we perceive causality.[9]

The research in science education suggests that the tendency to privilege active, intentional agency persists as we get older.[10] When asked why the liquid rises when they drink from a straw, students say, "I suck on the straw and I pull the liquid up."[11] This fits with their earliest conceptions of cause and effect—a simple linear causality with a strong grounding in their own agency.

So we give them three flasks of juice with straws, two of which have been modified slightly. They find that they can drink easily from the first flask. When they discover that the second one has a hole in the straw, they say that they "just couldn't suck hard enough." But the third flask has a stopper at the top and it is what gets students to revise their explanation. They are able to drink a little juice from the flask and then they cannot get any more.

This is puzzling to many people—students, teachers, and administrators—with whom we have worked. Armed with an agency-oriented and intentional notion of causality, they suck as hard as they can on the straw—sometimes hard enough to pull their tongues into the top of the straw. As one group of students commented, "We knew that the one with the stopper looked hard so we gave it to the strongest kid in our group so that he could suck really hard and get the juice out—but he couldn't!"

The scientific explanation is a form of relational causality. Once you have removed a little juice, the air inside the container spreads out in the available space. Since no air can take the place of the juice that has been removed, it effectively lowers the air pressure inside the container. Equilibrium is reached between the air pressure in the straw and in the container and there is no differential to push the liquid up the straw. Juice moves up the straw due to higher air pressure outside than inside the straw—a non-obvious cause.

If you try to remove more, it results in lower pressure in the flask and the feeling that your tongue is being pulled in. As active and intentional as you are, without that imbalance you can't get the juice to come up the straw. The scientific explanation is very different from our agency-oriented expectations.

Some students begin to realize that they have experienced this before, for instance, when drinking from a juice box, when they had to stop sucking and let more air into the container. Interestingly, they dealt with the problem without revising their agency-oriented explanations. Enterprising students then figure out that they can raise the pressure inside the container by blowing into it. This creates enough of a differential to spew juice across the room!

Intentional reasoning is common among all ages. Young children make distinctions between internally and externally caused movement [12] and between animate and inanimate things. [13] This relates to the capacity for intentional behavior. Adults often use intentional explanations—in appropriate and inappropriate contexts. [14] For instance, they struggle to view natural selection as nonpurposeful. They tend to say that organisms evolve characteristics to fill certain needs as in "giraffes have long necks to eat leaves from trees" rather than randomly generated variation being selected by environmental pressures. [15]

The close relationship between causality and agency actually can serve us well in some cases. Much of our causal reasoning and learning about causality in our world depends upon our ability to intervene in situations and make things happen. In fact, a whole body of research on causal learning focuses on exactly that type of learning—how we can thoughtfully intervene in controlled ways to assess the outcome of doing so and what it tells us about the causality in play.

This is a version of testing and screening off different variables to see what might happen that is similar to that of scientific isolation and control of variables. [16] Intervention allows us to manipulate and learn about causal systems to assess how they work. The difficulty comes when we start characterizing causality as having an active agency orientation in instances when it does not.

NON-AGENTIVE CAUSALITY AND PASSIVE CAUSES

Agency is not a key feature of all causal systems. Systems in steady state, as discussed in chapter ten, provide good examples. In the bridge example, the balanced forces just continue keeping the bridge up. Typically, we don't think of it as *doing* anything besides standing there and we are unlikely to focus on it unless something disrupts its balance. It is not characterized by agency.

Many forms of causality are not characterized by action—an active sense that someone or something is doing something. When riding in a car at fifty miles per hour, everything in the vehicle is moving at fifty miles per hour, including us. The car has brakes to stop it. What stops us? As long as the stopping of the car is gradual, we might not notice the role that our seatbelt plays in holding us in our seats. It is a passive restraint system.

When a car stops very hard (amplifying the effect), we are more likely to recognize our seatbelt as a cause that keeps us from lurching forward when the car stops. A more active causal agent might have a greater chance of being recognized. For instance, if a hand came out of the dashboard and pushed passengers into their seats each time the car came to a stop, we would quickly recognize it as a causal factor in the system.

Some causes have a passive nature. For instance, protons and electrons are attracted to each other and electrons are believed to move. However, both are a part of the causal equation. Consider a social example. If someone's persona inspires others to behave in certain ways, even if the person's behavior is passive, they are still part of the causal equation.

When asked about instances of passive causality, students often characterize it as agency oriented. For instance, Rich Lehrer and Leona Schauble, in a study of children's conceptions of gears, found that approximately half of the second and fifth graders in their sample typically consider the driving gear as active and the other gears in the train as passive recipients of motion.[17] Few children (9 percent of second graders and 25 percent of fifth graders) described a more sophisticated, interactive, or reciprocal causality where the gears pushed against each other.

The type of causal pattern that we recognize often depends upon whether or not we recognize steady state or passive causes. Unaware of ambient air pressure, we focus on a linear explanation for why juice rises in the straw when we suck on it instead of a relational one. The symbiotic act of the bee taking nectar could well be viewed as one act with one outcome (nectar for the bee) instead of two outcomes (nectar for the bee and pollination of the flower). Thus we reduce the causal pattern to a simple linear one instead of a mutual one.

INTENTIONS, OURS AND OTHERS

People are generally quite willing to reason about the intentions of others.[18] According to Fundamental Attribution Theory, we tend to ascribe the behaviors of others to internal causes that we cannot see—traits, dispositions, intentions, character.[19] With ease, we label others as hardworking, lazy, smart, mindful, and so on to attribute their successes or failures. We tend to think that people intend to do what they do. Imagine how different driving would be if we assumed less intentionality on behalf of other drivers. "Hmm . . . maybe they didn't intend to cut me off, but they had to dodge that other vehicle?"

On the other hand, Fundamental Attribution Theory (or "Error" as it is often called) also reveals that we are more likely to ascribe our own behaviors to situational factors—conditions of the moment, events that occurred, what others did, and so on.[20] So while we think that people are cutting us off on the highway, we know that we are just merging or getting out of the way of that ambulance back there.

There appears to be a cultural aspect to this tendency in which cultures that emphasize individual over group appear to make more trait- or disposition-based attributions than other cultures.[21] Even so, Fundamental Attribution Theory is a robust finding in social psychology and has been found by many experimenters across many cultures.

Why might we engage in attributions of this sort? There's no general agreement on what compels us to assess others differently than ourselves. In fact, given that we have more data about our own intentions and inner states, it is somewhat puzzling that we don't attribute more to them.

Dan Gilbert and Patrick Malone have argued that situational factors actually suffer from an invisibility problem in that they often have no physical manifestation. For instance, he argues, you can't see (smell, hear, or taste) "audience pressure" or things like a coach's instructions.[22] Interestingly, when people are given information about why people might adopt a certain perspective—hidden causes are unpacked for them—they often still make the attributions, only they tend to make ones that are less strong.

One explanation of the Fundamental Attribution Theory suggests that our perspective is largely responsible.[23] When watching someone else handle a situation, they are largely the focus of our attention, but when attending to our own actions, we are the constant and the situational variables become more salient. We also have far more data about ourselves and so we are willing to reason about our own patterns over time while we take the given instance as data about others whom we observe.

These explanations make sense in light of what we know about non-obvious causes. Intentions can be viewed as non-obvious causes and, as discussed in the last chapter, we can have trouble with non-obvious causes. However, our difficulty is typically in identifying them when there is nothing to call our attention to them or when there is a competing obvious explanation. Situational factors have different levels of non-obviousness depending upon whose role you are in.

LEARNING TO MIND THE PASSIVE AND NONINTENTIONAL

So how does the tendency to look for active, intentional causal agents, as opposed to passive, nonintentional ones, impact learning? Here is an example from our work in science classes. The eighth graders studying air pressure were unlikely to recognize air-pressure-related phenomenon that were not "event-like." Secondly, when they did attempt to reason about air pressure, they tended to characterize it as an active causal agent—substituting notions of force for pressure. Let's consider each conception in turn.

Air pressure is an ambient variable that is typically always present. When air pressure is balanced, it doesn't appear to "do" anything. However, when the balance shifts, it results in events or changes (ears popping, balloons expanding, liquid rising, and so on) that make it appear active. Analogous to the bridge example above, disrupting the balance of the system results in a dramatic event that fits with students' expectations about what constitutes a cause-and-effect relationship (that something acts on something else to make something obvious happen). They then notice air pressure as a relevant causal variable.

Students typically characterize air pressure as an active push in one direction, a unidirectional force that pushes down. This can result from substituting a force conception for pressure. However, air pressure acts omnidirectionally.

In order to grasp that air pressure acts omnidirectionally, one also has to realize that molecules that make up the air are randomly bouncing around and can bounce in all directions. Instead of one force pushing down, one has to visualize the collective effect of many different molecules bouncing all around (actively, but nonintentionally) and a collective impact of air pressure. This is a different idea than how many students think of pushing or force—to which they attach intentionality. As with air pressure, the idea of water pressure existing equally in all directions is counterintuitive to students. [24]

One further source of students' confusion may generate from reasoning about air- pressure-related phenomena at different levels. We do speak of individual molecules that make up the air as forceful—bumping into and bouncing off of things. The ambient, omnidirectional aspects of air pressure are due to the collective effect of individual molecules colliding and bouncing around. As discussed in chapter fourteen, it is well documented that students have difficulty reasoning about collective behaviors, and moving back and forth between levels of individual interaction and the collective, emergent outcomes. [25]

Learning to mind passive and nonintentional causes involves learning to recognize our tendency toward active and intentional explanations and examining where they do and do not apply. This is important because many concepts elicit notions of action or doing that we may otherwise not be aware of. Consider the case of hurricanes.

Hurricanes have powerful winds and therefore imprint a forceful, unidirectional notion in students' minds. Students confuse the forcefulness of the direction of the winds with the omnidirectional, pressure-related cause of the wind. Even if students learn that winds are the result of air moving from areas of higher pressure toward areas of lower pressure, the wind moves in a specific direction and therefore exerts force in that direction. Teasing apart the aspects that fit with students' agentive notions and those that do not is challenging.

PICTURES OF PRACTICE: WHAT DOES IT LOOK LIKE TO HELP STUDENTS LEARN TO EXPLICITLY CONSIDER THE POSSIBILITY OF NONINTENTIONAL AND PASSIVE CAUSES?

The third grade is talking about the story *The Lorax* by Dr. Seuss. They are discussing the many effects from the Once-ler's decision to start a Thneed Factory and start cutting down the Truffula Trees. There are many domino and radiating effects. A student mentions how bad the Once-ler was and how sorry he was at the end.

Her teacher introduces the question about intention and effect. "Did the Once-ler mean to hurt the brown Bar-ba-Loots or the Swomee Swans? In the end, does it matter?" "Did you ever cause harm that you didn't mean to 'cause because you didn't realize what would happen?" The Lorax told the Once-ler that he was hurting the Bar-ba-Loots and the Swomee Swans and still he didn't change his actions. "Is what he did worse because he knew that it was bad for them and ignored the Lorax?" The students realize that the outcome is just as bad but that we are usually more forgiving if something was an accident.

The fifth graders are considering the difficulties that the colonists faced when King George imposed additional taxes that led up to the protests of the Boston Tea Party. Events such as these were critical in the path to the American Revolution. But in trying to understand what colonial life was like, there were many more powerful, nonintentional difficulties imposed upon the colonists such as harsh weather and crop failures. These were significant factors in the success of the new colonies and in the course of history.

Ms. Jackson asks her students to consider both kinds of events in painting a fuller sense of colonial life. She presents our tendency to focus on intentional causes. She asks why we might have this tendency in history to focus more on decisions such as those of King George or those at Plymouth Colony when the colonists attacked the indigenous peoples than on nonintentional causes of difficulty for the colonists.

The students have many ideas. "Well, King George made a decision, he controls what he does, but weather isn't controlled." "We don't think of nature as bad." Another student realizes, "But when nature brings bad storms, we act like she's an angry person saying things like 'Mother Nature unleashes her wrath on us.'" "You have to focus your attention on fighting the British, with nature there's not really much that you can do so it makes sense to pay attention to the things people do."

The twelfth graders are discussing how we often "put a face" on events— for instance, the face of Hitler on the events during the Third Reich and the face of Osama Bin Laden on the events of 9/11. We also react with greater vigor when someone is acting to hurt us versus effects that are nonintentional.

"It's like, it took us much longer to pay attention to climate change than to terrorism," says one student. "Well, with climate change, we are doing it to ourselves, but with terrorism there is an enemy," responds another. "But think about Hurricane Katrina. We didn't prepare for it the way that we did prepare for the possibility of another terrorist attack. We knew that hurricanes like Katrina were possible. But if Katrina was a terrorist plot, we would have done more, I think."

NOTES

1. For research on children's tendency to overascribe intentionality, see Berndt & Berndt, 1975; Miller & Aloise, 1989, and Smith, 1978.

2. Bakalar, 2009

3. http://www.geology.sdsu.edu/how_volcanoes_work/Nyos.html; [accessed: 8-11-2009; http://natgeotv.com/uk/killer-fog [accessed: 7-5-2011]

4. Sunstein, 2002

5. Lagnado & Channon, 2008

6. Mann, 2004

7. Meltzoff, 2007

8. Carey, 2009

9. Meltzoff, 2007; Sommerville, 2007

10. Andersson, 1986; Basca & Grotzer, 2003; Brown, 1995; Gomez-Crespo & Pozo, 2004; Talanquer, 2002

11. Engel Clough and Driver (1985) also found that students bring a simple linear interpretation to their explanations of drinking from a straw.

12. e.g., Gelman, Durgin & Kaufman, 1995; Premack & Premack, 1995; Spelke, Phillips & Woodward, 1995

13. e.g., Gelman & Gottfried, 1996; Golinkoff et al.,1984; Legerstee, 1994

14. e.g., Murayama, 1994

15. Ohlsson, n.d.

16. e.g., Hitchcock, 2007; Schulz, Kushnir & Gopnik, 2007; Woodward, 2007

17. Lehrer & Schauble, 1998

18. Rossett, E. (2008). It's no accident. Our bias for international explanations. *Cognition* 108 (3), 771–80.

19. Ross, 1977

20. Ross, 1977

21. Miller, 1984

22. Gilbert & Malone, 1995

23. Jones & Harris, 1967; Ross, 1977; Ross & Nisbett, 1991

24. Engel Clough & Driver, 1985; Giese, 1987

25. e.g., Wilensky & Resnick, 1999

Chapter Thirteen

Step by Step . . . or Not:
The Mind-bending Concept of
Simultaneous Causality

"Just take it one step at a time."

*"If you break it down into steps,
it will be easier to understand."*

"But he did it first!"

Imagine watching a row of dominoes and suddenly the fifth one falls over before the third one. You wonder, "What strange force is at work?" Or a fifth grader comes in from recess insisting that Tommy pushed him on the playground. "What did you do first?" his teacher asks. A friend announces that she is engaged and begins to tell her friends about the big moment. "No, no, start at the beginning, we want to hear how it all happened," they insist.

Consider the intrigue of some movies that have drawn box-office success in recent years. In *Sliding Doors*, we witness the simultaneous living out of two possible lives of the character played by Gwyneth Paltrow. After accidentally traveling back in time and interfering with his parents' first meeting in *Back to the Future*, Marty McFly must get his parents to meet and fall in love, or his current-day existence is threatened. Movies like *The Terminator* and *The Matrix* also play with time in intriguing ways. [1]

Contrast this to more familiar types of sequential narrative. At age seven, my daughter wrote the following story, "Once there was a ball. A girl opened her toy chest. She played with the ball. Then her mom called her. And then the ball rolled away. When she came back the ball was not there. She looked then she found the ball. She played with it again. Then she put it back in her toy chest. Then she went to eat." It reminded me of so many stories that I had read as a second-grade teacher years ago.

"Sequentiality" is a predominant feature of discourse in many cultures and an underlying assumption of our causal stories as well. In Western culture, children's early stories are often "this then that" stories—a running sequence of events. They don't always make explicit causal links, but they have clear actions that occur over time.

Our causal stories don't tend to be much different. We focus on causality as it exists within the "flow of time." As in the Borneo story in chapter four, the World Heath Organization sprayed DDT to kill mosquitoes, then the DDT poisoned geckoes, eating geckoes poisoned the cats who died, then the rats flourished and so on . . .

But many causal dynamics are best characterized by simultaneity. Consider the following examples:

- A set of gears all turn at once.
- You plug in the holiday lights and they all light up at the same time.
- A bee takes nectar from a flower and simultaneously the flower receives the pollen that enables it to bear fruit.
- An arch bridge, a balance of forces, stands in the skyline.
- A satellite circles the earth in constant orbit.

Each of these examples involves causality, yet does not call to mind a temporal sequence between causes and effects. Visualize the set of gears turning. You could argue that there is a moment that lapses as the gears all begin to push on each other, but the essence of what happens is simultaneity, not sequentiality.

Chapter ten considered steady states which involves considering dynamics across time. Here, I consider the counterintuitive notion that causality can be simultaneous and explore simultaneity as a characteristic of a more expansive notion of causality—one that looks beyond temporally sequenced forms. Then I consider what we know about how children reason about simultaneous causality, why it is so hard to wrap our minds around, as well as the intrigue that it offers.

THE MIND-BENDING NOTION OF SIMULTANEOUS CAUSALITY

Can effects happen at the same time as their causes? Most of us would say no. The very idea of cause and effect requires that something happens in response to something else and for most of us that means first the cause and then the effect. This question that most of us answer with ease has raised the interest of many a philosopher, among them David Hume and Immanuel Kant. Hume argued that temporal precedence between causes and effects is one of the basic principles of causality. Certainly this fits with the strong prototypical concept that many of us think of when contemplating cause and effect.[2]

However, as gears are turning, it is meaningless to say one turned and then the other turned, and then the next—tracking causes and effects across time. It *is* possible to detect which gears interlock with which others to trace a causal path—but not a temporal causal path. What about the holiday lights?[3] When it comes to simple circuits, a common misconception is that the circuit is empty and that it fills sequentially with electrons causing the bulb(s) to light.[4]

With the right support, students can reason their way beyond this idea. They realize that a circuit can't be empty as electrons are part of what make up the wire. They learn that the cyclic movement of electrons, like the spinning of a bicycle wheel, is what enables bulbs along the circuit to light.[5] The lighting of the bulbs is essentially simultaneous with the completing of the circuit and the bulbs don't light one at a time in sequence along the wire— they light all at once.

UNPACKING SIMULTANEOUS CAUSALITY

Some of the causal patterns presented in part two are more easily character-ized by either sequentiality or simultaneity. For instance, domino causality has a strong sequential characterization. This is also the case in escalating causality. Because the escalation plays out over time, there is an inherent temporal sequence.

However, some of the causal patterns are strongly characterized by simul-taneity. Mutual causality often involves simultaneous, bi-directional out-comes. This is the case in many instances of attraction. The Earth and the moon are simultaneously attracted to each other. So are protons and elec-trons. Relational causality is characterized by simultaneity. Something sinks or floats due to the relationship between the liquid and the object or between two liquids. Which direction a seesaw tilts depends upon the balance be-tween the weights of the kids sitting on it.

One *could* argue that neither the holiday lights or the gears are indeed simultaneous, that there's a transient delay of under a nanosecond for the holiday lights to get up to a steady state where they all light or for the gears to all start moving, following the initial turning of a crank. Indeed, whether we view something as simultaneous depends, in part, upon the time scale that we employ. What appears to be simultaneous on a geologic scale would be eternities apart on a nanoscale.

Another way to avoid simultaneity is to redefine what is cause and effect. For instance, one could focus on the kids getting onto a seesaw and the tipping one way or the other as a result. However, that shifts what is being explained. In one case, it is why the seesaw tips in the direction that it does, while in the other, it is that there is an effect at all. In each of these cases, it's not that one interpretation is right and the other is wrong, it's that different levels of analysis fit different situations. A strong bias toward assuming temporality shifts what we see and attend to in any given situation.

Whether simultaneous causality is a possibility has been long argued by philosophers. The discussions debate the physics of certain events, such as if a train were pulling a caboose, are the cause (train pulling) and effect (caboose moving) simultaneous? Often the question is reduced to whether or not one can discount tension on the bar, and so forth.[6]

However, some schools of thought allow for simultaneous causality. For example, the Sarvastivada Buddhist School includes six types of causality, including "co-existent cause" which allows for simultaneous forms of causality. While the philosophical question is intriguing, a more relevant question from a teaching and learning perspective is how a default assumption of sequentiality impacts our reasoning in the world.

How does it get us in trouble to reduce simultaneous causality to sequential? Does it really matter? Casting simultaneity into a sequential mold can lead us to take isolated actions. We think that we can take things one step at a time and believe that there is time to revise our actions and that there are multiple points for intervention. If something doesn't unfold as we hoped, we can just stop it at a further point along the road.

An assumption of sequentiality can be comforting in a number of ways. There's an appealing, ordered quality to sequential causality. There is a sense that we can untangle events and emerge with clear knowledge of how things played out. We prefer to believe that if we can just "rewind the tape" we'll know what happened or at least who was at fault. This is every kid's intention when he says, "But he did it first!" Sequential causality brings the sense that you can deal with one thing at a time—that perhaps one can stop a cascade of events by stopping the next domino in the line.

But often events are not sequentially timed, actions overlap, effects occur all at once. There's that disquieting feeling that things didn't go quite right— like when letters cross in the mail—a miscommunication of sorts or like too much is happening at once. Consider the simultaneity of the effects of global warming—weather changes, species loss, land loss, economic impacts, and so on. If our attention is drawn by events, then simultaneous causes and effects are most frustrating because we have no opportunity for intervention between when our attention is captured and effects are noticed.

During the Cold War, there was always the uncomfortable, perilous question—if one of the superpowers pushed the button, would the other follow suit? There was a sense that the response would be automatic—if one superpower pushed the button, the other would do so reflexively. It is not quite the same thing as simultaneous causes and effects, yet it condenses time, and makes outcomes essentially inevitable. It is a game changer.

Casting simultaneity into a sequential mold can get us in trouble inside the classroom as well. It certainly matters in science class. Imposing sequentiality on a phenomena better characterized as simultaneous can result in focusing on isolated parts of a system and missing what is going on across the system.

Envisioning the electrical circuit sequentially filling with electrons and then returning to the battery to be recycled (as many students and teachers do) results in a number of misconceptions. It leads to reasoning about the circuit in terms of isolated parts instead of as a system making it hard to apply Ohm's Law (which addresses the constraint-based relationship between current, voltage, and resistance).[7] In reasoning about parallel and series circuits, students incorrectly think that the first light in a string of lights wired in series will either come on first or get more power and be brighter than the others.

Breaking things down into steps is a common reaction to complexity and is often a very good idea. From a psychological standpoint, it makes difficult tasks approachable. From a cognitive perspective, it minimizes the load in our minds, helping us to grasp more information. Sequential causality can be easier to think about because there is less dynamic information to hold in your head at once. But, as a fourth grader remarked when learning about simple circuits, "When you learn something new, you break it down into steps to learn it,[8] but with all-at-once causality, if you break it down, then you have the wrong idea."

WHY DO WE DEFAULT TO SEQUENTIAL PATTERNS?

So why do we make the default assumption that causes must always occur sequentially before effects and therefore lose the simultaneous causal features of some problems? What makes us tend to view things sequentially?[9] Think back to our baby in the crib. As he or she reaches out and perhaps inadvertently bats at a toy and a bell rings, cries in distress and mom or dad comes, or drops a rattle and hears it hit the floor, the baby gains a sense of agency and learns, "If I do something, something else follows."[10]

Summing across these co-varying events, in a Bayesian fashion, we notice causal patterns and we intervene to assess causality. Batting a bell is followed by a sound. Without temporal precedence between causes and effects, figuring out causal patterns through intervention can become quite complicated.

As discussed in chapter nine, temporal information plays an important role in our causal reasoning. Children learn to interpret causal chains of events and to reason about what is causal and what is temporal by as early as fifteen months of age. Researchers used a sequence where the intermediate steps were visible and found that by fifteen months old, babies interpreted causal chains (A causes B causes C) as adults do.[11]

Merry Bullock, Rochel Gelman, and colleagues conducted a series of experiments to study how children reason about temporal order—the sequence between events. They found that preschoolers use temporal precedence in addition to the plausibility of the mechanism.[12] In one study, they showed children an apparatus with two mirror-image runway boxes with a jack-in-the-box in the middle. Balls were dropped into either side before or after the jack-in-the-box popped up. Five-year-olds consistently selected the ball that rolled down just before the clown popped up as the cause. Three- and four-year-olds selected it most of the time.

Without a sequential relationship between causes and effects, which is a "cause" and which is an "effect" can become blurred—at least without careful attention to the mechanisms involved. Children attend to causes and effects differently and afford different status to each. As early as seven months, infants pay attention to what is a cause and what is an effect.[13] By ten months of age, they afford a special status to "causes" and expect that certain kinds of agents are responsible for certain kinds of actions.[14]

LEARNING TO MOVE BEYOND SEQUENTIAL PATTERNS

Children have many experiences with sequential phenomena, but one can argue that they also have experiences with simultaneous causality. When they make a mark with a crayon, the act of marking and the resulting line are perceptibly simultaneous. When they push a toy car across the room, they are making the car move and it moves with their hand motion. In each example, there is a clear cause, a clear effect, and they are essentially simultaneous.

Even though we tend to focus on sequential causality, a small body of emerging research suggests that even young children can be taught about nonsequential causality. These studies suggest that children (and adults) can reason about causality even when causes and effects are simultaneous.

Gopnik and colleagues showed four-year-olds two puppets that moved simultaneously (nonvisibly moved by the researcher).[15] They said that the puppets move together and stop together, but that one is special and that the special puppet always makes the other move.[16] Then, they showed the puppets moving and said, "I'm moving X, and X is making Y move. Which is the special puppet?" Children who chose "X" continued on. Then the puppets moved together and stopped together four times and then the experimenter visibly moved Y, but X did not move. Children chose X as the special puppet 78 percent of the time.

Similarly, Laura Schulz showed adults and children two objects that moved together and that intervening on one impacted the movement of the other, but not vice versa. With that information, they were able to infer which object was causal.[17]

PICTURES OF PRACTICE: WHAT DOES IT LOOK LIKE TO HELP STUDENTS LEARN TO EXPLICITLY CONSIDER SIMULTANEOUS CAUSATION?

The fourth graders are drawing models of what happens in a series circuit. They know that the circuit is a circle—a closed system—and the electrons are recycled by the battery. But most still hold sequential models for how the electrons flow. They think of the circuit as empty and that it fills sequentially with electrons such that the bulb should light as the electrons reach it. So what is going on? Given their sequential model, one bulb should light first or only one should light or at least be brighter than the other. But they both appear to light to the same brightness and they both appear to light at the same time.

Their teacher challenges them to consider whether the circuit starts out empty. Setting out a white shower curtain with a circuit drawn on it, she contrasts two different ideas, one starts with an empty circuit and the other with electrons all along it. What if all the electrons move at once—repelling those in front of them while being repelled by those behind them? The students line up along the circuit to try it. One of them can't move until the others do; they all must move at once. The teacher presents this "all at once" causality in contrast to "step-by-step" causality. The students consider whether either one helps them to explain what they observe with a series circuit.[18]

The sixth graders are mapping out the causes of the American Revolution. Mrs. Hamid notices that as students explain their mappings, they give domino-like causal narratives of how events unfolded over time where first one thing happened and then that caused the next thing and so on. They have been talking in past weeks about how one's perspective impacts the historical narrative that gets told—how some events stand out as relevant from certain perspectives and not others.

She decides to engage the class in thinking about the sequential features of their narratives. "I'm noticing that many of you have drawn lines showing what happened in a domino pattern where one thing causes another thing which causes another thing to happen. This emphasizes how both sides acted in reaction to the other."

Mrs. Hamid sets out a new focus, "For the last part of class, I'd like you to try a different focus, one that will let you see other sides of what might be happening and to see issues and tensions instead of just actions in response to each other." She asks them to consider if they can find any events or ongoing problems that were happening at the same time and to think about how these things happening all at once might change what is important to show in their pictures. She encourages them to draw a concept mapping.

She offers an example, "So the British were trying to find ways to deal with large amounts of debt following the French and Indian War, including considering new taxes, and were also trying to keep down costs of protecting the Indians from encroachment by the colonists. At the same time, the colonists were trying to expand to establish the colonies and make economic gains. These things were happening at the same time and indeed impacting each other. How might this shift how you view the situation?"

NOTES

1. *Sliding Doors* (1998), Intermedia Films/Miramax; *Back to the Future* (1985), Universal Pictures; *The Terminator* (1984), Hemdale Film; *The Matrix* (1999), Warner Bros.

2. For more information, see the writings of A. David Kline (e.g., 1985) and Jay F. Rosenberg (e.g., 1998).

3. Unlike older versions, which were wired in series, newer holiday lights are often a combination of parallel and series circuits; thus if one bulb burns out, they don't all go out at once and they make for a less straightforward example in science class!

4. Shipstone, 1984, 1985

5. In a simplified model.

6. e.g., Kline, 1980

7. Rather than addressing this underlying mental model, high school teachers often teach constraint-based models about the relationship between voltage, current, and resistance. However, problems arise when students try to reconcile their different pieces of knowledge and the underlying mental model interacts with how they interpret and remember the algorithms.

8. This is what Feltovich, Spiro & Coulson (1989) have referred to as an "acquisition bias."

9. It is possible that sequential causality is a more predominant feature of Western thought than that of other cultures, given the focus on linearity and sequential narrative.

10. Lakoff and Johnson (1980) first called this the "experiential gestalt of causation (EGC)." Andersson (1986) has argued that as children act upon their environments, they learn that actions by an agent (themselves) can impact objects (such as toys, blankets, bottles, and parents).

11. Cohen et al., 1999; Research is divided on how adults attribute causal chains, with some researchers suggesting that they attribute it to the earliest event in the chains (e.g., Johnson et al., 1989; Vinokur & Ajzen, 1982), others saying the latest event is viewed as causal (e.g., Miller & Gunasegaram, 1990), and others saying that the event that co-varies most consistently (Mandel & Lehman, 1996) or without which the event probably would not have occurred (Spellman, 1997). (See Cohen et al., 1999, for a discussion.)

12. Bullock & Gelman, 1979

13. Golinkoff, 1975

14. Cohen & Oakes, 1993

15. Gopnik et al., 2004

16. Thus the framing may have enabled children to separate the notion of the "special status" afforded to causes from temporal precedence.

17. Schulz, 2001

18. This lesson is available as part of the Simple Circuits unit available on the Understandings of Consequence Project web site.

Chapter Fourteen

Figuring Out What to Count On: Dealing with Stochastic Causality

*"One time at a store, my brother put a quarter in
the gum-ball machine and he got NOTHING."*

*"My sister finally said that it made her mad when I used
her markers. How was I supposed to know? She acted
like it was okay, and then said stop once or twice."*

You turn the key and the car starts, but then one morning, it doesn't. You text a friend and get an immediate reply . . . most of the time. Sometimes you don't get one at all. You push a button on a game board and sometimes a card shoots out and sometimes it doesn't. You slide your credit card across a swipe pad in the department store and usually it reads the information, but sometimes you have to swipe it again and perhaps again. How do we respond when a cause does not reliably lead to an effect? It actually happens quite often. In this chapter, I consider what has been called stochastic or probabilistic causation, using the terms interchangeably.

Research suggests that we hold a strong expectation of determinism—that causes reliably lead to effects.[1] When we set our alarm clock each night, we expect that it will go off each and every morning. When we turn the key in the ignition of the car, we expect it to start. In deterministic causality, there is a consistent, reliable relationship between causes and effects. Each time a cause occurs, the effect follows. One can depend upon it.

This chapter explores our tendencies toward determinism and the understandings that we need to achieve to manage well in a probabilistic world. It considers what research says about our ability to understand and act upon probabilistic causal contexts. What do we know about how and when these understandings are learned? How do things seen and unseen—the age of the car or how cold it is—impact our expectations for whether it will reliably start? How does the context impact our assumptions? Is it different for people— when we call to our mothers, spouses, or colleagues, do we expect a reliable response?

STEP ON A CRACK, BREAK YOUR MOTHER'S BACK

Our strong expectation of determinism is not surprising. Philosopher David Hume considered determinism to be a fundamental feature of causality.[2] Albert Einstein, who studied complex, seemingly probabilistic phenomena, refused to believe that "God plays dice" with the universe. According to Susan Carey, "Humans are theory builders; from the beginning we construct explanatory structures that help us find the deeper reality underlying surface chaos."[3] This sense that we understand how our world works and can know what to expect helps us to feel empowered and in control.

Our need to make sense and to know what we can expect sometimes reveals itself in superstitions. We avoid the cracks in the sidewalk "just in case it matters." We blow on the dice for good luck. Sometimes these are private gestures, and other times, they are part of a larger, socially constructed reality.

In the 2004 baseball season, when Red Sox fans were hoping that their team would finally win the pennant after eighty-six years, the entire city of Boston engaged in rituals to "impact" the luck of the team. Some fans didn't shave or change their socks for weeks. One man plowed down a house that had formerly belonged to Babe Ruth who, legend had it, left "the Curse of the Bambino" when he was traded from the Red Sox to the New York Yankees.

These responses to uncertainty are not surprising. We all like to think that the events in our world are under our control and we find ways to convince ourselves that we have that control. But even setting aside the complex topics that Einstein studied, such as quantum mechanics and chaos theory, people actually do entertain concepts of uncertainty in how effects follow from causes every day. Serendipity, probability, and spurious events shape much of the fabric of our lives. We come into contact with a sick person and sometimes we get sick, sometimes we don't. We head to work, suddenly finding ourselves in a traffic jam.

PROBABILISTIC CALCULATIONS IN A CLOAK OF DETERMINISM?

Interestingly, even though we hold an expectation of determinism, recent research also suggests that our everyday mode of causal inference works probabilistically.[4] As discussed in depth in chapter three, one of the ways that we infer causality is through a statistical summing across of events in relation to plausible causes. We sum across instances to infer the existence of a causal relationship and are able to do so even if the causes and effects do not reliably co-occur.

One could argue that few causal patterns in our world truly are probabilistic in nature. If we follow a reductionist path, we can often get to an explanation of why an effect did not occur as expected. If the car does not start, we can go through a process of figuring out why (and are pretty frustrated if that process does not lead to a clear answer). If our spouse does not come when we call, we assume that he or she is out of earshot, is busy, or perhaps has intentionally decided to ignore us.

However, many patterns regularly give the appearance of being probabilistic or at least do *not* give the appearance of being deterministic. The same causal event, such as pushing a button in a game or calling out to a friend, can lead to a specific outcome sometimes, but not others. Further, the patterns of contingency can vary. One push on a game may lead to an outcome, yet at other times three pushes may be necessary. Going beyond this appearance can require dogged determinism that may lead to an answer or not. For instance, we may never have the information that helps us to figure out why a particular seed did not grow or what compelled our teenage son not to call when he said he would.

Sometimes these patterns fall within the boundaries of what we attend to so we notice what the contingencies are. However, just as often, they fall beyond our attentional boundaries. Seeds take a long time to grow thus introducing time delays; the intricacies of a social interaction increase in cognitive load until it is difficult to reason well about them; plausible mechanisms can become increasingly non-obvious such that detecting them invites a long, reductionist investigation.

We may shift our attention to other stimuli in our environment, no longer noticing the nature of the contingencies within the patterns. We may substitute our assumptions for what generally happens with what actually happens in a given instance if we do not have access to all of the information, don't have it all in mind, or simply have stopped attending.

TURNING THE PROBLEM INSIDE OUT LEADS
TO A BIGGER SET OF ISSUES

Most of the research on how people reason about stochastic or probabilistic causes focuses on instances where the causes and effects are in the same attentional set (for instance, as in the research study mentioned in chapter three where a stuffed monkey is shown to sneeze when it puts its face into a set of flowers)[5] or where we have the effect to be explained—such as feeling sick or the car not starting. But how might stochastic causality interact with our reasoning when we aren't trying to explain an effect—*before* we are aware that one exists?

The title of this chapter refers to figuring out what to count on. However, the issues are actually significantly broader than that. Turn the problem inside out for a moment. Consider the quote above from the child whose sister finally got mad that he took her markers. He had no idea that a cause-and-effect relationship existed. Unreliable effects are hard to notice if the causal link isn't already expected because the inconsistent co-variation readily escapes detection. And a strong expectation of determinism dictates that if she was going to get angry, she should have done it already.

The less reliable the cause-and-effect relationship, the less likely we are to detect it. Combine this with our deterministic stance and the more we engage in an action without an obvious effect, the less likely that we'll even notice clues that suggest that it leads to a certain effect. It's a little like the adage, "If you've gotten away with something once . . ." except that you didn't explicitly realize that you were getting away with anything. It is not that we can't sum across instances or screen off potential causes to figure out what is going on; we are unlikely to be sensitive to the need to do so.

One could certainly argue that taking your sister's markers is the kind of offense that can get you in trouble. The boy could have reasoned from similar cases (as in "taking things can make someone else mad"). However, in novel cases where you don't have a strong set of cases to reason from, it might take a very long time to notice an effect.

Mixing bleach and dish soap can make you very sick, but the connection between getting sick and mixing the chemicals may be hard to detect if you have mixed them many times before and not breathed enough of the resulting gases to get sick. Here, even if you notice an effect to be explained, summing across the negative cases works against recognition, so you aren't likely to include the mixture in the sink as a plausible cause. It's not new or different.

Now let's further complicate matters. Most of the research has focused on how we respond when we see a possible cause that only sometimes leads to a possible effect in the same attentional set. But what if they are not in the same attentional set? The difficulty of linking causes and effects within different attentional sets becomes even more problematic when we turn the problem inside out. It makes it unlikely that we will even pursue the possibility of a causal link, and because we expect a deterministic relationship, we might not even attach salience to the occasional instances that do draw our attention.

Imagine for example, that you are at the cause end of things. Each time you put fertilizer on your lawn, you may not know that an occasional result is that the eggs of baby birds are too soft to survive. Or if you were at the effect end of things and you occasionally found unhatched eggs containing dead birds you would not likely connect it to applying lawn fertilizer. Even if you found each instance of weakened bird eggs, it would not have a one-to-one or even discernible relationship with fertilizer applications.

If we are at the possible effect end of things, we see potential outcomes, but they unreliably co-vary with anything within our attention set that we might call a possible cause. Working from the direction of the effect to discerning potential causes presents us with the challenge of figuring out that there even is an effect. Tolerating unreliable cause- effect relationships when we are cued to their existence is one thing, but we aren't likely to detect stochastic event structures in the first place with so little to suggest their existence.

Why does our ability to detect stochastic event structures matter? In a complex world, it is easy to lose sight of the impact of particular choices, individual and societal, when we cannot detect an effect following an action. Many patterns present themselves stochastically. This includes instances of slow accumulation, when no observable outcome exists prior to "tipping points," when detecting connections involves extended reduction, or in cases of actual stochasticity. These characterize some of the most recalcitrant problems of our time, such as climate change, ecosystems decline, and global disease transmission.

When we know the causal link, dealing with probabilistic outcomes is not so problematic for everyday causal reasoning. However, the big problems come into play in detecting effects that need explaining when they are probabilistic—because we just don't notice them well. Even when we are aware of the relationship, it is difficult to keep them on our radar when they happen only occasionally. Our office has a doorbell that works much of the time, but not all of the time. This makes it really easy to forget to fix it!

HOW DO WE DEAL WITH UNRELIABLE CAUSAL RELATIONSHIPS?

Next, I tease apart concepts related to stochastic or probabilistic causality and how we understand them. The first links back to chapter three—addressing research on whether we use a statistical summing across process to arrive at everyday causal inferences. The second considers how children learn to reason about concepts of uncertainty, both subjectively and objectively. The third further considers the research on the development our implicit, and in some cases, explicit expectation of determinism even if we use an implicit probabilistic mechanism to arrive at many of our causal inferences (perhaps unbeknownst to us).

Bayesian Statistical Summing across Probabilistic Causality

Probabilistic causation deeply interests researchers for the reasons presented in chapter three. It has the potential to reveal aspects of how people determine the existence of a causal relationship.[6] An abundance of research shows that children use co-variation data in combination with spatial and temporal proximity[7] and information about plausible mechanisms in assessing causality.[8] However, this is a very active area of research and we are continuing to learn a lot about how they use this data.

Earlier research suggested that children expect reliable cause-effect relationships[9] and that they use consistent co-variation between causes and effects to determine whether or not a causal relationship exists.[10] The tendency appeared to be age-related, with the youngest children accepting less than perfect correlation, presumably due to the cognitive load of tracking perfect correlation.[11]

However, recent research by Alison Gopnik and colleagues argues that young children are actually following Bayesian rules for summing across experiences in their causal reasoning. They argue that preschoolers can override imperfect correlation and that they use different patterns of probability in how consistently causes and effects are correlated to make accurate causal inferences.[12]

Gopnik and her colleagues showed preschoolers a block that activated a detector three out of three times and a second block that activated the detector only two out of three times.[13] Most of the children said that both had causal power despite the probabilistic nature of the second block relationship. When Kushnir and Gopnik showed them an object that activated a novel toy either 33 percent or 66 percent of the time, children could make appropriate inferences based upon causal reliability.[14]

Further support for this idea comes from research on what happens when unreliable causal connections are juxtaposed against gaps in space and time. Preschoolers are more likely to choose inconsistent events that were closely connected in space and time over events that consistently co-varied but were not closely connected in space or time. [15]

An even stronger form of the argument put forth by Kushnir and Gopnik suggests that preschoolers use statistical contingency data to overcome spatial gaps. [16] Preschoolers could use probabilistic data about cause-and-effect relationships to figure out if a toy could be activated by placing objects on or over it. However, children were more likely to be correct in the condition where the object touched the toy and when there was a gap; they were able to override it more often when the relationship was deterministic.

One of the questions that this research raises is whether young children are actually overriding imperfect correlation or not tracking correlation well enough such that they make probabilistic choices. [17] Earlier research suggested that as children got older, by eight or nine years old, they were less accepting of probabilistic causation in their predictions. [18]

Even if older students are less accepting of probabilistic causation than their younger counterparts, it would not necessarily signal that three-year-olds are not subconsciously screening off. It is possible that eight- and nine-year-olds are bringing other learning to bear on the tasks such as the importance of scientific tests being replicable. As discussed below, some recent research suggests that older children may hold ideas pertaining to reasoning about evidence in science that could impact their answers to tasks with probabilistic outcomes. [19]

Developing Understanding of the Concepts Related to Uncertainty

Reasoning about probabilistic causation (despite whether one does not effectively track the relationship or overrides it) involves grasping a number of concepts related to certainty, uncertainty, determinate, and indeterminate outcomes, randomness, and so forth. What do we know about the development of these concepts?

Uncertainty is a multifaceted concept. [20] Children grasp some aspects of the concept of uncertainty by five years of age. However, the concept is fragile and children's ability to apply it depends upon the context. [21] Other aspects appear to emerge much later and continue to be difficult through the adult years. [22]

There is evidence that by four and five years of age, children are beginning to correctly identify situations when they can be certain or predict an outcome as compared to ones that are uncertain and that they cannot predict.[23] Five- to seven-year-olds knew that the marble could either follow one of two different, but equally likely, paths on a marble track even if they could not explain why.[24]

Sylvia Kuzmak and Rochel Gelman ran a study that asked children whether they knew what the next outcome would be for a random and a determined event and why. The task with the random event asked which color marble would emerge from a spinning cage that allowed one marble to escape every so often; the determined event asked which color marble would emerge next from a clear tube with a hole on the bottom. By three, children often made correct predictions on the deterministic task. By four, they knew that they could not predict the random outcome and by five, they gave adequate explanations of why. [25]

The research above focused on what the children knew. This relates to their knowledge of subjective probability—how confident one is that an outcome will occur. Researcher Kathleen Metz has argued that the research findings are very clear in showing that young children do understand subjective certainty/uncertainty. However, what about children's understanding of objective probability—the concept that it is possible to know some outcomes but not possible to know others? [26]

The idea that some phenomena are fundamentally uncertain at some levels is an important idea in reasoning about complexity. Figuring out whether it is *possible* to know something is not an internal assessment, but rather involves analyzing trends that emerge over the course of many observations, keeping in mind that the relative frequency of events in a large number of repetitions varies. All of this involves a lot to hold in one's mind and is subject to attentional factors—thus is much harder to grasp explicitly.[27]

The research is mixed. Some research shows that children think that, if repeated enough times, they can control random events, for instance rolling dice.[28] When given a choice between a random and nonrandom sequence to the outcomes of coin flipping, seven- to eleven-year-olds assigned a nonrandom one. There was some improvement by adolescence. [29]

Other research found that second graders could distinguish between the indeterminate nature of rolling dice and more determinate actions (writing, doing arithmetic problems, etc.). However, many did not think of rolling the dice as completely random—they integrated elements of luck or wishing as "helping influences" upon the outcomes. By fourth grade, they did not integrate concepts of luck or wishing into their reasoning and viewed dice rolling as random.[30]

The research literature as a whole reveals some contradictions in performance. These appear to be related to differences in how tasks were posed and with what support, as well as differences in the specific concept being assessed. There was also the possibility that some of the tasks can be solved through much less sophisticated means.[31] Adults, too, often use simplified strategies.[32]

Kathleen Metz studied how different ages reasoned about randomness. She considered whether they integrated concepts of uncertainty with patterns of effects emerging over repeated instances (in a distributional mode). This bears on the important question above about what people do in thinking about probabilistic effects over time. However, in this case, the tasks were posed within the attention span of one study (thus simplifying the problem space over what the real world would demand).

Most kindergartners did not reveal a concept of randomness, and if they did, they rarely used it. They sometimes evoked uncertainty, but not in connection with the probabilistic patterns. Most third graders did grasp the concept of randomness, but used it rarely and depending upon the context. Adults revealed an integrated concept of uncertainty and probability, however, they, too, struggled with recognizing uncertainty. All three age groups overapplied determinism, which brings us to our next set of questions.[33]

Holding Implicit or Explicit Notions of Determinism

It is clearly very hard to extract information from the world when the relationship between causes and effects is stochastic. This relates to the questions in chapter three about the ontological problem—how we discern causes and effects in a world full of rich patterns that compete for our attention along with noise or chaotic stimuli that make it hard to detect the patterns. However, the research above also raises the question of whether we carry expectations of determinism that complicate the process.

When my son was two, we had the first of many conversations that could be characterized as "if it happens, there's a reason and I want to know why." We'd hear a small noise in the kitchen and he'd ask, "What was that noise?" "Oh just the refrigerator creaking." "What made it creak?" "Maybe it moved a little" "Why did it move a little?" "I don't know, maybe the floor shifted a little." "What made the floor shift?" And so on.

While a reason for the noise certainly existed, the connection between noise and cause was not easily traced. However, my son's questions revealed a fundamental human tendency—a reluctance to allow for causeless events. We typically assume that physical events are caused and expect causes to reliably lead to given effects—a key principle of determinism.

Hume argued that determinism is a fundamental, innate causal principle upon which we base our expectations of the world.[34] Bullock and colleagues also argued for determinism as a fundamental principle in children's causal reasoning.[35] An abundance of research suggests that we are pattern seekers and that we are oriented toward seeking regularities. Without this tendency, the world would be a chaotic and confusing place, what William James once called a world of "buzzing, blooming confusion."[36] So an orientation toward order and regularity is likely an adaptive stance in many respects.

The research certainly supports that children hold deterministic tendencies. Laura Schulz and Jessica Sommerville found that preschoolers prefer deterministic over probabilistic causality, at least in the instance of a machine-like toy-box mechanism.[37]

Charles Kalish investigated whether three- to five-year-olds view the cause of illness as probabilistic or deterministic. He argued that parents and teachers often tell children that conditions such as dirtiness, eating dirty food, and getting cold can cause illness, and that since none of these conditions are the underlying cause of illness (as is germ transmission), they give the impression of probabilistic causation.

He found that four- to five-year-olds felt very certain about their predictions of illness and viewed the causal relationship as similar to that of gravity. They expected deterministic and reliable causal relationships— that if all of the children in a classroom played with a sick child, all or none would get sick. This was even so when they were asked to assess "strong" and "weak" causes in an effort to see if less potent causes would be more likely to elicit probabilistic reasoning.[38]

My colleagues and I conducted microgenetic studies with students in kindergarten, second, fourth, and sixth grades to look very closely at children's reasoning across domains.[39] We examined whether students would behave deterministically or probabilistically in different contexts and whether their stance shifted across a period of four to six sessions.

We found that most students approached the tasks from a strongly deterministic stance across the domains tested. This was expected for mechanical devices, but not for games, biology, and social tasks. Most students even explained prior experiences such as planting seeds deterministically and in a reductionist manner. They treated the tasks as puzzles to be solved in terms of the patterns.

However, there was some variation. A subset of students across grades, including kindergarten, approached the tasks in a more open manner—allowing for the possibility of probabilistic or deterministic responses. They gave significantly more balanced answers and shifted the type of explanations in response to particular domains, giving more probabilistic statements to social tasks and games. These students introduce a different growth pattern and, perhaps, points of leverage that can be used in service of instruction.

Across all of the students, there were shifts in language toward recognizing the possibility of probabilistic causality, particularly when contrasting across examples from different domains. For instance, a sixth grader shifted from 90 percent deterministic statements across multiple sessions to 57 percent deterministic and 43 percent probabilistic and began to introduce the language of probabilities and uncertainty into his explanations. This shift, however, appeared to pull against his reasoning about evidence in science. Sixth graders talked about needing to "follow the evidence in science" in explaining their deterministic responses.[40]

One of the puzzles about holding an implicit assumption of determinism is that we appear to hold it at the same time that we implicitly use a Bayesian "summing across process" to arrive at causal connections. While this would appear to be in contradiction, it is possible that the Bayesian mechanism for summing across statistical instances works implicitly at a very basic level, even without an explicit concept of probabilistic causation.

What about learning to suspend our deterministic stance in relevant instances? Laura Schulz has argued that causal determinism is an adaptive stance because it sends you looking for causes—even if it is long, reductive search.[41] One can certainly see many reasons why this is so. A deterministic stance can help us to notice discrepancies in outcomes and sometimes these discrepancies hold important information that can inform our causal models.[42]

However, determinism can also work against us if we don't notice causal contingencies because we assume determinism and therefore miss stochastic events that fall outside our attentional parameters. It encourages risk taking in situations that we may not even realize involve risk. While a deterministic stance might be more adaptive than a sense that our world is entirely probabilistic, a reflective stance on our determinism that considers the possibility of probabilistic causation might be the most adaptive in the bigger picture.

PICTURES OF CLASSROOM PRACTICE: WHAT DOES IT LOOK LIKE TO HELP STUDENTS LEARN TO EXPLICITLY CONSIDER THE POSSIBILITY OF PROBABILISTIC CAUSATION?

Having finished up a unit on static electricity, the fourth graders are discussing lightning. They are trying to figure out if the explanation given in their textbook makes sense to them. Part of the explanation argues that lightning results in an imbalance of charge between electrons and protons and that a buildup of charge in the sky repels electrons in high spots on the ground, leaving the protons without "partners" so the electrons in the sky and protons on Earth are attracted to each other. The students discuss how it does make sense and consider various aspects of the explanation.

A student puts her hand up and says, "I was at camp once and we got stuck in a storm and were sitting on the highest part of the hill and we didn't get struck, so that can't be right." Other students agree that this contradicts their explanation and decide that they need a better one. The teacher steps in and asks them to consider whether the explanation meant that being in a high spot always resulted in lightning or just much of the time.

A heated discussion ensues about whether evidence needed to show that the described situation led to lightning every time for it to be part of a causal story. "We learned in science that you should be able to repeat an experiment and the same thing should happen each time." "But some things happen some of the time and not others, but it doesn't mean that the cause is not the cause." "Sometimes the cause doesn't work and we just don't know why not. Like I might get sick if you sneeze on me but he might not, but maybe I didn't have some immunity that he has but we didn't know."

In health class, the tenth-grade girls are talking about the practice of sharing combs and brushes. "Mr. Thompson says that we'll get lice, but I've done it before and I've never gotten lice," remarks Alicia. Ms. Rodriguez raises a question and asks everyone to think about it and formulate their own reaction before she calls upon anyone: "If you do something multiple times and there are no clear consequences, should you decide that it is okay to do it in the future?"

The students ponder the question and start to share examples. "Well, remember when we were younger and we used to do that thing where we pricked our fingers and mixed our blood to be 'blood sisters'? I think that we were just lucky, we could have gotten AIDS or something," says Dinesha. "But grown-ups always tell you all this bad stuff is gonna happen and it like never does, they're just trying to scare us," says Precious.

Tanya interjects, "Well, but some things don't always happen, but they could and you guys walk around like you're immortal, some kinda special, that like you're not gonna get some disease and die or get pregnant, that just happens to other people. It can happen to you too. Your number is going to come up, girl, just like it can happen to all of us."

"Okay," says Ms. Rodriguez, reeling the conversation back in, "so we started talking about lice, but it's really about anything where there's chance involved and the behavior sometimes has consequences and sometimes doesn't. Tanya is asking you to think about whether you should be taking those risks with your life. If you're gonna test it out, I'd rather you test it out on getting lice than more serious consequences." The girls make faces about the idea of getting lice, but the point is well taken.

NOTES

1. Bullock, Gelman & Baillargeon, 1982; Gelman, Coley & Gottfried, 1994; Schulz & Sommerville, 2006
2. Hume, 1739–1740

3. Carey, 1985, p. 194
4. e.g., Gopnik et al., 2001
5. Schulz & Gopnik, 2004
6. e.g., Einhorn & Hogarth, 1986; Kahneman et al., 1982
7. Borton, 1979; Leslie, 1982, 1984; Leslie & Keeble, 1987; Oakes, 1993; Spelke, Phillips & Woodward, 1995; Van de Walle & Spelke, 1993
8. e.g., Bullock, 1979; Baillargeon, Gelman & Meck, 1981
9. e.g., Bullock, 1985; Bullock, Gelman & Baillargeon, 1982; Shultz, 1982
10. Borton, 1979; Leslie, 1982, 1984; Leslie & Keeble, 1987; Oakes, 1993; Spelke, Phillips & Woodward, 1995; Van de Walle & Spelke, 1993
11. Shultz & Mendelson, 1975; Siegler, 1976; Siegler & Liebert, 1974
12. Gopnik et al., 2004; Kushnir & Gopnik, 2007
13. Gopnik et al., 2004
14. Kushnir & Gopnik, 2005
15. Mendelson & Shultz, 1976
16. Kushnir & Gopnik, 2007
17. The rates that preschoolers detect correlate with the probabilistic causality which suggests that they are tracking. However, as designed the research does not definitively answer this question.
18. Shultz & Mendelson, 1975; Siegler, 1976; Siegler & Liebert, 1974
19. Grotzer, Tutwiler, Solis, & Duhaylongsod, 2011
20. Metz, 1998b
21. e.g. Byrnes & Beilin, 1991; Metz, 1998b
22. Metz, 1998a
23. Fay & Klahr, 1996; Kuzmak & Gelman, 1986
24. Fischbein, Pampu & Minzat, 1975
25. Kuzmak & Gelman, 1986
26. Metz, 1998a, 1998b; Huber & Huber, 1987
27. Serrano as cited in Batanero et al., 1998
28. Fischbein & Gazit, 1984
29. Green, 1983
30. Horvath & Lehrer, 1998; Lehrer, Horvath & Schauble, 1994
31. Byrnes & Beilin, 1991; Metz, 1998b
32. e.g., Kahneman, Slovic & Tversky, 1982; Konold, 1991
33. Metz, 1998b
34. Hume, 1739–1740
35. Bullock, Gelman & Baillargeon, 1982
36. James, 1890, p. 488
37. Schulz & Sommerville, 2006
38. Kalish, 1998
39. Grotzer, Duhaylongsod & Tutwiler, 2011; Grotzer, Tutwiler, Solis & Duhaylongsod, 2011
40. A related body of research looks at how students interpret co-variation data where students are asked to reason about instances where the outcomes are contingent with a certain set of conditions when they are not. This research shows age-related increases in correct causal responses, but also a tendency to over-attribute causality. Adults pay special attention to exceptions to see if there is something to be learned from them. See Shaklee and Goldston (1989) for further information.
41. Schulz, personal communication, July 14, 2010.
42. Grotzer & Tutwiler, forthcoming

Chapter Fifteen

Isn't Anybody in Charge around Here?: Attending to Distributed Causality and Emergence

"I don't know why everybody has to stay in from recess. We weren't the ones who were being noisy!"

"Suddenly, long established dictators started to fall as pro-democracy movements rose up from the people."

Recall sitting in the school cafeteria trying to talk to those around you? As you tried to be heard by the kid next to you, you had to talk a little louder and a little louder to be heard over the escalating noise as each kid talked louder and louder to be heard by others. This is a spiraling causal pattern as discussed in chapter six, but that's not all that's going on. Soon, the lunch monitor is telling the whole group that there'll be no recess because you've all been too noisy. There are indignant responses as no one wants to own the outcome. "It wasn't my fault," they exclaim!

Imagine living in a community where everyone is quite pleasant to each other. They greet each other on the street, stop to let others go first when they arrive at a door, and if someone needs help, there are always willing neighbors to pitch in. It just seems like each individual follows rules of engagement that lead to a deep community feeling. As new individuals move to town, the patterns of engagement are soon contagious.

On your way home from work, there's a spot along the way where if there's enough traffic, things get snarled. The lanes are clearly marked and if all the cars turning left stay to the left lane and all the cars turning right stay right, things move along with only a brief delay. However, the left lane of traffic is typically shorter than the right and some drivers play by different

147

rules. They take the left lane to turn right despite the clearly marked lanes. They gain time but to the disadvantage of all of the other drivers in the right lane. A brief delay quickly turns into a complicated snarl.

These are all stories about distributed causality. Instead of a top-down, centralized causality, the patterns are bottom-up, decentralized forms of causality. There's no centralized structure or person in charge, and effects at the systems level are emergent—they emerge from the interactions between individuals. Here I use the terms decentralized causality and distributed causality interchangeably, often using the first in contrast to centralized causality and the second to emphasize the "spread out" nature of the actors.

Sometimes we recognize decentralized, distributed causality for what it is, but often we don't. Distributed causality has been studied by Mitch Resnick, Uri Wilensky, and others. This research shows that people tend to expect centralized causal structures. Mitch Resnick has described what he calls the "centralized mindset." People often assume an orchestrated leader or some preexisting, built-in "inhomogeneity" in the environment is responsible for complex patterns (what Resnick refers to as "created by lead or by seed").

Resnick is not talking only about students and the lay population, but also accomplished scientists. He offers examples from the history of science where these assumptions have led scientific discourse. For instance, scientists believed that a specialized founder or pacemaker cell directed the clustering of the individual organisms that make up the larger entity that we call a "slime mold." This belief is characterized by centralized causality. However, scientists Evelyn Keller and Lee Segel illustrated that clustering can occur without a centralized process. [1]

According to Resnick, many phenomena that people have experience with are designed by a centralized process—watches, the ballet, families, and school systems. We are familiar with the concept of a planful designer that sets out to create some entity, product, or otherwise. So one might argue that we have more experience with centralized than decentralized causal structures, but it's not clear that this is the case.

DISTRIBUTED CAUSALITY IS ALL AROUND US

Distributed causality is everywhere around us. The Internet is a prime example of distributed causality for the sharing of information. Wikipedia illustrates that products, in this case, an encyclopedia of knowledge, can be constructed and vetted through distributed means. Individual buying behaviors collectively have a profound effect on the stock market and the economy.

Driving behavior, purchasing choices, where we throw our garbage, how many of us tune into a certain televised event, and so on, are all examples of distributed behaviors that lead to emergent outcomes.

Together we shape our collective reality to a large extent every day. The power of the people, community watch, ballot initiatives, open-source computing, and civil disobedience, for example, have a significant impact on our world. And we have terminology for decentralized causal patterns. We talk about "grassroots efforts," "bottom-up initiatives," "crowd mentality," and so forth.

Children also have plenty of experiences with aspects of distributed causality. Whole-school assemblies are opportunities to observe that the room doesn't get quiet until the students' actions collectively produce the result, as opposed to the direct result of the principal's actions. Any teacher who has stood in front of a group of noisy students knows that slightly powerless feeling. Even Halloween depends upon distributed causality. If the people in your neighborhood don't light their doorsteps and put out candy, there is no trick-or-treating. And nothing but the calendar tells them to do so.

The power of distributed causality was demonstrated in the pro-democracy movements in the Middle East during the spring of 2011. Protesters were able to organize their grassroots efforts through distributed communication devices and to mount successful and empowering resistance. The contagion spread to new countries as efforts met with success, such as President Hosni Mubarak stepping down in Egypt in February of 2011 after thirty years in power.[2]

Often, everyday phenomena have both centralized and decentralized aspects. For instance, a centralized view of why communities are civilized might say that the police keep people in line, whereas a decentralized view would argue that it is the civilized behavior of individuals that gives rise to an emergent civilization. An economic crisis demands that effective and fair legislation is put in place with proper incentives to encourage distributed emergent behaviors that support a healthy economy. Thoughtful leadership attends to both aspects and considers how they interact.

Terrorism is a particularly interesting case. Distributed throughout many countries and homegrown, it is incredibly resistant. Characterizing it as top-down and centralized captures certain aspects of it, but misses other fundamental aspects of how it has grown. Following 9/11, much of the government rhetoric positioned Osama Bin Laden as a centralized leader and focused on getting him. At the same time, many of our actions fueled discontent and hatred of the West, breeding new terrorists in a decentralized way.

It was believed that the highly organized interactions in an anthill or beehive were all the direct result of chemical signals communicated from the queen. Now, scientists consider much of this organization emergent—due to the individual rules that particular ants and bees follow. (They acknowledge though, that without the queen, the community will fail.) According to E. O. Wilson, the social context was always considered a very important aspect of life in ant communities. A balanced view that acknowledges the strong social context and distributed causality alongside the important role of the queen attends to the diversity of dynamics in play. [3]

Further, centralized actions can lead to new distributed behaviors. Without a good predictive model of what those might be and how they might play out, it is very hard to predict the outcomes of many choices. This is a feature that makes many complex systems, like the economy, political system, etc., so difficult to understand and manage.

Given the prevalence of decentralized causality in our lives, it makes sense to ask why so often we attend to the centralized aspects of systems and miss the decentralized ones. In the past, I pondered whether it has its roots in a family structure where parents are typically in control and make many decisions. Now with my own children, that argument seems less compelling and there are days when the dynamics are much more bottom up. Of course, the prevalent patterns of one generation may be different from that of another.

In the following paragraphs, I explore the features of distributed causality and the ways in which it can be hard to wrap our minds around it. I consider how children engage with it, what we know about learning it, and why it's critical that we all learn to understand and to reason about it. The research on children's developing understanding of distributed causality is lean and more research is clearly needed. However, research strands on related aspects contribute to our understanding and I draw upon these as I discuss the conceptual challenges. Finally, I offer suggestions for ways to help students learn it.

THE FEATURES OF DISTRIBUTED CAUSALITY: WHAT MAKES IT SO HARD?

Thinking at Multiple Levels

A key challenge in reasoning about distributed causality involves thinking about causes and effects at different levels. One must monitor individual and systems-level outcomes. Thinking about effects at different levels often results in confusion about levels of description and what is an "object" at different levels.

Wilensky, Resnick, and colleagues have written about these confusions. [4] For instance, they argue that in a traffic jam the cars are the objects at one level but at another level, the jam acts as the object. Similar difficulties have been seen in reasoning about ecosystems. Students often have difficulty reasoning about ecosystems interactions at the level of populations because they try to apply the population dynamics to individuals. This complicates their ability to reason about population-level effects such as balance and flux.[5]

With different outcomes on different levels, it can be challenging to monitor both. For instance, the children in a cafeteria are focused on being heard by their friends, however, they may not think about monitoring the systems-level effect—the noise in the cafeteria. When it gets so noisy that it breaks through and captures their attention or it is brought to their attention by the lunchroom monitor, they may try to find ways to impact it.

One approach is bottom-up. If enough children start to change their individual actions and speak more softly, the noise level will begin to de-escalate. Another is top- down. As many of us will recall from our cafeteria days, a centralized cause can step in, such as a kid who can shout loudly telling everyone to be quiet or the lunch monitor blinks the lights to quiet everyone down.

Monitoring on two levels can be especially challenging when outcomes on the systems level don't capture our attention. In the cafeteria example, the high noise level exists in a fairly confined space and eventually gains the attention of the individuals in the room.

However, accumulating greenhouse gases responsible for global warming are less likely to be noticed and the causes are much more distributed. When I jump into my car to go buy groceries, I am focused on the outcome of bringing food home to my family. The distributed, emergent effect of increased carbon from the emissions of all of the individual vehicles with owners focused on accomplishing some immediate task does not make it onto most people's radar screen. Not being able to directly perceive greenhouse gases (see chapter eleven on non-obvious causes) makes it harder to attend to the causal patterns involved.

Mitch Resnick has also argued that there is relatively lower salience to the many fine-grained actions, such as those of worker bees compared to the individualized actions of a single queen bee, as a reason for our centralized mindset.[6] One can extend this argument to include the actions of the many individuals deciding to drive their cars or not in contrast to the obviousness of an action like signing the Kyoto Accord to cut back on greenhouse gases. The centralized actions often demand our attention more easily than the distributed ones.

It is difficult enough to reason about both levels when they are "under our nose" so to speak. Distributed causality often involves actors spatially distributed well beyond our attentional space. It is possible to have actors that are far-flung and thus they are not easily discerned as contributors to an emergent outcome. They may not be coordinated in time either (emergent effects may arise over time and coordination failures can be due to time lags.)[7]

The Counter-intuitive Notion of Emergence

In distributed causality, outcomes at the systems level are often characterized by emergence. Emergence refers to the concept that complex patterns can arise from multiple simple interactions and that the result cannot be reduced to the sum of its parts. The interactions give rise to a new essence.

The concept of emergence departs so significantly from our traditional notions of cause and effect that cognitive science researcher Michelene Chi has considered them to be acausal.[8] Some of the characteristics that she underscores as departing from direct forms of causality are the simultaneous, continuous nature of the interactions in terms of time. She also focuses on the unconstrained (random) and independent nature of the components that interact to lead to an emergent phenomenon.

Chi argues that this makes them very hard to map in the traditional sense of a causal connection. Predicting how these components will interact is very difficult especially given the synergistic interactions involved. Indeed, research shows that students reduce emergent phenomena and interactions in self-organizing systems either to a linear causality, a centralized model, and/or a deterministic framework.[9]

Michael Jacobson has described complex, organic systems as being non-reductive, decentralized with multiple causes. They can have big effects from small actions and complex behavior from simple rules.[10] The action of the agents can be random and stochastic. There is a focus on equilibration processes rather than events. He compares this to a "Clockwork Mental Model" that characterizes phenomena as reductive, with centralized control and single causes. It involves predictable actions with the magnitude of effects consistent with the magnitude of the action and a focus on static structures and events.[11]

Emergent phenomena are not reducible to the sum of their parts, and predicting from those parts to an outcome—reasoning about so many interacting actors, far-flung or not—is nearly impossible. Imagine the challenges. One must hold in mind the most likely actions of many individuals and imagine how, collectively, they interact, reasoning about it synergistically and dynamically. This amount of mental work or "cognitive load" requires a lot of processing capacity. Researchers Cindy Hmelo-Silver and Roger Azevedo argued that even if secondary school students could do this, they are unlikely to be inclined to.[12]

How does one deal with so much cognitive load? One possibility is to download it in some way, such as to a computer model. StarLogo is a programmable computer modeling environment developed by Mitch Resnick and colleagues at MIT[13] that enables one to model distributed causal patterns. It uses massively parallel processing or many microprocessors to reveal how many lower-level interactions give rise to emergent outcomes at the systems level. Students can program assumptions about how the individuals behave and then observe what these individual rules of engagement predict for systems-level patterns.

Consider an example from a project from Resnick's lab. It modeled the behavior of termites based upon the following simple rules. "Each termite starts wandering randomly. If it bumps into a wood chip, it picks the chip up, and continues to wander randomly. When it bumps into another wood chip, it finds a nearby empty space and puts its wood chip down. With these simple rules, the wood chips eventually end up in a single pile."[14] Star Logo downloads the cognitive load and enables students to learn about distributed causality and emergent outcomes.

Some educators may be familiar with NetLogo developed by Uri Wilensky at the Center for Connected Learning and Northwestern University. Inspired by the original StarLogo, NetLogo grew out of StarLogoT, a Mac-based version of StarLogo developed by Wilensky in 1997.[15] It includes a programming environment in which it is possible to develop multiuser participatory simulations so that interacting groups can reason about collective actions in contrast to individual ones.

One of the most challenging aspects of reasoning about emergence is predicting the outcome of changes at the individual level on emergent outcomes at the systems level. What is most startling to many people is how relatively small changes in individual behavior can lead to large and often unexpected emergent outcomes.

Wilensky and Resnick probed students' ideas while they worked with StarLogo.[16] Having students work on projects ranging from the interaction of cars on a highway to termites gathering wood chips, they investigated how students construe the relationships and what they expect the outcomes of collective behaviors to be. Students were shocked to see how individual rules of interaction at one level lead to emergent effects at another level. Students (and adults) find it very difficult to predict collective behavior. Across a number of topics that students find it difficult to reason about macro-level properties that emerge in systems as a result of micro-level interactions.[17]

Models such as StarLogo and NetLogo can help people to realize that minor changes to individual rules can lead to big changes in emergent-systems behavior. This helps us to become aware of just how complicated prediction can be. There are many instances in life when actions are happening in real time and there is little opportunity to reflect upon the patterns, for instance swerving to avoid another car in traffic. However, modeling programs can certainly help us to learn about and reflect upon actions that recur or play out over time, such as global warming.

One of the biggest challenges is to realize that the actions of many are more than just a collection of actions. The actions involved are not always homogeneous. And they can result in aggregate effects or can interact to result in synergistic effects. We can often predict actions of termites, ants, and other members of the animal world—predictable instincts that guide behavior. Sometimes we can reason about the incentives that will lead to fairly predictable human behavior. But often we cannot, and as individuals begin modifying their behaviors in response to each other, the results become very complex indeed.

If everyone follows rules that we know or at least the same rules, despite the difficulties, it enables some level of prediction. Unlike StarLogo, which allows you to model the same assumptions into each type of actor, the real world often is less predictable. Anyone who has tried to maneuver out of an impending traffic accident realizes the complexity involved (despite only a few interacting actors). You assume that certain rules are in play (we are both trying not to hit each other; stopping or swerving might be in order, etc.), but it is very hard to predict how the other driver will react to your reactions.

It is especially challenging to think about individual agency and emergent collective results in systems with trigger effects where the magnitude of the resulting effect comes about suddenly and at a point where the action that triggers it couldn't have triggered it without the collective contributions of earlier actors. The idea is analogous to games that children play such as the one where they slide out certain sticks and then eventually one is removed and a whole pile of marbles falls down. It gives the appearance that the last actor "caused" the collapse, when indeed all of the players took part.

The Puzzling Role of Agency and Intentionality in Distributed Causality

Decentralized causality is also challenging because it introduces puzzling separations between intentionality and outcome. We know that agency, goals, and intentions are a compelling part of our causal repertoire as discussed in chapters three and twelve. While we do realize instances where we did something "by accident," we typically think of actions connected with outcomes that we intend. With distributed causality, intention is typically linked to actions at the individual level, but not to the emergent outcomes. The emergent outcomes are often treated as one big "oops!"

Decentralized intent refers to a lack of a centralized goal that arises from an intentional leader. The distributed agents may or may not be coordinated in a group-level intent and may not share individual goals or intent. For instance, in pro-democracy movements, they share group-level intent, but in our collective contributions to global warming, we are all engaged in individual actions with different intents and purposes and none of us intend global warming to occur.

Often emergent effects are treated as "not my fault" because people fail to see the connection between their actions and the collective result. A Calvin and Hobbes cartoon, by Bill Watterson, where Calvin has learned about the greenhouse effect and is berating his mom for the planet she is leaving to him, illustrates this. When she counters, "This from the kid who wants to be chauffeured any place more than a block away." Calvin responds, "Hey, nobody told me about the ice caps, all right?"[18] Similarly, students are indignant when held accountable for the cafeteria noise level—usually blaming it on the loudest kid.

Adults are not so different from kids in this regard. Enlightened leadership around issues of global warming is critical. However, we are all part of the problem and we all have the capacity to contribute to a solution without waiting on our legislators. Even if we didn't intend to contribute to the problem, we did. Blaming government is just one way of not taking responsibility.

The importance of agency and intention in our causal repertoire is discussed at length in chapters three and twelve.[19] Differentiating instances when intentionality does and does not play a role in agency is an important developmental task. Research suggests that children tend to link intention and agency, yet they reveal developing understanding of instances where the two are separate. They make distinctions between animate and inanimate objects and between parents and the family dog in terms of the type of actions associated with each.[20]

These may be early building blocks for reflecting upon intentionality. However, understanding distributed causality and emergence introduce considerable new challenges for mapping intentionality and outcomes at different levels. Much more research is needed for understanding how intentionality, agency, and responsibility for outcome interact in how children reason about distributed causality.

LEARNING ABOUT DISTRIBUTED CAUSALITY

An important question for education relates to how students attempt to build models of emergence and whether these relate to the ways that experts think about emergence. The forms of thinking involved in emergence depart dramatically from students' typical default patterns. Frederica Raia found that college students attempted to use what she called a linear-mono-causal approach that was characterized by simple linear chains and unidirectionality rather than one that recognized the complex relations between different levels.[21]

This raises the question of whether the students' approach is a productive path or whether "you can't get there from here." Concepts related to emergence within distributed causality are some of the most difficult as compared to those related to decentralization. Raia found that focusing on the structures of how something is organized can help students develop more sophisticated notions of emergence and document how one student's reasoning shifts. [22]

Researchers who write about helping students to learn about complex systems that are characterized by emergence have stressed how challenging the endeavor is and that more research is needed. [23] However, they also suggest that it is important to help students gain experience with concepts related to emergence and to make the organizing conceptual framework explicit. They stress the need for students to engage in modeling to test out their theories and revise them as needed. [24]

Reflecting on the structure of everyday experiences that students are familiar with through a "distributed causality lens" can help them to begin to build a richer repertoire for understanding emergence. Take the cafeteria example for instance. One can reenact it in the classroom and have students see what happens when they modify the rules slightly. What if each time it starts to get too noisy, they each start talking a little softer instead of a little louder? How does that rule change impact the outcome?

What other experiences do students have that already use forms of distributed causality? For instance, many schools encourage kids to put two fingers in the air to signal quiet when it gets too loud. Soon other kids notice and do this too. In what ways does this solution involve distributed causality?

Sharona Levy and Uri Wilensky explored ways to build upon sixth graders' current experience and reasoning in order to address their difficulties reasoning between levels, from agent-based causality to aggregate forms of causality involving emergence. [25] Seeking the compatibility between the levels, they sought ways to create bridges for students between them. They interviewed students about the common P.E.-class activity called "scattering."

In the scattering activity, teachers commonly say, "Spread out so that you all have enough room without bumping into each other." When one student tests the limit by spreading out much too far, the teacher sets a new parameter by telling him or her not to go "too far' and that everyone should spread as far apart as they need to have enough room, but not more room than they need. The scattering activity simulates individual agents acting but with a collective, emergent effect at the systems level.

Levy and Wilensky then used an interviewing approach to engage the students in reflecting upon what happened in scattering. The interview levels went from less to more scaffolded, eventually encouraging reflection on both the agent-based and aggregate levels. They included "what if?" questions that tapped knowledge students were likely to have of the given situation, such as what if there was a puddle or the room was smaller.

They found that students engaged in "Mid-Level Model Construction" to reason between levels of complexity.[26] Students consistently developed subgroupings to help them in reasoning dynamically about what happened. Levy and Wilensky argue for the importance of viewing agent-based models as developmentally prior to aggregate ones.

There are certainly many opportunities to consider decentralized causality in the curriculum. For example, there are instances in science, from how slime molds aggregate and behave to the gas laws. Social insects, such as termites, bees, and ants offer a great opportunity to talk about decentralized causes. When studying ecosystems, there are many opportunities to explore how rules of behavior, shifted so slightly, could impact the amount of available resources, the size of populations, and ultimately the survival of species.

History and current events include examples such as the causes of the Revolutionary War to civil disobedience in support of racial equality to discussion of current events, including the green movement in business and the rise of blogging and its impact on politics. Taking ownership for actions that occur at the micro-level that impact the macro-level is important for a healthy planet and healthy communities.

Ronald Heifeitz, at Harvard's Kennedy School of Government has contrasted approaches to leadership that are in part top-down or bottom-up in their features. He compares the peaceful, collective approach of Martin Luther King Jr. and the voting rights march into Selma, Alabama, in 1965 to the "lone ranger" approach of the sheriff at the time as a key in the success of King and the demonstrators.[27]

Modeling programs like StarLogo and NetLogo can be an important teaching scaffold. One can program the individual rules of interaction to reflect what is known about behavior in the real world. The Understandings of Consequence Project Ecosystems Curriculum[28] uses StarLogo to help students think about how the behaviors that rabbits and foxes engage in impact the population levels of each. David Penner found that students using StarLogo did, to some extent, come to a better understanding of the relationship between the patterns on different levels.[29]

There is a catch about using such modeling programs in service of learning. Without knowledge of the phenomenon being modeled, students cannot judge the authenticity of the emergent relationships.[30] A former graduate student of mine, Doug Krause, brought his deep knowledge of marine biology to bear as he programmed the behaviors of sea urchins and otters at the level of individuals into StarLogo. As the program then ran, it replicated the way that sea urchin beds form in nature. Unlike most students, he was in a good position to judge what he was seeing against evidence from real sea urchin beds.

Efforts to teach distributed causality often involve simulation games where students can take on roles and then consider the emergent effects. Eric Klopfer at MIT has used handheld computers for students to communicate with one another to reveal the emergent outcomes of distributed individual interactions.

In one game, "Big Fish, Little Fish," students take on the role of either a big fish or little fish and how they interact—leading to population effects—which can be graphed in real time as the game goes on. The handheld devices are programmed to assume that, as a big fish, you need to eat at certain intervals to stay alive, and as a little fish, you need to try not to get eaten. The basic goal of trying not to get eaten leads to certain kinds of behaviors, for instance schooling together, hiding under the most rock-like object you can find (in this case, a classroom desk!) and so forth. [31]

PICTURES OF PRACTICE: WHAT DOES IT LOOK LIKE TO HELP STUDENTS LEARN TO EXPLICITLY CONSIDER THE NATURE OF DISTRIBUTED CAUSALITY?

The first grade is learning about their community. They have learned a lot about the various structures in their town—that the people elect a mayor, there's a police commissioner, and so forth. Their teacher engages them in a conversation about "what makes their community work." The children focus on the structures that they have learned about—that the mayor runs things and the police make sure that everyone does what they are supposed to.

Their teacher tries to get them to think about distributed causes as well as centralized one. She asks them to think about the job chart in the classroom and what would happen if people didn't do their jobs. A student responds, "You would make them." "That's true," responds their teacher, "but what if no one did their job?" "Our classroom would get really messy and things wouldn't work right." "That's right, I would try to get you all to do your jobs, but it takes all of us working together to make our classroom run well."

She helps them to see that communities are like that, too; the mayor and the police can help guide and enforce the rules, but everyone has to do their part. It's not just one thing on the top making everything else happen—like the mayor making the town run. Lots of things happening out here in the community—like every one of us following the rules and treating each other nicely—also makes the town run.

A high school class is reasoning about population-level effects in disease transmission. The teacher poses a question, "Right now we have made the assumption in our model that each person will interact with at least four to five others in the course of a day and that approximately half of those people will become infected. How would the emergent outcomes change if we modify the individual rules of interaction, so that each person interacts with fifteen to twenty people a day and still approximately half become ill? What might that pattern look like?"

A student interjects, "I think that the model needs to take into account the variations in how people behave. For instance, some people interact with more than a few people, especially if you live in a city, and others interact with a lot less." "Okay, so let's gather some other ideas about what types of variation in individual interactions should we try to model?"

A second student says, "Right now, we're just talking about the distributed behavior of individuals. If this was a really serious disease, wouldn't there also be centralized rules that might change how individuals act?" "That's an important thing to think about in our model, you can have centralized structures, laws, or mandates that impact distributed behavior. Let's decide on two or three patterns and model them to see what happens."

NOTES

1. Resnick, 1996; Keller & Segel, 1970
2. CBS News, Feb. 11, 2011
3. Foster, 1999
4. Wilensky & Reisman, 2006; Wilensky & Resnick, 1999
5. e.g., Driver, Leach, Scott, & Wood-Robinson, 1994b; Grotzer, 2002a; Wilensky & Resnick, 1999
6. 1996
7. Frey & Goldstone, 2010
8. Chi, 1993, 2000; Hmelo-Silver & Azevedo (2006) have argued that a complex system can be emergent at one level and causal at another.
9. e.g., Drummond, 2001; Penner, 2000; Raia, 2008; Wilensky & Resnick, 1999
10. Casti, 1994
11. Jacobson, 2001
12. 2006
13. Resnick, 1994; 1996
14. StarLogo Termite Project, http://education.mit.edu/starlogo/ [accessed: 10-3-08].
15. http://ccl.northwestern.edu/netlogo/docs/faq.html#diff
16. 1999
17. e.g., Penner, 2000; Resnick, 1994; Wilensky & Resnick, 1999
18. Bill Watterson, Calvin and Hobbes comic strip, Sept. 4, 2009, http://www.gocomics.com/calvinandhobbes/2008/09/04/ [accessed: 7-6-2011].
19. e.g., Andersson, 1986; Kelemen, 1999
20. e.g., Gelman, Durgin & Kaufman, 1995; Legerstee, 1994
21. Raia, 2008
22. Ibid.
23. Hmelo-Silver & Azevedo, 2006; Jacobson & Wilensky, 2006

24. Jacobson & Wilensky, 2006

25. Levy & Wilensky, 2008

26. Ibid.

27. Lambert, 1995

28.   For more information, go to Causal Patterns in Science web site: http://www.pz.harvard.edu/ucp/causalpatternsinscience/

29. Penner, 2000

30. Personal communication, Nick Haddad, July 21, 2011.

31.   PDA Participatory Simulations: Big Fish, Little Fish: http://education.mit.edu/pda/ifish.htm [accessed July 6, 2011].

Part 4: Summing Up: The Implications for Helping a New Generation Understand Causal Complexity

Thus far, I have set out arguments that suggest a challenging endeavor—though one with significant promise and possibility. In this final chapter, I summarize the broad argument that everyday causal reasoning alone is not enough to enable sophisticated complex causal explanation. I then offer techniques that may help us to make the journey between the two and examples of projects that are attempting to help educators make the trip with their students.

Chapter Sixteen

Putting It All Together: Teaching for Causal Complexity

"We realized that we couldn't just find out what happened on the days before. We needed to look at a longer amount of time."

"I was sucking so hard to make the juice come up that my cheeks hurt. I found out that air pressure needs to push on the other side."

This book offers ample evidence of the challenges of reasoning about complex causality. Yet, it also gives examples of how researchers are investigating the puzzles of learning it. Some of these, such as StarLogo, also offer promising ways of teaching it. It includes examples of how teachers have guided students in the specific causal challenges outlined in each chapter through activities and explicit causal discussion. In this final chapter, I sum up the nature of the challenges; offer some helpful techniques; and provide fuller examples of promising work that puts these approaches together.

BUILDING COMPLEX CAUSAL COGNITION FROM EVERYDAY CAUSAL REASONING: CAN IT BE DONE?

It is clear that everyday causal reasoning helps us to discern a lot about our environment. We notice patterns over time and we seek out explanations for them. From an early age, we begin building a causal repertoire to help us understand how our world works. As the preceding chapters detail, we understand some very complex concepts—that causes can be non-obvious, action can occur at a distance, the reliability between causes and effects can vary,

163

and so forth. We also learn a lot about particular causal mechanisms and what they do, such as remote controls, germs, and air pressure differentials. That's a pretty impressive repertoire.

While young children show great promise in understanding isolated complex causal concepts in the laboratory, these are confounded in the real world in ways that vastly complicate the story. Often multiple forms exist in complex, interacting instances.

Consider the example of climate change. Dealing with climate change involves reasoning about domino and cascading causal patterns that have tipping points; and cyclic and escalating causal patterns with inherent feedback loops. We must analyze complex patterns of space and time: at different scales; with gaps and delays; and monitor steady states rather than focusing on event-based causality. We must reason about non-obvious causes and think about causality at different levels—mapping between levels to consider how actions at one level may have emergent effects on another.

Further, I have argued throughout this book that our tendencies stop short of the ability promised by the laboratory research. We typically stop seeking causes once we detect a salient plausible cause, tending to notice obvious ones over non-obvious ones, and single causes over multiple sufficient or interacting causes. Unless there is reliable enough co-variation to signal that a relationship exists, we miss probabilistic relationships that are not right under our noses, as in a lab setting. We are unaware of effects at an attentional distance. If we weren't told about the impact of global warming on polar bears, the general population would never have discerned it through our everyday causal reasoning!

Further, as argued in chapter three, everyday causal reasoning engages us in a process of summing across. When we do so, we miss the information provided by critical exceptions.[1] In summing across instances to search for statistical regularities, we may sum over those that we most need to know about. In retrospect, we can often figure out that a person was behaving oddly after it led to tragic consequences. Or that the best way to teach our students certain concepts can't necessarily be gleaned by what most of them do—that exceptions to the norm offer important information to guide teaching even if these exceptions don't gain much attention in normative research.

Yet, these tendencies aren't capricious—they are a reaction to a busy world full of stimuli that pulls our attention in different directions. We filter out information and prune how extended our attention is as part of our cognitive survival. Taking in all that there is to take in is neither adaptive nor possible.

So how do we help learners to see the more complex patterns in their world? How do we help them attend to the other side of the tensions presented in this book? I think that the two tales of development presented here—that young children are more capable than we realize, and yet in elementary school and beyond they struggle when reasoning about complexity—invite us to rethink what the problem is. The findings here suggest that we consider what is possible with optimal scaffolds for building upon the early promise that children show.

The prevailing message is that children hold a lot of implicit knowledge from which we can build more sophisticated understandings. In the examples above, we asked kindergartners about the voice coming out of the loudspeaker in their room—building explicit awareness of action at a distance. Sharona Levy and Uri Wilensky interviewed students on concepts from gym class related to building greater understanding of emergence. I believe that we are just beginning to figure out how to build upon children's knowledge to teach explicit understanding of complex causal concepts and have yet to mine the possibilities.

Of course, there are a few caveats to this enterprise that bear mention. There are discipline-specific versions of the causal concepts. For instance, ecosystem scientists discuss "pulse" and "press" disturbances to balance and flux over time in a kind of resilience model that influences reasoning about steady states and processes. Pulse disturbances are short-term oscillations where the system undergoes sudden changes and may return to the earlier state, and press disturbances are continuous disturbances resulting in more permanent change.[2] These versions add considerable texture and nuance.

Also, reasoning modes about a phenomenon might depart from the mental models that one holds for how the phenomenon works. For instance, one can reason about simple circuits as having an electrical differential that results in flow—a kind of relational causality—and yet analyze circuit flow using a constraint-based model that calculates current as a result of resistance and voltage.

Also, I reiterate an earlier warning. It would be unfortunate to teach these causal patterns as if they are *the* causal patterns. This displaces an attempt at a more expansive repertoire by further reductionism. Offering initial patterns for students to reason about must be balanced against enabling emergent and organic structures to arise.

In moving forward, it is important to frame the teaching and learning problem in a *dispositional* rather than an *ability* approach to thinking. I will elaborate on a concept introduced in the introduction to part three. David Perkins, Shari Tishman, and Eileen Jay introduced a triadic notion of thinking dispositions. They argued that it was not enough to have the ability to think in certain ways, but that one needed a triad approach that focuses on sensitivity, ability, and inclination.[3] When it comes to dealing with causal complexity, each of these is hugely challenging.

Sensitivity refers to noticing opportunities to engage particular forms of thinking. Perkins and colleagues found that it was often the greatest challenge of the three.[4] It is especially complicated when the environment does not offer external cues, such as in the case of non-obvious causes and action at a distance, where a more salient plausible cause attracts attention or an effect occurs beyond our attentional boundaries. Further, cognitive neuroscience suggests that our minds are designed to behave in a reinforcing pattern—once we notice a pattern we are more likely to discern it in the future at the expense of others. This makes sensitivity to new patterns even more challenging.[5]

Ability refers to actually having the capacity to enact the thinking. When it comes to constructing complex causal explanations from everyday causal inference, ability becomes a huge problem. There is simply too much information to hold in our heads. As much as we might wish, we are simply not supercomputers. Our brain structures evolved to prioritize certain kinds of events over others and emotion points us in certain directions as a matter of survival. Once our amygdala gets in the act, we may find ourselves reacting in ways that made sense in a much less complex world.[6]

Inclination refers to the tendency to actually follow through with the reasoning once an occasion is detected and the ability is available to be deployed. With two of the three challenges in place, it would seem that inclination would be easy. The problem is that follow-through requires inclination in the moment, not the type with a capital "I" in which we decide once to make a big and critical change. It is less like the moment of making a New Year's resolution and more like trying to keep it in every moment.

Follow-through can pull against efficiency and agency at the lowest levels of processing—just not investing the cognitive effort to go beyond. It is hard to attend to complexity in the moment—it can be paralyzing and involves extraordinary commitment.

TECHNIQUES FOR BUILDING BRIDGES THAT CAN GET YOU THERE

So, given these challenges, what are some steps in the right direction? How can we begin to help the next generation build bridges between their everyday causal reasoning and the forms of complexity that they will need to reason in a complex world? Next, I discuss approaches that offer leverage on the problem—ones that have a significant research supporting the value of their use. In the concluding paragraphs, I discuss two promising examples of programs that address causal complexity. Each one has teaching resources behind it and I encourage you to pursue these as a way to start on this journey.

The Power of Narrative and Case-based Reasoning

Stories are a powerful means to communicate information about causal complexity. I have used this technique throughout the book to encourage you to view causality in new ways. Research shows that we often use available instances or stories from our own lives to guide our reasoning even when these overly simplify the causal dynamics. But we can offer compelling narratives that address greater complexity so that they can, at best, replace these simplified stories and, at the least, live beside them and perhaps offer some competition.

Stories have the advantage of communicating important information about "what happens" and to do so in a way that anchors cognition and can be returned to in the future. Stories such as that of Lake Nyos, cats being parachuted into Borneo, and the dynamics of the meltdown at Chernobyl provide powerful images of a world that is more complex than we often treat it. A body of research on "case-based reasoning" shows that powerful, anchoring cases can often be used to reason from and to be extended to new instances.[7]

Systems-thinking educator Linda Booth-Sweeney has developed some useful resources for teachers who are interested in using stories to teach various causal dynamics. As a graduate student, she worked with the Understandings of Consequence Project team in the early days of the project (and later with MIT's Society for Organizational Learning). Subsequently, she developed a guide to teach a variety of causal patterns, including some of those from the project and earlier supporting work.[8] She followed up that book, *When a Butterfly Sneezes*, with a later volume entitled *Connected Wisdom: Living Stories for Living Systems*.[9]

Stories are a kind of testimony about what has happened and what might happen. Paul Harris has argued persuasively that testimony from others is an important means of learning about science and the world. While some causal relationships can be discovered, many of the forms presented in this book require some type of testimony to learn. Action at an attentional distance and non-obvious, abstract, inferred causes are two such examples. Harris and his colleagues have studied how children learn from the testimony of others and the sophistication with which they evaluate what to attend to or discount.[10] Such testimony can make an important contribution to learning to reason about complex causality.

However, stories or cases alone are not enough. Significant research suggests that the power of stories also invites us to reason from these salient single cases more than we should without attending to statistical regularities that may also be an important part of the context.[11] So what else can we do?

Metacognition and Reflective Processing

Metacognition engages learners in active reflection upon the causal models that they employ. Thus, it has the potential to invite shifts from a low level of processing to a higher level that engages an evaluative stance on the choice of models and the subsequent fit of those models. Since so many of these default assumptions are "below the radar," so to speak, higher-level reflection can influence how students structure their ideas and can invite them to expand their repertoire of causal models.

A study carried out with my colleague Sarah Mittlefehdlt found that actively engaging students in metacognitive reflection both deepened understanding of science concepts and enhanced students' ability to transfer them to new topics.[12] This is not surprising given the rich literature on the power of metacognition for enhancing learning.[13]

Building a Language of Causality

Developing causal vocabulary goes hand in hand with the other techniques here. Our language does not always offer easy terminology for talking about the most counterintuitive forms of causality in this book. However, building that terminology with students is a way to make it explicit and encourage reflection upon it. As mentioned above, much of the terminology used in this book came from the K–12 students with whom we have worked.

Research by Maureen Callanan and colleagues[14] demonstrates that, in everyday contexts, parents scaffold their children toward more complex causal mechanisms and that they adjust this language to the age of their child. Introducing a broader repertoire of terminology can be a way of further building and elaborating children's understanding.

Opportunities to Explore Causal Structure

Offering rich opportunities to explore the causal patterns and features described here provide important instances for students to discuss and to be metacognitive about. For example, as discussed in chapter fifteen, playing with StarLogo models offered students concrete experiences with the causal dynamics that enabled them to see what happens in different cases and to explicitly discuss these.

Examples often exist in the everyday experiences of students. I have offered many of them in the context of this book—the fight on the playground, escalating noise in the cafeteria, considering the risk of different choices, and so on. It merely takes a discerning ear to pull them out and use them as teachable moments. Scaffolding students' conversations and helping them draw out the relevant principles in play can go a long way toward helping them learn to understand complex causal dynamics.

These opportunities can be enhanced by technology. Throughout the book, I offered many examples to illustrate how. For instance, technology enabled students to see microscopic worlds in a water drop, to engage in action at a distance as they work a webcam halfway around the world, or to experience the distributed causality of the Internet. These are rich affordances for helping students learn to conceptualize complex causality. Below, I discuss a curriculum called EcoMUVE, where scaffolding is built into a virtual world to allow students to investigate the causal dynamics in ways that they normally could not.

RECASTing

A concept developed in the Understandings of Consequence Project called RECASTing can also be helpful. As discussed in chapter eight, it stands for revealing causal structure and refers specifically to activities that surprise students because the outcomes are discrepant with what they expect, but in ways that convey important information about the nature of the underlying causality. We have found these kinds of activities to be important means to starting the conversation—to really catching students' attention and helping them to realize that the structure of their explanation is wanting.

A number of activities discussed in this book involve RECASTing. This includes the candle activity discussed in chapter eight and the surprise that Wilensky and Resnick found when teaching students how individual agents often behave very differently than the aggregate, systems-level behaviors.

In part, RECASTing works because it draws attention to critical distinctions that are otherwise overlooked in everyday causal reasoning. As we sum across instances, we may fail to attach importance to data that falls outside normative patterns.[15] Let's consider some examples.

In sinking and floating, one can only recognize the importance of the relationship between the density of the object and that of the liquid when one experiences an object floating in one liquid and sinking in another (or a liquid that floats on one liquid and sinks on another). The intensive quantity that is density can only be recognized by holding either mass or volume constant, otherwise density will be confounded with mass or weight. In the three-flask example from chapter twelve, the pull of agency is so powerful that it is difficult to let go of it until one confronts the rare instance when they cannot pull the liquid up the straw. These are critical, yet not common distinctions.

EXAMPLES OF GOOD BRIDGES

Here I discuss two examples of curricula that offer rich opportunities to build bridges between what students understand about causality to greater complexity. The first is from Facing History and Ourselves, an organization started over thirty years ago to encourage rigorous investigation of historical events to further democracy and fight bigotry. While not designed specifically for the purpose, it invites discussion of complex causal dynamics. [16] The second, EcoMUVE, is a recent project funded by the Institute for Education Sciences that my colleague Chris Dede and I started with others here at the Harvard Graduate School of Education. It was designed to teach complex causal reasoning in the context of ecosystems science and to make both explicit in the discussion.

Facing History and Ourselves

The "Facing History and Ourselves" curriculum materials offer a critical antidote to simplified versions of history that reduce "what happened" to a single story line from a predominant perspective. The materials invite students into the complexity of historical perspectives, reasoning, and dynamics. Students build from their own experiences to consider historical events, relating the events to knowledge that they hold from their own social interactions.

The curriculum offers rich opportunities to consider the nature of causality, for instance, that while events are often a focus in history, these are snapshots of an instance in a much longer set of dynamics; or that there are typically multiple contributing causes to any outcome. It specifically addresses the tendency to be reductive in thinking about the causal dynamics involved.

Taking any one of the many valuable lessons and modules offered on the Facing History and Ourselves website, one could tease out how it offers a strong bridge for students. For instance, one module, called "Bullying: A Case Study in Ostracism," looks at a middle school incident that occurred within a group of girls and quickly got out of control. [17] The perspectives of the girls involved is offered as well as a teacher perspective and outside perspectives from educators on what happened.

The issues invite consideration of group dynamics, inclusion and exclusion, charismatic leaders, and how dynamics can play out over time. The language of situations that "snowball" out of control and "tipping points" is introduced. It also invites consideration of distributed causal agency—even though there was a charismatic leader, many of the hurtful behaviors were not explicitly directed. The actions of individuals interacted to give rise to the situation.

The curriculum engages students in metacognition as they reflect upon the causal dynamics and to try to explain what happened. It also asks them to connect back to their own experiences and what about the situation might seem familiar to them. Comparison to other powerful narratives, such as *The Crucible* by Arthur Miller and that of Hitler and the Holocaust can further anchor understanding of the dynamics. Introducing multiple perspectives on what happened RECASTs the narrative into multiple stories with multiple causes and counters the reductive tendency to frame what happened from one perspective.

While explicit discussion and naming of the causal dynamics is not incorporated into the materials, one can easily see how they might become part of the language in the classroom, as terms such as "snowballing" or "tipping point" have become part of our cultural language. Introducing the features of domino and spiraling causality would offer the students broader terminology to discuss the causal dynamics.

EcoMUVE

EcoMUVE is a virtual computer world that invites students to explore ecosystems but offers them affordances to help them discover the inherent causal complexity. MUVE stands for "multiuser virtual environment." My colleague Chris Dede has studied MUVEs for over a decade and has demonstrated their power for engaging students in learning and enjoying science.[18] Together, with the project team of Shari Metcalf, Amy Kamarainen, and M. Shane Tutwiler, we developed EcoMUVE as a means of teaching ecosystems dynamics and causal complexity.[19]

What does it look like? Picture a class of students, each working within a virtual world at computers. When students enter the pond EcoMUVE, they see an overview of a realistic pond ecosystem. They see through the eyes of an avatar who can walk around in the world (even under the water!) and can gather information. The students can use a camera tool to take pictures of the organisms that they find as they walk around. However, just as in the real world, many of the animals respond to the students—the fish swim away and the birds take off in flight.

So far, the students' experiences in the world are not so different from one's experience walking around a real pond. And it's not a substitute for visiting a real pond—it sounds like one, but the smells and textures are missing. But soon, the affordances of EcoMUVE become clear.

Students realize that they can descend into the pond in a submarine that offers levels of zoom and allows them to discover a whole world of non-obvious, microscopic organisms. They can time-travel between different dates on the calendar. They can take measurements and graph out their results or collect information about organisms and put them into a log book. They also can learn from the testimony of the park ranger and others whom they meet in the environment.

The importance of these affordances becomes abundantly clear when they travel to the middle of the summer and find many dead fish around the banks of the pond! They typically respond to this event within the parameters described in this book—now that an event has occurred, they begin searching for a cause. They often begin by treating the problem as intentional—they search for who might have done this. They look locally within the edges of the pond for an answer and they search the few days before the problem for indications as to why it happened.

It isn't until students find that there are no ready answers that they start to look for non-obvious causes, that they begin to wander beyond the banks of the pond, and consider a longer span of time. Because they can travel back and forth in time, they start to realize that there had been subtle changes in the pond all along. The water was getting a bit greener and more turbid; phosphate, nitrate, and dissolved oxygen levels were shifting and impacting algae growth in the pond. The importance of monitoring steady states over time starts to become apparent.

As students explore, they begin to see that the pond ecosystem extends well beyond the edges of the pond and they come to realize that actions taken at a distance—in this case, in the housing development to the west—are impacting the pond. They eventually make a connection between all those green lawns, the fertilizer that they saw in the truck of a landscaper, and the complex patterns set in motion that resulted in dead fish.

EcoMUVE aims to develop the ability to understand the causal dynamics in ecosystems. Teachers can invite explicit discussion of the realizations that students make in MUVE and help them to transfer these understandings to other contexts. Because EcoMUVE invites observation the way that one would engage in the real world but offers additional affordances, it enables students to see missed opportunities thus encouraging greater sensitivity to occasions to reason in more complex ways.[20] It does not replace experiences in the natural world, rather it makes explicit what nature does not, helping to illuminate and encourage greater understanding of ecosystems patterns.[21]

How does EcoMUVE invite the use of the bridging techniques above? EcoMUVE offers rich opportunities to draw out students' causal assumptions—in this case, that intentional, local, immediate causality is in play. These assumptions become explicit in how students explore the EcoMUVE—inviting opportunities for explicit discussion about causal patterns. Teachers can engage the students in metacognitive reflection on how they are framing their causal explanations.

As their initial causal models fail to explain the available evidence for what happened to the fish, this invites students to RECAST their causal framing with support from the affordances of time travel, ability to zoom in and out, and to examine nonlocal possible causes. Powerful stories included in the teaching guide help students to see the importance of the particular causal dynamics in ecosystems more broadly.

EcoMUVE also provides evidence that teaching causal complexity and the concepts that teachers are responsible for in the standards is not an either/ or proposition. It is designed to address ecosystems concepts in the national standards for middle school *and* the complex causal dynamics. Research on the achievement of students who used the EcoMUVE offers evidence that they made significant gains in both.[22]

CONCLUDING THOUGHTS

Notice that the examples here and throughout the book use learning about causal complexity in the service of deeper understanding of the curriculum. Instead of becoming an "add-on," they work in service of the context that they are embedded within. Thus they become a part of better teaching instead of overburdening the curriculum.

I close this book with a sense of optimism. Causality is a part of our everyday lives. We can learn to avoid the reasoning pitfalls that plague us and can build more sophisticated understandings of consequence. We can learn about extended and nonlinear causalities, action at a distance, temporal complexities, and non-obvious causes and so on. Instead of waiting for our political leaders or our scientists to create change, we can take responsibility for the roles that we play as distributed causal agents that lead to emergent outcomes. We can collectively become better citizens of our complex world and contribute to a better tomorrow for all of us and for future generations.

NOTES

1. Grotzer & Tutwiler, forthcoming. This makes it likely that we will ignore anomalous cases (Chinn & Brewer, 1993, 1998) because we will not notice them. However, in cases of probabilistic causality, it makes sense to sum across cases. As argued by Grotzer and Tutwiler, the difficulty arises because we can't know a priori which cases involve critical distinctions to be learned and which do not, as in the example of the fourth graders reasoning about lightning in chapter fourteen. For our students, this argued for carefully mediated curriculum and exploration that is guided even for constructivist approaches.
2. Bender, Case & Gilpin, 1984
3. Perkins, Tishman & Jay, 1993
4. Perkins et al., 2000

5. Grotzer, Miller & Lincoln, 2011; Grotzer, 2011

6. e.g., Damasio, 1994; LeDoux, 2000, 2007

7. See, for example, Kolodner, 1992

8. Grotzer, 1989; 1993

9. Booth-Sweeney, 2001, 2008

10. e.g., Corriveau & Harris, 2009; Koenig & Harris, 2005; Pasquini et al., 2007

11. See, for instance, Kahneman, Slovic & Tversky, 1982; Sunstein, 2002

12. Grotzer & Mittlefehldt, 2011

13. e.g., White & Frederiksen, 2005; Zohar & Dori, 2011

14. Callanan & Oakes, 1992

15. Grotzer & Tutwiler, forthcoming.

16. http://www.facinghistory.org/ [accessed: 5-20-2011].

17. http://ostracism.facinghistory.org/ [accessed: 5-20-2011].

18. See Chris Dede's work on the River City Project at http://muve.gse.harvard.edu/river-cityproject/ [accessed 7-6-2011]. Also see Clarke et al., 2006

19. More information on the EcoMUVE Project and Team can be found at www.ecomuve.org

20. Perkins et al., 2000

21. More information on EcoMUVE, both the Pond Module and a Forest Module, can be found at www.ecomuve.org. Papers explaining the research findings can also be found there.

22. See Grotzer, Tutwiler, Dede, Kamarainen & Metcalf, 2011; Metcalf et al., 2011. Visit the EcoMUVE website at www.EcoMUVE.org for further research findings.

References

Ahn, W., Kalish, C. W., Medin, D. L., & Gelman, S. A. (1995). The role of covariation versus mechanism information in causal attribution. *Cognition 57*, 299–352.

Alloy, L., & Tabachnik, N. (1984). Assessment of covariation by humans and animals: The joint influence of prior expectations and current situational information. *Psychological Review 91*, 112–49.

Andersson, B. (1986). The experiential gestalt of causation: A common core to pupils' preconceptions in science. *European Journal of Science Education 8*(2), 155–71.

Andersson, B., & Karrqvist, C. (1979). Electric circuits, EKNA Report No. 2, Gotesberg University, Molndal, Sweden.

Astington, J. W. (1993). *The child's discovery of the mind.* Cambridge, MA: Harvard University Press.

Atran, S. (1995). Causal constraints on categories and categorical constraints on biological reasoning across cultures. In D. Sperber, D. Premack & A. J. Premack (eds.), *Causal cognition* (pp. 205–233). Oxford, UK: Clarendon.

Au, T., Sidle, A., & Rollins, K. (1993). Developing an understanding of conservation and contamination: Invisible particles as a plausible mechanism. *Developmental Psychology 2*, 286–99.

Baillargeon, R., & Gelman, R. (1980, Sept.). *Young children's understanding of simple causal sequences: Predictions and explanations.* Paper presented at a meeting of the American Psychological Association (APA), Montreal.

Baillargeon, R., Gelman, R., & Meck, E. (1981, April). *Are preschoolers truly indifferent to causal mechanism?* Paper presented at the biennial meeting of the Society for Research in Child Development (SRCD), Boston.

Bakalar, N. (2009). What really killed Mozart? Maybe strep, *New York Times*, Aug. 18.

Baldwin, C. P., & Baldwin, A. L. (1970). Children's judgments of kindness. *Child Development 41*, 29–47.

Baldwin, D. A., Baird, J. A., Saylor, M. N., & Clark, M. A. (2001). Infants parse dynamic action. *Child Development 72*, 708–17.

Bang, M., Medin, D. L., & Atran, S. (2005). Cultural mosaics and mental models of nature. *Proceedings of the National Academy of the Sciences, 1–7.*

Banyai, I., (1998). *Zoom.* New York: Puffin Books.

Bar, V. (1986). *The development of the conception of evaporation.* Unpublished paper, Hebrew University of Jerusalem.

Barker, M., & Carr, M. (1989). Teaching and learning about photosynthesis. *International Journal of Science Education 11*(1), 48–56.

Barman, C. R., Griffiths, A. K., & Okebukola, P. A. O. (1995). High school students' concepts regarding food chains and food webs: A multinational study. *International Journal of Science Education 17*(6), 775–82.

Barman, C. R., & Mayer, D. A. (1994). An analysis of high school students' concepts and textbook presentations of food chains and food webs. *American Biology Teacher 56*(3), 160–63.

Bartsch, K., & Wellman, H. M. (1995). *Children talk about the mind.* New York: NYU.

Basca, B., & Grotzer, T. A. (2001, April). *Focusing on the nature of causality in a unit on pressure: How does it affect students' understanding?* Paper presented at the American Educational Research Association (AERA) Conference, Seattle, WA.

Basca, B. B., & Grotzer, T. A. (2003). *Causal patterns in air pressure-related phenomena: Lessons to infuse into air pressure units.* Cambridge, MA: Harvard University Press.

Belluck, P. (2009). Tick-borne illnesses have Nantucket considering some deer-based solutions, *New York Times*, Sept. 6.

Berndt, T. J., & Berndt, E. J. (1975). Children's use of motives and intentionality in person perception and moral development. *Child Development 46*, 904–12.

Bindra, D., Clarke, K. A., & Shultz, T. R. (1980). Understanding predictive relations of necessity and sufficiency in formally equivalent "causal" and "logical" problems. *Journal of Experimental Psychology 4*, 422–43.

Birkland, T. A. (1998). Focusing events, mobilization, and agenda setting. *Journal of Public Policy 18* (1): 53–74

Bojcyk, K. E., & Corbetta, D. (2004). Object retrieval in the first year of life: Learning effects of task exposure and box transparency. *Developmental Psychology 40*, 54–66.

Booth-Sweeney, L. (2001). *When a butterfly sneezes.* Waltham, MA: Pegasus.

Booth-Sweeney, L. (2008). *Connected wisdom: Living stories about living systems.* White River Jct., VT: Chelsea Green.

Borton, R. W. (1979, March). *The perception of causality in infants.* Paper presented at a meeting of the Society of Research in Child Development (SRCD), San Francisco.

Boyes, E., & Stanisstreet, M. (1991). Development of pupils' ideas of hearing and seeing: The path of light and sound. *Research in Science and Technology Education 9*, 223–44.

Bracy, G. W. (1998). Tips for readers of research: No causation from correlation. *Phi Delta Kappan 79*(9), 711–12.

Bradt, S. (2010). I'll get mine, Jack: Self-interest wins out over mutually beneficial, study says. *Harvard Gazette*, August 31.

Brinkman, F., & Boschhuizen, R. (1989). Pre-instructional ideas in biology: A survey in relation with different research methods on concepts of health and energy. In M. T. Voorbach & L. G. M. Prick (eds.), *Research and developments in teacher education in the Netherlands* (pp. 75–90). London: Taylor & Francis.

Brown, D. E. (1995, April). *Concrete focusing and re-focusing: A cross-domain perspective on conceptual change in mechanics and electricity.* Paper presented at the American Educational Research Association (AERA) Conference, San Francisco, CA.

Brown, D. E., & Clement, J. (1987). Misconceptions concerning Newton's law of action and reaction: The underestimated importance of the third law. In J. D. Novak (ed.), *Proceedings of the Second International Seminar: Misconceptions and Educational Strategies in Science and Mathematics*, vol. 3, Ithaca, NY (pp. 39–53).

Browne, C. A., & Woolley, J. D. (2004). Preschoolers' magical explanations for violations of physical, social, and mental laws. *Journal of Cognition and Development 5*(2), 239–60.

Bruner, J. (1991). The narrative construction of reality. *Critical Inquiry 18* (1), 1–21 .

Bullock, M. (1979). *Aspects of the young child's theory of causation.* Unpublished doctoral dissertation, University of Pennsylvania.

Bullock, M. (1984). Preschool children's understanding of causal connections. *British Journal of Developmental Psychology 2*, 139–48.

Bullock, M. (1985). Causal reasoning and developmental change over the preschool years. *Human Development 28*, 169–91.

Bullock, M., & Gelman, R. (1979). Preschool children's assumptions about cause and effect: Temporal ordering. *Child Development 50*, 89–96.

Bullock, M., Gelman, R., & Baillargeon, R. (1982). The development of causal reasoning. In W. J. Friedman (ed.), *The developmental psychology of time* (pp. 209–54). New York: Academic.

Burke, J. (1978). *Connections*. Boston: Little, Brown.

Callanan, M.A., & Oakes, L.M. (1992). Preschoolers' questions and parents' explanations: Causal thinking in everyday activity. *Cognitive Development, 7*, 213–233.

Camp, C., Clement, J., & Brown, D. (1994). *Preconceptions in mechanics: Lessons dealing with students conceptual difficulties.* Dubuque, IA: Kendall-Hunt.

Carey, S. (1995). On the origin of causal understanding. In D. Sperber, D. Premack & A. J. Premack (eds.), *Causal cognition* (pp. 268–302). Oxford, UK: Clarendon.

Carey, S. (2009). *The origin of concepts*. New York: Oxford University Press.

Case, R. (1991). *The mind's staircase: Exploring the conceptual underpinnings of children's thought and knowledge.* Hillsdale, NJ: Erlbaum.

Casti, J. L. (1994). *Complexification: Explaining a paradoxical world through the science of surprise.* New York: Harper Collins.

CBS News (2011). Egyptian President Hosni Mubarak resigns, Feb. 11. Available: http://www.cbsnews.com/stories/2011/02/11/501364/main20031504.shtml [accessed: 7-6-2011].

Chandler, M. J., & Boutilier, R. G. (1992). The development of dynamic system reasoning. *Human Development 35*, 121–37.

Chi, M. T. H. (1997). Creativity: Shifting across ontological categories flexibly. In T. B. Ward, S. M. Smith & J. Vaid (eds.), *Creative thought: An investigation of conceptual structures and processes* (pp. 209–34). Washington, DC: APA.

Chinn, C. A., & Brewer, W. F. (1993). The role of anomalous data in knowledge acquisition: A theoretical framework and implications for science education. *Review of Educational Research 63*, 1–49.

Chinn, C. A., & Brewer, W. F. (1998). An empirical test of a taxonomy of responses to anomalous data in science. *Journal of Research in Science Teaching 35*(6), 623–54.

Clarke, J., Dede, C., Ketelhut, D., & Nelson, B. (2006). A design-based research strategy to promote scalability for educational innovations. *Educational Technology 46*(3), 27–36.

Clement, J. (1982). Students' preconceptions in introductory mechanics. *American Journal of Physics 50*(1), 66–71.

CNN (2007). Divers face dangerous conditions as river search continues, Aug. 2.

Cohen, L. B., & Amsel, G. N. (1998). Precursors to infants' perception of the causality of a simple event. *Infant Behavior & Development 21*, 713–31.

Cohen, L. B., Amsel, G. N., & Casasola, M. (1997, April). *Precursors to infants' perception of causality.* Paper presented at a meeting of the Society for Research in Child Development (SRCD), Washington, DC.

Cohen, L. B., & Oakes, L. M. (1993). How infants perceive a simple causal event. *Developmental Psychology 29*(3), 421–33.

Cohen, L. B., Rundell, L. J., Spellman, B. A., & Cashon, C. H. (1999). Infants' perception of causal chains. *Psychological Science 10*(5), 412–18.

Corrigan, R. (1995). How infants and young children understand the causes of events. In N. Eisenberg (ed.), *Social Development: Review of Personality and Social Psychology*, vol. 15. Thousand Oaks, CA: Sage.

Corrigan, R., & Denton, P. (1996). Causal understanding as a developmental primitive. *Developmental Review 16*, 162–202.

Corriveau, K. H., & Harris, P. L. (2009) Choosing your informant: Weighing familiarity and past accuracy. *Developmental Science 12*, 426–37 .

Crocker, J. (1981). Judgment of covariation by human perceivers. *Psychological Bulletin 80*, 272–92.

Damasio, A. (1994). *Descartes' error: Emotion, reason, and the human brain.* New York: Putnam.

Dearborn, H. (2007). WaterWaves, *Fryeburg's Citizen's Newsletter*, March, 2007.

deBerg, K. C. (1995). Student understanding of the volume, mass, and pressure of air within a sealed syringe in different states of compression. *Journal of Research in Science Teaching 32*(8), 871–84.

diSessa, A. A. (1993). Toward an epistemology of physics. *Cognition & Instruction 10*(2 & 3), 105–226.

diSessa, A. (2006). A history of conceptual change research: Threads and fault lines. In R. K. Sawyer (ed.), *The Cambridge handbook of the learning sciences* 16 (pp. 265–82). New York: Cambridge University Press.

Dorfman, J., Shames, V. A., & Kihlstrom, J. F. (1996). Intuition, incubation, and insight: Implicit cognition in problem-solving. In G. Underwood (ed.), *Implicit cognition* (pp. 257–296). Oxford, UK: Oxford University Press.

Dorner, D. (1989). *The logic of failure: Why things go wrong and what we can do to make go right.* New York: Metropolitan Books.

Driver, R., Guesne, E., & Tiberghien, A., eds. (1985). *Children's ideas in science.* Philadelphia: Open University.

Driver, R., Squires, A., Rushworth, P., & Wood-Robinson, V. (1993). *Making sense of secondary science.* New York: Routledge.

Drummond, C. N. (2001). Immanence and configuration: The quest for a cause. *Journal of Geoscience Education 49,* 329.

Dweck, C. (2006). *Mindset: The new psychology of success.* New York: Random House.

Eastwood, J. D., Smilek, D., & Merikle, P.M. (2001). Differential attentional guidance by unattended faces expressing positive and negative emotion. *Perceptual Psychopsychology 63*(6), 1004–13.

Edwards, B. J., Burnett, R. C., & Keil, F.C. (2008). *Structural Determinants of Interventions on Causal Systems.* Proceedings of the Cognitive Science Society.

Einhorn, H. J., & Hogarth, R. M. (1986). Judging probable cause. *Psychological Bulletin 99*(1), 3–19.

Energy Policy Act of 2005, Wikipedia, http://en.wikipedia.org/wiki/Energy_ Policy_Act_of_ 2005 [accessed 6-15-09].

Engel Clough, E., & Driver, R. (1985). What do students understand about pressure in fluids? *Research in Science & Technological Education 3*(2), 133–44.

Erickson, G., & Tiberghien, A. (1985). Heat and temperature. In R. Driver, E. Guesne & A. Tiberghien (eds.) *Children's ideas in science* (pp. 52–84). Milton Keynes, UK: Open University.

Fallon, A. E., Rozin, P., & Pliner, P. (1984). The child's conception of food: The development of food rejections with special reference to disgust and contamination sensitivity. *Child Development 55,* 566–75.

Feinfeld, K. A., Lee, P. P., Flavell, E. R., Green, F. L., & Flavell, J. H. (1999). Young children's understanding of intention. *Child Development 14,* 463–86.

Feltovich, P. J., Spiro, R. J., & Coulson, R. L. (1989). The nature of conceptual understanding in biomedicine: The deep structure of complex ideas and the development of misconceptions. In D. Evans & V. Patel (eds.), *Cognitive Science in Medicine: Biomedical Modeling* (pp. 115–72). Cambridge, MA: MIT.

Feltovich, P. J., Spiro, R. J., & Coulson, R. L. (1993). Learning, teaching, and testing for complex conceptual understanding. In N. Frederiksen & I. Bejar (eds.), *Test theory for a new generation of tests* (pp. 181–217), Hillsdale, NJ: Erlbaum.

Feng, J., Spence, I., & Pratt, J. (2007). Playing an action videogame reduces gender differences in spatial cognition. *Psychological Science 18*(10), 85–855.

Finucane, M. L., Alhakami, A., Slovic, P., & Johnson, S. M. (2000). The affect heuristic in judgments of risks and benefits. *Journal of Behavioral Decision Making 13*(1), 1–17.

Fosgate, H. (2002). *Gulf Lumber: A family affair.* University of Georgia, Daniel B. Warnell School of Forest Resources Alumni Association Publication, Spring/Summer.

Foster, D. (1999). Bugged: A biologist challenges the basic assumptions of what makes an ant colony work and rankles the reining king of the hill, Edward O. Wilson, *New York Times,* Oct. 31.

Francis, E. (2000). *Dioxindorms: One in a million. Chronogram,* December 2000.

Frederiksen, J., & White, B. (2000, April). *Sources of difficulty in students' understanding causal models for physical systems.* Presented at a meeting of the American Educational Research Association (AERA), New Orleans.

Fredette, N., & Lochhead, J. (1980). Student conceptions of simple circuits. *The Physics Teacher 18,* 194–98.

Friedman, W. (2001). The development of an intuitive understanding of entropy. *Child Development 72*(2), 460–73.

Gelman, R. (1990). First principles organize attention to and learning about relevant data: Number and the animate-inanimate distinction as examples. *Cognitive Science 14,* 79–106.

Gelman, R., Durgin, F., & Kaufman, L. (1995). Distinguishing between animates and inanimates: Not by motion alone. In D. Sperber, D. Premack, & A. J. Premack (eds.), *Causal cognition* (pp. 150–84). Oxford, UK: Clarendon.

Gelman, S., Coley, J., & Gottfried, G. (1994). Essentialist beliefs in children: The acquisition of concepts and theories. In L. Hirschfeld & S. Gelman (eds.), *Mapping the mind: Domain specificity in cognition and culture* (pp. 341–65). New York: Cambridge University Press.

Gelman, S., & Gottfried, G. M. (1996). Children's causal explanations of animate and inanimate motion. *Child Development 67,* 1970–87.

Gelman, S., & Kremer, K. E. (1991). Understanding natural causes: Children's explanations of how objects and their properties originate. *Child Development 62,* 396–414.

Gelman, S. A., & Welman, H. M. (1991). Insides and essence: Early understandings of the non-obvious. *Cognition 38,* 213–44.

Giese, P. A. (1987, June). *Misconceptions about water pressure.* Proceedings of the Second International Seminar: Misconceptions and Educational Strategies in Science and Mathematics, vol. 2, Ithaca, NY, Cornell University.

Gilbert, D., & Malone, P. (1995). The correspondence bias. *Psychological Review 117*(1), 21–38.

Gilbert, D. T., Pelham, B. W., & Krull, D. S. (1988). On cognitive busyness: When person perceivers meet persons perceived. *Journal of Personality and Social Psychology 54,* 733–40.

Gladwell, M. (2000). *The tipping point.* New York: Little, Brown.

Goldman, A. (1989). Interpretation psychologized. *Mind and Language 4,* 161–85.

Golinkoff, R. M. (1975). Semantic development in infants: The concept of agent and recipient. *Merrill-Palmer Quarterly 24,* 53–61.

Golinkoff, R. M., Harding, C. G., Carlson, V., & Sexton, M. E. (1984). The infant's perception of causal events: The distinction between animate and inanimate objects. In L. P. Lipsett (ed.), *Advances in infancy research, vol. 3* (pp. 145–65). Norwood, NJ: Ablex.

Gomez-Crespo, M. A., & Pozo, J. I. (2004). From everyday knowledge to scientific knowledge. *International Journal of Science Education 26*(11), 1325–43,

Gopnik, A., & Glymour, C. (2002). Causal maps and Bayes Nets: A cognitive and computational account of theory formation. In P. Carruthers, S. Stich, & M. Siegal (eds.), *The Cognitive Basis of Science* (pp. 117–32). New York: Cambridge University Press.

Gopnik, A., Glymour, C., Sobel, D. M., Schulz, L. E., Kushnir, T., & Danks, D. (2004). A theory of causal learning in children: Causal maps and Bayes Nets. *Psychological Review 111*(1), 3.

Gopnik, A., & Schulz, L. (2007). Introduction. In A. Gopnik and L. Schulz (eds.), *Causal learning.* Oxford, UK: Oxford University Press.

Gopnik, A., & Sobel, D.M., (2000). Detecting blickets: How young children use information about novel causal powers in categorization and induction. *Child Psychology 71*(5), 1205–22.

Gopnik, A., Sobel, D., Schulz, L., & Glymour, C. (2001). Causal learning mechanisms in very young children: Two, three, and four-year-olds infer causal relations from patterns of variation and covariation. *Developmental Psychology 37*(5), 620–29.

Goswami, U., & Brown, A. (1989). Melting chocolate and melting snowmen: Analogical relations and causal relations. *Cognition 35,* 69–95.

Green, C. S., & Bavelier, D. (2003). Action video games modify visual selective attention. *Nature 423,* 534–37.

Green, D. W. (1997). Explaining and envisaging an ecological phenomenon. *British Journal of Psychology 88,* 199–217.

Greenwald, A. G. (1992, June). Unconscious cognition reclaimed. *American Psychologist*, 776–79.

Griffiths, A. K., & Grant, B. A., (1985). High school students' understanding of food webs: Identification of a learning hierarchy and related misconceptions. *Journal of Research in Science Teaching 22*(5), 421–36.

Grotzer, T. A. (1989). *Can children learn to understand complex causal relationships?: A pilot study.* Unpublished qualifying paper, Harvard University, Cambridge, MA.

Grotzer, T. A. (1993). *Children's understanding of complex causal relationships in natural systems.* Unpublished doctoral dissertation, Harvard University, Cambridge, MA.

Grotzer, T. A. (2000, April). *How conceptual leaps in understanding the nature of causality can limit learning: An example from electrical circuits.* Paper presented at the American Educational Research Association (AERA) Conference, New Orleans.

Grotzer, T. A. (2003). Learning to understand the forms of causality implicit in scientific explanations. *Studies in Science Education 39*, 1–74.

Grotzer, T. A. (2004, Oct.). Putting science within reach: Addressing patterns of thinking that limit science learning. *Principal Leadership*.

Grotzer, T. A. (2005, April). *Transferring structural knowledge about the nature of causality to isomorphic and non-isomorphic topics.* Paper presented at the American Educational Research Association (AERA) Conference, Montreal.

Grotzer, T. A. (2011, April). *Building the understanding of our youngest scientists in a complex world.* Science Teachers' Association of New York State Newsletter.

Grotzer, T. A. (2011). Public understanding of cognitive neuroscience research findings: Trying to peer beyond enchanted glass. *Mind, Brain, and Education 5*(3), 108–14.

Grotzer, T. A. (forthcoming). The role of causal complexity in learning progressions: Exploring student learning of simple circuits.

Grotzer, T. A., & Basca, B. B. (2003). How does grasping the underlying causal structures of ecosystems impact students' understanding? *Journal of Biological Education 38*(1) 16–29.

Grotzer, T. A., Basca, B., & Donis, K. (2002). Causal patterns in ecosystems: Lessons to infuse into ecosystems units. Cambridge, MA: Harvard University Press.

Grotzer, T. A., Basca, B., & Donis, K. (2011). *Causal patterns in ecosystems: Lessons to infuse into ecosystems units,* 2nd ed. Cambridge, MA: Harvard University Press.

Grotzer, T. A., Duhaylongsod, L., & Tutwiler, M. S. (2011, April). *Developing explicit understanding of probabilistic causation: Patterns and variation in young children's reasoning.* Paper presented at the American Educational Research Association (AERA) Conference, New Orleans.

Grotzer, T. A., Miller, R. B., & Lincoln, R. A. (2011). Perceptual, attentional, and cognitive heuristics that interact with the nature of science to complicate public understanding of science, in M. S. Khine (ed.), *Advances in the nature of science research: Concepts and methodologies.* (pp. 27–50). New York: Springer.

Grotzer, T. A., & Mittlefehdlt, S. (2011). Students' metacognitive behavior and ability to transfer causal concepts. In A. Zohar & J. Dori (eds.), *Metacognition in science education: Trends in current research.* New York: Springer.

Grotzer, T. A., Solis, S. L., & Tutwiler, M. S. (forthcoming). *Action at an attentional distance.*

Grotzer, T. A., & Sudbury, M. (2000, April). *Moving beyond underlying linear causal models of electrical circuits.* Paper presented at a meeting of the National Association for Research in Science Teaching (NARST), New Orleans.

Grotzer, T. A., & Tutwiler, M. S. (forthcoming). *Critical exceptions: Why Causal Bayesian induction may not lead to deep understanding in science.*

Grotzer, T. A., & Tutwiler, M. S. (forthcoming). *Learning the nature of complex causality from Causal Bayes Nets reasoning: An impossible journey?*

Grotzer, T. A., Tutwiler, M. S., Dede, C., Kamarainen, A., & Metcalf, S. (2011, April). *Helping students learn more expert framing of complex causal dynamics in ecosystems using Eco-MUVE.* Paper presented at a meeting of the National Association of Research in Science Teaching (NARST), Orlando, FL.

Grotzer, T. A., Tutwiler, M. S., Metcalf, S., Kamarainen, A., & Dede, C. (forthcoming). *Learning to focus on processes and steady states in ecosystems dynamics using a virtual environment.*

Grotzer, T. A., Tutwiler, M. S., Solis, S. L., & Duhaylongsod, L. (2011, April). *Interpreting probabilistic causal outcomes in science: A microgenetic study of sixth graders' patterns of reasoning.* Paper presented at a meeting of the National Association of Research in Science Teaching (NARST), Orlando, FL.

Harris, P. L. (1989). *Children and emotion.* Oxford, UK: Blackwell.

Harris, P. L. (1997). The last of the magicians?: Children, scientists, and the invocation of hidden causal powers. *Child Development 68*(6), 1018–20.

Harris, P. L. (2002). What do children learn from testimony? In P. Carruthers, S. Stich & M. Siegal (2002). *The cognitive basis of science* (pp. 316–34). New York: Cambridge University Press.

Harris, P. L. (2006). Social cognition. In W. Damon, R. Lerner, D. Kuhn & R. Siegler (eds.), *Handbook of Child Psychology: Cognition, Perception, and Language,* 6ᵗʰ ed. (pp. 811–58). New York: Wiley.

Harris, P. L., & Koenig, M. (2006). Trust in testimony: How children learn about science and religion. *Child Development 77,* 505–24.

Hitchcock, C. (2007). On the importance of causal taxonomy. In A. Gopnik & L. Schulz (eds.), *Causal Learning* (pp. 101–14) New York: Oxford University Press.

Hmelo-Silver, C. E., & Azevedo, R. (2006). Understanding complex systems: Some core challenges. *Journal of the Learning Sciences 15,* 53–61.

Hmelo-Silver, C. E., Marathe, S., & Liu, L. (2007). Fish swim, rocks sit, and lungs breathe: Expert-novice understanding of complex systems. *Journal of the Learning Sciences 16,* 307–31.

Holding, B. (1987). *Investigation of school children's understanding of the process of dissolving with special reference to the conservation of matter and the development of atomistic ideas.* Unpublished PhD thesis, University of Leeds.

Honda: *The Cog,* YouTube video: Available: http://www.youtube.com/watch?v=_ve4 M4UsJQo [accessed 6-23-2011].

Honey, R., & Grotzer, T. (2008, August). *Tacit assumptions that limit ecosystems understanding.* Paper presented at a meeting of the Ecological Society of America (ESA), Milwaukee, WI.

Houghton, C., Record, K., Bell, B., & Grotzer, T. A. (2000, April). *Conceptualizing density with a relational systemic model.* Paper presented at a meeting of the National Association for Research in Science Teaching (NARST), New Orleans.

Huang, I. (1943). Children's conception of physical causality: A critical summary. *Journal of Genetic Psychology 64,* 71–121.

Hume, D. (1739–1740). *A treatise of human nature.* D. F. Norton & M. J. Norton (eds.), New York: Oxford University Press, 2000.

Jackson R. (2000). Guidelines on preventing cardiovascular disease in clinical practice. British Medical Journal *320* , 659–61.

Jacobson, M. J. (2001). Problem-solving, cognition, and complex systems: Differences between experts and novices. *Complexity 6* (3), 41–49.

Jacobson, M. J., & Wilensky, U. (2006). Complex systems in education: Scientific and educational importance and implications for the learning sciences. *Journal of the Learning Sciences 15* (1), 11–34.

Jacoby, J. (2008). *Br-r-r!: Where did global warming go? Boston Globe* , Jan. 6.

James, W. (1890). *The principles of psychology* . Cambridge, MA: Harvard University Press, 1983.

Janovic, B., Kiraly, I., Elsner, B., Gergely, G., Prinz, W., & Aschersleben, G. (2007). The role of effects for infants'perception of action goal. Psychologia 50, 273–90.

Johnson, J. T., Ogawa, K. H., Delforge, A., & Early, D. (1989). Causal primacy and comparative fault: The effect of position in a causal chain on judgments of legal responsibility. *Personality and Social Psychology Bulletin 15,* 161–74.

Jones, E. E. & Harris, V. A. (1967). The attribution of attitudes. *Journal of Experimental Social Psychology 3* , 1–24.

Kahneman, D., Slovic, P., & Tversky, A. (eds.) (1982). *Judgment under uncertainty: Heuristics and biases.* Cambridge, UK: Cambridge University Press.

Kalish, C. (1996). Causes and symptoms in preschoolers' conceptions of illness. *Child Development 67*, 1647–70.

Kalish, C. (1997). Preschooler's understanding of mental and bodily reactions to contamination. *Developmental Psychology 33*(1), 79–91.

Kalish, C. (1998). Reasons and causes: Children's understanding of conformity to social rules and physical laws. *Child Development 69*(3), 706–20.

Karniol, R., & Ross, M. (1976). The development of causal attributions in social perception. *Journal of Personality and Social Psychology 34*, 455–64.

Keil, F.C. (1994). The birth and nurturance of concepts by domains. In L. Hirschfield & S. Gelman (eds.), *Domain specificity in cognition and culture* (pp. 234–54). New York: Cambridge University Press.

Keil, F. C., & Lockhart, K. L. (1999). Explanatory understanding in conceptual development. In E. K Scholnick, K. Nelson, S. A. Gelman, & P. H. Miller (eds.), *Conceptual development: Piaget's legacy* (pp. 103–29), Hillsdale, NJ: Erlbaum.

Kelemen, D. (1999). Why are rocks pointy? Children's preferences for teleological explanations of the natural world. *Developmental Psychology 35,* 1440–52.

Keller, E. F., & Segel, L. (1970). Initiation of slime mold aggregation viewed as an instability. *Journal of Theoretical Biology 26,* 399–415.

Kelley, H. H. (1973). The processes of causal attribution. *American Psychologist 28*(2), 107–28.

Kim, N. S., & Keil, F. C. (2003). From symptoms to causes: Diversity effects in diagnostic reasoning. *Memory & Cognition 31* (1), 155–65.

Kline, A. D. (1980). Are there cases of simultaneous causation? In P. D. Asquith & R. N. Giere (eds.), *PSA* , vol. 1. East Lansing, MI, 292–301.

Kline, A. D. (1985). Humean causation and the necessity of temporal discontinuity, *Mind XCIV* (376), 550–56.

Koenig, M. A., & Harris, P. L. (2005). Preschoolers mistrust ignorant and inaccurate speakers. *Child Development 76*, 1261–77.

Kolodner, J. L. (1992). An introduction to case-based reasoning. *Artificial Intelligence Review 6*, 3–34.

Koplowitz, H. (1984). A projection beyond Piaget's formal-operations stage: A general stage theory and a unitary stage. In M. L. Commons, F. A. Richards & C. Armon (eds.), *Beyond formal operations* (pp. 272–96). New York: Praeger.

Koslowski, B. (1976). *Learning about an instance of causation.* Unpublished manuscript, Cornell University.

Koslowski, B., & Masnick, A. M (2002). Causal reasoning. In Goswami, U. (ed.), *Handbook of childhood cognitive development* (pp. 257–81). Malden, MA: Blackwell.

Koslowski, B., & Okagaki, L. (1986). Non-Humean indices of causation in problem-solving situations: Causal mechanism, analogous effects, and the status of rival alternative accounts. *Child Development 57,* 1100–1108.

Koslowski, B., & Snipper, A. (1977). *Learning about an instance of non-mechanical causality.* Unpublished manuscript, Cornell University.

Koslowski, B., Spilton, D., & Snipper, A. (1981). Children's beliefs about instances of mechanical and electrical causation. *Journal of Applied Developmental Psychology 2,*189–210.

Kosugi, D., Ishida, H., Murai, C., & Fujita, K. (2009). Nine to 11-month-old infants' reasoning about causality in anomalous human movements. *Japanese Psychological Research 51*(4) 246–57.

Kraus, N., Malmfors, T., & Slovic, P. (2000). Intuitive toxicology: Expert and lay judgments of chemical risks. In R. Slovic (ed.), *The perception of risk* (pp. 285–315). London: Earthscan.

Kristof, N. D. (2008). Where breathing is deadly. *New York Times,* May 25.

Kron, J. (2009). Deadly gas flows add to a lake's list of perils. *New York Times,* Nov. 6.

Kuhn, D., & Angelev, J. (1977). An experimental study of the development of formal operational thought. *Child Development 47*, 697–706.

Kuhn, D., & Ho, V. (1977). The development of schemes for recognizing additive and alternative effects in a "natural experiment" context. *Developmental Psychology 13*, 515–16.

Kuhn, D., Phelps, E., & Walters, J. (1985). Correlational reasoning in an everyday context. *Journal of Applied Developmental Psychology 6*, 85–97.

Kun, A., Parsons, J. E., & Ruble, D. N. (1974). Development of integration processes using ability and effort information to predict outcome. *Developmental Psychology 10*, 721–32.

Kun, A., & Weiner, B. (1973). Necessary versus sufficient causal schemata for success and failure. *Journal of Research in Personality 7*, 197–207.

Kushnir, T., & Gopnik, A. (2005). Young children infer causal strength from probabilities and interventions. *Psychological Science 16*(9), 678–83.

Kushnir, T., & Gopnik, A. (2007). Conditional probability versus spatial contiguity in causal learning: Preschoolers use new contingency evidence to overcome prior spatial assumptions. *Developmental Psychology 43*(1), 186–96.

Kushnir, T., Gopnik, A., & Schaefer, C., (2005, April). *Children infer hidden causes from probabilistic evidence.* Paper presented at a meeting of the Society for Research in Child Development (SRCD), Atlanta, GA.

Kushnir, T., Gopnik, A., Schulz, L. E., & Danks, D. (2003). Inferring hidden causes. In R. Alterman & D. Kirsh (eds.), *Proceedings of the Cognitive Science Society,* Austin, TX.

Lagnado, D. A., & Channon, S. (2008). Judgments of cause and blame: The effects of intentionality and foreseeability. *Cognition 108*, 754–70

Lakoff, G., & Johnson, M. (1980). *Metaphors we live by.* Chicago: University of Chicago.

Lambert, C. (1995, March-April). Leadership in a new key. *Harvard Magazine*, 28–33.

Leach, J., Driver, R., Scott, P., & Wood-Robinson, C. (1992). *Progression in conceptual understanding of ecological concepts by pupils aged 5-16,* Centre for Studies in Science and Math Education, University of Leeds.

LeDoux, J. (1996). *The emotional brain* . New York: Simon & Schuster .

LeDoux, J. (2000). Emotion circuits in the brain . *Annual Review of Neuroscience 23* , 155 –84 .

LeDoux, J. (2007). The amygdala. *Current Biology 17*(20), R868–R874.

LeDoux, J. (n.d.). Fearful brains in the age of terror. Available: http://www.cns.nyu. edu/ledoux/slide_show/Slide_show_age_of_terrow.htm [accessed: 9-20-2010].

Legerstee, M. (1994). Patterns of 4-month-old infant responses to hidden silent and sounding people and objects. *Early Development and Parenting 3*(2), 71–80.

Lehrer, R., & Schauble, L. (1998). Reasoning about structure and function: Children's conceptions of gears. *Journal of Research in Science Teaching 35*(1), 3–25.

Lehrer, R., & Schauble, L. (2004). Modeling natural variation through distribution. *American Educational Research Journal 41*(3), 635–79.

Leslie, A. M. (1982). The perception of causality in infants. *Perception 11*, 173–86.

Leslie, A .M. (1984). Spatiotemporal continuity and the perception of causality in infants. *Perception 13*, 287–305.

Leslie, A. M. (1988). The necessity of illusion: Perception and thought in infancy. In L. Weiskrantz (ed.), *Thought without language.* Oxford, UK: Clarendon.

Leslie, A. M. (1995). A theory of agency. In D. Sperber, D. Premack, & A. J. Premack (eds.), *Causal cognition* (pp. 121–41). Oxford, UK: Clarendon.

Leslie, A. M., & Keeble, S. (1987). Do sixth month old infants perceive causality? *Cognition 25*, 265–88.

Lesser, H. (1977). The growth of perceived causality in children. *The Journal of Genetic Psychology 130,* 142–52.

Levin, A. (2007). New bridge monitoring devices go unused, *USA Today*, Aug. 6.

Levy, S. T., & Wilensky, U. (2008). Inventing a "mid-level" to make ends meet: Reasoning through the levels of complexity. *Cognition & Instruction*: 1–47.

Liu, L., & Hmelo-Silver, C. E. (2009). Promoting complex systems learning through the use of conceptual representations in hypermedia. Journal of Research in Science Teaching 46, 1023–40.

Longden, K. A. (1984). Understanding of dissolving shown by 1–12-year-old children. Unpublished MS thesis, University of Oxford.

Mack, A., & Rock, I., (1998). *Inattentional Blindness*. Cambridge, MA: MIT Press.

Macy, J. (1991). *Mutual causality in Buddhism and General Systems Theory: The dharma of natural systems* (Buddhist Studies Series). Albany, NY: SUNY Press.

Mandel, D. R. & Lehman, D. R., (1996). Counterfactual thinking and ascriptions of cause and preventability. *Journal of Personality and Social Psychology 71,* 450–63.

Mann, C. C. (2004). Unnatural abundance, *New York Times*, Nov. 25.

Meltzoff, A. N. (2007). Infants' causal learning: Intervention, observation, imitation. In A. Gopnik & L. Schulz (eds.), *Causal learning* (pp. 37–47) New York: Oxford University Press.

Meltzoff, A. N. & Blumenthal, E. J. (2006, April). *Causal monitoring*. Paper presented at the meeting of the McDonnell Foundation Causal Learning Workshop, Pasadena, CA.

Mendelson, R., & Shultz, T. R. (1976). Covariation and temporal contiguity as principles of causal inference in young children. *Journal of Experimental Child Psychology 22,* 408–12.

Metcalf, S. J., Kamarainen, A., Tutwiler, M. S., Grotzer, T. A., & Dede, C. J. (2011). Ecosystem science learning via multi-user virtual environments. *International Journal of Gaming and Computer-Mediated Simulations 3*(1), 86–90.

Metz, K. E. (1991). Development of explanation: Incremental and fundamental change in children's physics knowledge. *Journal of Research in Science Teaching 28*(9), 785–97.

Metz, K. E. (1998a). Emergent ideas of chance and probability in primary-grade children. In S. P. Lajoie (ed.), *Reflection on statistics: Learning, teaching, and assessment in grades K–12* (pp. 147–73). Mahwah, NJ: Erlbaum.

Metz, K. E. (1998b). Emergent understanding and attribution of randomness. *Cognition & Instruction 16*(3), 285–365.

Michotte, A. (1963). *The perception of causality*. (T. R. Miles & E. Miles, trans.). New York: Basic Books. (Original work published 1946.)

Miller, D. T., & Gunasegaram, S. (1990). Temporal order and the perceived immutability of events: Implications for blame assignment. *Journal of Personality and Social Psychology 59,* 1111–18.

Miller, J. G. (1984). Culture and the development of everyday social explanation. *Journal of Personality and Social Psychology 46*, 961–78.

Miller, P. H. & Aloise, P. A. (1989). Young children's understanding of the psychological causes of behavior: A review. *Child Development 60,* 257–85.

Moray, N. (1959) Attention in dichotic listening: Affective cues and influence of instructions. *Quantitative Journal of Experimental Psychology 11*(1), 56–60.

Morrison, P., & Morrison, P. (1982). *Powers of ten: A book about the relative size of things in the universe and the effect of adding another zero* with the Office of Charles and Ray Eames, NY: W. H. Freeman.

Morrone, C. & Burr, D. (2006). Visual stability during saccadic eye movements. In M. S. Gazzaniga (ed.), *The Cognitive Neurosciences*, 4ᵗʰ ed. (pp. 511–24), Cambridge, MA: MIT.

Murayama, I. (1994). Role of agency in causal understanding of natural phenomena. *Human Development 37*, 198–206.

Naskrecki, P. (2005). *The smaller majority*. Cambridge, MA: Belknap.

Nisbett, R., & Ross, L. (1980). *Human inference: Strategies and shortcomings of social judgment*. Englewood Cliffs, NJ: Prentice-Hall.

Nisbett, R. E., Peng, K., Choi, I., & Norenzayan, A. (2001). Culture and systems of thought: Holistic versus analytic cognition. *Psychological Review 108*(2), 291–310.

Nuridsany, C., & Pérennou, M (1996). *Microcosmos*. Miramax Films.

Oakes, L. M. (1993, March). *The perception of causality by 7- and 10-month-old infants*. Paper presented at a meeting of the Society for Research in Child Development (SRCD), New Orleans.

Oakes, L. M., & Cohen, L. B. (1990). Infant perception as a causal event. *Cognitive Development 5*, 193–207.

Ohlsson, S. (n.d.). *Acquiring an explanatory schema: A preliminary model and related data*. Unpublished paper.

Ohman, A., Flykt, A., & Esteves, F. (2001). Emotion drives attention: Detecting the snake in the grass. *Journal of Experimental Psychology 130*(3), 466–78.

Osborne, R. & Gilbert, J. K. (1980). A method for investigating concept understanding in science. *European Journal of Science Education 2*(3), 311–21.

Osborne, R. J., & Cosgrove, M. M. (1983). Children's conceptions of the changes of state of water. *Journal of Research in Science Teaching 20*(9), 825–38.

Palmer, D. H. (1996). Students' application of the concept of interdependence to the issue of preservation of species. *Journal of Research in Science Teaching 34*(8), 837–50.

Pasquini, E., Corriveau, K., Koenig, M., & Harris, P. L. (2007). Preschoolers use past reliability in deciding which informant to trust. *Developmental Psychology 43*, 1216–26.

Penner, D. (2000). Explaining systems: Investigating middle school students' understanding of emergent phenomena. *Journal of Research in Science Teaching 37*(8), 784–06.

Pepine, C. J. (2003). Optimizing lipid management in patients with acute coronary syndromes. *American Journal of Cardiology 91*(4A), 30B–35B.

Perkins, D., & Grotzer, T. A. (2005). Dimensions of causal understanding: The role of complex causal models in students' understanding of science. *Studies in Science Education 41*,117–65.

Perkins, D., Tishman, S., Ritchhart, R., Donis, K., & Andrade, A. (2000). Intelligence in the wild: A dispositional view of intellectual traits. *Educational Psychology Review 12* (3), 269–93.

Pomerantz, C. (1971). *The day they parachuted cats on Borneo: A drama of ecology.* Reading, MA: Young Scott.

Premack, D. (1990). The infant's theory of self-propelled objects. *Cognition, 36* 1–16.

Premack, D., & Premack, A. J. (1995). Intention as psychological cause. In D. Sperber, D. Premack & A. J. Premack (eds.), *Causal cognition* (pp. 185–99). Oxford, UK: Clarendon.

Raia, F., (2008). Causality in complex dynamic systems: A challenge in earth systems science education. *Journal of Geoscience Education 56*(1), 81–94.

Resnick, M. (1994). *Turtles, termites, and traffic jams.* Cambridge, MA: MIT.

Resnick, M. (1996). Beyond the centralized mindset. *Journal of the Learning Sciences 5*(1), 1–22.

Revkin, A. C. (2009). U.S. curbs use of endangered species act in protecting polar bear, *New York Times*, May 9.

Roberts, N. (1978). Teaching dynamic feedback systems thinking: An elementary view. *Management Science 24*(8), 836–43.

Rosenberg, J. F. (1998). Kant and the problem of simultaneous causation. *International Journal of Philosophical Studies 6*(2), 167–88.

Rosset, E. (2008). It's no accident: Our bias for intentional explanations. *Cognition 108*(3), 771–80.

Ross, L. (1977). The intuitive psychologist and his shortcomings: Distortions in the attribution process. In L. Berkowitz (ed.), *Advances in experimental social psychology*, vol. 10. New York: Academic.

Ross, L., & Nisbett, R. E. (1991). *The person and the situation: Perspectives of social psychology.* New York: McGraw-Hill.

Rozin, P. (1990). Development in the food domain. *Developmental Psychology 26*, 555–62.

Rozin, P., Fallon. A. E., & Augustoni-Ziskind, M. L. (1986). The child's conception of food: The development of categories of acceptable and rejected substances. *Journal of Nutrition Education 18*, 75–81.

Rutherford, F. J. & Ahlgren, A. (1990). *Science for all Americans.* New York: Oxford University Press.

Sander, L. W. (1975). Infant and caretaking environment: Investigation and conceptualization of adaptive behavior in a system of increasing complexity: Explorations in child psychiatry. New York: Plenum.

Scheines, R., Easterday, M., & Danks, D. (2007). Teaching the normative theory of causal reasoning. In A. Gopnik and L. Schultz (eds.), *Causal learning* (p.119). New York: Oxford University Press.

Schlottmann, A. (1999). Seeing it happen and knowing how it works: How children understand the relation between perceptual causality and underlying mechanism. *Developmental Psychology 35*(5), 303–17.

Schlottmann, A., Allen, D., Linderoth, C., & Hesketh, S. (2002). Perceptual causality in children. *Child Development 73*(6), 1656–77.

Schulz, L. (2001). *Do-calculus: Adults and preschoolers infer causal structure from patterns of outcomes following interventions.* Presented at the Cognitive Development Society Conference, Virginia Beach, VA.

Schulz, L., & Gopnik, A. (2004). Causal learning across domains. *Developmental Psychology 40*(2), 162–76.

Schulz, L, Gopnik, A., & Glymour, C. (2007). Preschool children learn about causal structure from conditional interventions. *Developmental Science 10*(3) 322–32.

Schulz, L., & Sommerville, J. (2006). God does not play dice: Causal determinism and preschoolers' causal inferences. *Child Development 77*(2), 427–42.

Scott, S. (2002, April 19). Importers of mongoose ignored voice of caution.http://www.susanscott.net/Oceanwatch2002/apr19-02.html[accessed 6-15-09].

Sedlak, A.J., & Kurtz, S.T. (1981). A review of children's use of causal inference principles. *Child Development 52*, 759–84.

Shaklee, H., & Goldston, D. (1989). Development in causal reasoning: Information sampling and judgment rule. *Cognitive Development 4*, 269–81.

Shaw, J. (2007). The undiscovered planet: Microbial science illuminates a world of astounding diversity. *Harvard Magazine*, (Nov.-Dec.).

Shipstone, D. (1984). A study of children's understanding of electricity in simple DC circuits. *European Journal of Science Education 6*(2), 185–98.

Shipstone, D. (1985). Electricity in simple circuits. In R. Driver, E. Guesne & A. Tiberghien (eds.), *Children's ideas in science* (pp. 33–51). Philadelphia: Open University.

Shultz, T. R. (1982). Rules of causal attribution. *Monographs of the Society for Research in Child Development 47*(1, 194), 1–51.

Shultz, T. R., Fisher, G. W., Pratt, C. C., & Rulf, S. (1986). Selection of causal rules. *Child Development 57*, 143–52.

Shultz, T. R., & Kestenbaum, N. R. (1985). Causal reasoning in children. *Annals of Child Development 2*, 195–249.

Shultz, T. R., & Mendelson, R. (1975). The use of covariation as a principle of causal analysis. *Child Development 46*, 394–99.

Shultz, T. R., Pardo, S., & Altmann, E. (1982). Young children's use of transitive inference in causal chains. *British Journal of Psychology 73*, 235–41.

Siegal, M., & Share, D. L. (1990). Contamination sensitivity in young children. *Developmental Psychology 26,* 455–58.

Siegler, R. S. (1975). Defining the locus of developmental differences in children's causal reasoning. *Journal of Experimental Child Psychology 20*, 512–25.

Siegler, R. S. (1976). The effects of simple necessity and sufficiency relationships on children's causal inferences. *Child Development 47*, 1058–63.

Siegler, R., & Liebert, R. (1974). Effects of contiguity, regularity, and age on children's causal inferences. *Developmental Psychology 10*(4), 574–79.

Simons, D. J. (1996). In sight, out of mind: When object representations fail. *Psychological Science 7,* 301–5.

Simons, D. J., & Levin, D.T. (1998). Failure to detect changes to people during a real-world interaction, *Psychonomic Bulletin & Review 5*(4), 644–49.

Sloman, S. (2005). *Causal models: How people think about the world and its alternatives.* New York: Oxford University Press.

Smith, C., Carey, S., & Wiser, M., (1985). On differentiation: A case study of the concepts of size, weight, and density. *Cognition 21*, 177–237.

Smith, C., Maclin, D., Grosslight, L., & Davis, H. (1997). Teaching for understanding: A study of students' preinstruction theories of matter and a comparison of the effectiveness of two approaches to teaching about matter and density. *Cognition & Instruction 15*(30), 317–93.

Smith, E., & Anderson, C. (1986, April). *Alternative conceptions of matter cycling in ecosystems*. Paper presented at a meeting of the National Association of Research in Science Teaching (NARST), San Francisco.

Smith, M. C. (1975). Children's use of multiple sufficient cause schema in social perception. *Journal of Personality and Social Psychology 32*, 737–47.

Smith, M. C. (1978). Cognizing the behavior stream, *Child Development 49*, 736–43.

Sobel, D. (2004). Exploring the coherence of young children's explanatory abilities: Evidence from generating counterfactuals, *British Journal of Developmental Psychology 22*, 37–58.

Sobel, D. M., & Buchanan, D. W. (2009). Bridging the gap: Causality-at-a-distance in children's categorization and inferences about internal properties. *Cognitive Development 24*(3), 274–83.

Sobel, D. M., & Kushnir, T. (2003). *Interventions do not solely benefit causal learning: Being told what to do results in worse learning than doing it yourself*. Proceedings of the Cognitive Science Society, Boston, MA.

Sobel, D., Tenebaum, J., & Gopnik, A. (2004). Children's causal inferences from indirect evidence: Backwards blocking and Bayesian reasoning in preschoolers. *Cognitive Science 28*, 303–33.

Sommerville, J. A. (2007). Detecting causal structure: The role of interventions in infants' understanding of psychological and physical causal relations. In A. Gopnik & L. Schulz (eds.), *Causal learning* (pp. 48–57). New York: Oxford University Press.

Sommerville, J. A,. & Woodward, A. L., (2005). Infants' sensitivity to the causal features of means-end support sequences in action and perception. *Infancy 8*, 119–45.

Sommerville, J. A., Woodward, A. L., & Needham, A. (2005). Action experience alters 3-month-old infants' perception of others' actions. *Cognition 96*, B1–B11.

Spelke, E. S., Phillips, A., & Woodward, A. L. (1995). Infants' knowledge of object motion and human action. In D. Sperber, D. Premack, & A. J. Premack (eds.), *Causal cognition* (pp. 44–78). Oxford, UK: Clarendon.

Spellman, B. (1997). Crediting causality. *Journal of Experimental Psychology 126*, 1–126.

Springer, K., & Belk, A. (1994). The role of physical contact and association in early contamination sensitivity. *Developmental Psychology 30*, 864–68.

Springer, K., & Keil, F. C. (1991). Early differentiation of causal mechanisms appropriate to biological and nonbiological kinds. *Child Development 62*, 767–81.

Steyvers, M., Tenenbaum, J., Wagenmakers, E. J., Blum, B. (2003). Inferring causal networks from observations and interventions. *Cognitive Science 27*, 453–89.

Sunstein, C. R. (2002). *Risk and reason*. Cambridge: Cambridge University Press.

Talanquer, V. (2002). Minimizing misconceptions: Tools for identifying patterns of reasoning. *The Science Teacher* (Nov.), 47–49.

Tamir, P. (1985). Causality and teleology in high-school biology. *Research in Science and Technology Education 3*, 19–28.

Thierry, B. (2005). Integrating proximate and distal causes. *Current Science 87*(7).

Tiberghien, A., & Delacotte, G. (1976). Manipulations et representations de circuits electrique simples chez les infants de 7 a 12 ans. *Revue Francais de Pedagogie 34*.

Treisman, A. (2009). Attention: Theoretical and psychological perspectives. In M. S. Gazzaniga (ed.), *The Cognitive Neurosciences*, 4ᵗʰ ed. (pp. 189–204) Cambridge, MA: MIT.

Tytler, R. T. (1998). Students' conceptions of air pressure: Exploring the nature of conceptual change. *International Journal of Science Education 20*(8), 929–58.

Van de Walle, G., & Spelke, E. S. (1993, March). *Integrating information over time: Infant perception of partly occluded objects*. Paper presented at a meeting of the Society for Research in Child Development (SRCD), New Orleans.

Van Orden, G. C., & Paap, K. R. (1997). Functional neuroimages fail to discover pieces of mind in the parts of the brain. *Philosophy of Science 64* (Proceedings), S85–S94.

Vinokur, A., & Ajzen, I., (1982), Relative importance of prior and immediate events: A causal primacy effect. *Journal of Personality and Social Psychology 42*, 820–29.

Vuilleumier, P. (2005). How brains beware: Neural mechanisms of emotional attention. *Trends in Cognitive Science 9*(12) 585–94.

Waldmann, M. R., & Hagmayer, Y. (2005). Seeing versus doing: Two modes of accessing causal knowledge. *Journal of Experimental Psychology 31*, 216–27.

Walker, B., & Salt, D. (2006). *Resilience thinking: Sustaining ecosystems and people in a changing world.* Washington, DC: Island Press.

Webb, P., & Boltt, G. (1990). Food chain to food web: A natural progression? *Journal of Biological Education 24*(3), 187–90.

Wellman, H. M., & Gelman, S. A. (1988). Children's understanding of the nonobvious. In R. J. Sternberg (ed.), *Advances in the psychology of human intelligence,* vol. 4 (pp. 99–135). Hillsdale, NJ: Erlbaum.

Westbrook, S. L., & Marek, E. A. (1992). A cross-age study of student understanding of the concept of homeostasis. *Journal of Research in Science Teaching 29*(1), 51–61.

White, B. Y. & Frederiksen, J. R. (1998). Inquiry, modeling, and metacognition: Making science accessible to all students. *Cognition & Instruction 16*, 3–118.

White, B. Y. & Frederiksen, J. R. (2000). Metacognitive facilitation: An approach to making scientific inquiry accessible to all. In J. L. Minstrell & E. H. Van-Zee (eds.), *Inquiring into inquiry learning and teaching in science* (pp. 331–70). Washington, DC: AAAS.

White, B. Y., & Frederiksen, J. R. (2005). A theoretical framework and approach for fostering metacognitive development. *Educational Psychologist 40*(4), 211–23.

White, P. A. (1997). Naive ecology: Causal judgments about a simple ecosystem. *British Journal of Psychology 88,* 219–33.

Wilensky, U., & Resnick, M. (1999). Thinking in levels: A dynamic systems approach to making sense of the world. *Journal of Science Education and Technology 8*(1), 3–19.

Wilensky, U., & Reisman, K. (2006). Thinking like a wolf, a sheep or a firefly: Learning biology through constructing and testing computational theories. *Cognition & Instruction 24*(2), 171–209.

Wiser, M., & Carey, S. (1983). When heat and temperature were one. In D. Gentner & A. Stevens (eds.), *Mental models* (pp. 267–98). Hillsdale, NJ: Erlbaum.

Woodward, A. L. (1998). Infants selectively encode the goal of an actor's reach. *Cognition 69,* 1–34.

Woodward, A. L. (2003). Infants' developing understanding of a link between looker and object. *Developmental Science 6,* 297–311.

Woodward, J. (2007). Interventionist theories of causation in psychological perspective. In A. Gopnik & L. Schulz (eds.), *Causal learning* (pp. 19–36) New York: Oxford University Press.

Yamasaki, H., LaBar, K. S., & McCarthy, G. (2002). Dissociable prefrontal brain systems for attention and emotion. *PNAS, USA 99*(17) 11447–51.

Zohar, A., & Dori, J., eds. (2011). *Metacognition and science education.* New York: Springer.

Zohar, A., & Peled, B. (2008). The effects of explicit teaching of metastrategic knowledge on low- and high-achieving students. *Learning and Instruction,* 337–53.

Index

ability. *See* triadic notion of thinking dispositions
accumulation, 84, 100
acquisition bias, 130n8
action at a distance, 36n14, 75, 78, 79, 78, 79, 87n9, 80, 165, 169, 173. *See* also spatial gaps
agency, 20, 21, 24–26, 34, 43, 115–116, 127, 154, 167, 169
agentive framework, 25
air pressure, 102–103, 108, 109, 115, 119
albedo effect, 59, 61
American colonies, 47
American revolution, 130
amplification, 6, 45, 59
amygdala, 29, 166
angiogenesis, 80
An Inconvenient Truth, 92
anthropogenic causes, 1
archetypes, 7
Aristotle, 15n20, 74n7
Asian Long Horn Beetle, 1
attentional capture, 33, 90, 101
attentional distance, 81
Azevedo, Roger, 152

babesiosis, 45
Badui, China, 104
balance, 70
Bayesian causality, 91, 138–139. *See* also Causal Bayes Nets

Bayesian reasoning, 10, 26, 128, 135, 143
Because Brian Hugged his Mother, 46
The Bee Movie, 66
Big Fish, Little Fish, 158
Bin Laden, Osama, 121, 149
biodiversity, 1, 47
Biofuel Plan, 1
Booth-Sweeney, Linda, 167
Borneo, 41, 44, 48n1, 83, 124, 167
Boston tea party, 121
branching causal pattern, 42, 43, 48n16
Bruner, Jerome, 46
Buddhism and General Systems Theory, 65
bullies, 58, 170
Bullock, Merry, 128, 141
Burke, James, 102
The Butter Battle Book, 58

Callanan, Maureen, 168
Carey, Susan, 24, 115, 134
Case, Robbie, 74n5
case-based reasoning, 167
Causal Bayes Nets, 26, 28–29, 35n1
causal chain, 42, 45, 131n11
causal default assumptions, 6, 8, 10, 23, 75, 168
causal default patterns. *See* causal default assumptions
causal impact diagrams, 6
centralized causality, 147–158

65719660R00116

Made in the USA
Lexington, KY
22 July 2017